Art Therapy, Research and Evidence-based Practice

Art Therapy, Research and Evidence-based Practice

Andrea
Gilroy

S SAGE Publications
London ● Thousand Oaks ● New Delhi

First published 2006

SAGE Publications Ltd
1 Oliver's Yard
55 City Road
London EC1Y 1SP

SAGE Publications Inc.
2455 Teller Road
Thousand Oaks, California 91320

SAGE Publications India Pvt Ltd
B-42, Panchsheel Enclave
Post Box 4109
New Delhi 110 017

British Library Cataloguing in Publication data

A catalogue record for this book is available from the British Library

ISBN-10 0-7619-4113-4   ISBN-13 978-0-7619-4113-2
ISBN-10 0-7619-4114-2 (pbk)   ISBN-13 978-0-7619-4114-9 (pbk)

Library of Congress Control Number available

Typeset by C&M Digitals (P) Ltd., Chennai, India
Printed on paper from sustainable resources
Printed and bound in Great Britain by TJ Intenational Ltd, Padstow, Cornwall

For Joyce and Jock

Contents

Biography

Andrea Gilroy, PhD, is an experienced art therapy educator and researcher. She trained originally as a painter, then qualified as an art therapist in the mid 1970s and worked in acute psychiatry and with people who have learning disabilities. She gained her PhD in 1991 for research into the occupational choice and career development of art therapists that focused on the evolution of their art practice. She has taught at Goldsmiths College, University of London since 1979 and is currently Reader in Art Psychotherapy and the Programme Area Coordinator for Art Psychotherapy and Dance Movement Therapy, teaching across a range of programmes and short courses. She is involved in the development of art therapy in Australia through her continuing involvement as an educator and researcher at the University of Western Sydney, NSW. Her research interests include the development of an evidence base for art therapy and the interface between the theories and practices of visual art/visual culture and the theory and practice of art therapy. Her publications include *Pictures at an Exhibition: Selected Essays on Art and Art Therapy* (Routledge, 1989) with Tessa Dalley; *Art Therapy: A Handbook* (Open University Press, 1992) with Diane Waller; *Art and Music: Therapy and Research* (Routledge, 1995) with Colin Lee; and *The Changing Shape of Art Therapy: New Developments in Theory and Practice* (Jessica Kingsley, 2000) with Gerry McNeilly.

Foreword

It seems to me that Andy Gilroy has almost single-handedly taken on the research mantle for the art therapy profession. Having completed her doctorate on 'Art therapists and their art: from the origins of an interest in art to occasionally being able to paint', as Programme Area Director for Arts Psychotherapies at Goldsmiths College, she has taught and developed post-qualification, research-based programmes. In this way, Andy has driven forward the research agenda when many of us may have been somewhat reluctant to acknowledge its significance and importance, particularly in the current climate of waiting-list pressures and shrinking resources within the public sector.

The reality is that we are living and working in a new culture. Since the 1990s, government policies have required practice to be research based and practitioners to prove their clinical and cost effectiveness. There is 'evidence' that art therapy as a profession has progressed sufficiently to be granted State Registration in 1997 by the Council of Professions Supplementary to Medicine (now the Health Professions Council). However Andy argues that this is not enough – indeed she turns the question around suggesting that research has much to offer art therapy. Providing an evidence base for our discipline can develop theory and practice, and progress the recognition of art therapy as an effective and innovative treatment for a wide range of clients. Subjecting one's practice to research seems challenging but can be hugely helpful. This book goes a long way to help us understand how and why this is the case.

I remember discussing the idea of this book many years ago. It has long been an ambition of Andy's to bring these issues to the profession in a meaningful and manageable way. We now have the privilege of this book to help us all through the quagmire of the different research methodologies that are pertinent to our practice. In her paper written in 1992, Andy acknowledged the ambivalence of art therapists to research. The word 'evidence' elicits various responses ranging from alarm, anxiety and despondency to thoughtful engagement with the rigours of the research endeavour producing a growing body of empirical and qualitative evidence. Pointing out tensions in the process of art therapy becoming evidence based and the idea that research may demand conformity and prescriptive practice, she describes how art therapy can develop its own appropriate evidence base. This involves new work and different work. Essentially Andy is inviting us to think about research, open up the debate and produce a range of evidence tailored to our needs, that is, make our own evidence base that informs our discipline so that we can judge this for ourselves.

The argument is persuasive and is approached with optimism and enthusiasm. The thrust of this book is that art therapists certainly cannot afford to fall behind as evidence for all practices across all sectors is being developed. 'It is all about language, all about audience. Art Therapists have to think, act and write with a political purpose in mind' (p. 37). The challenge is to research the effectiveness of art therapy through both quantitative and qualitative means. In her personable and very readable style, Andy has certainly helped us rise to this challenge and this book will equip us to the task.

When mulling over these ideas, two main thoughts came to my mind. First, if we are to provide our own evidence base, do we need to provide the necessary 'evidence' that it is the 'art' in art therapy that is the worthwhile and effective component. Andy argues that the alternativeness of art therapy makes it unique and especially helpful for those who find it hard to engage with routine services. I would go further by suggesting that it is in the very nature of the non-verbal processes at the preconscious and unconscious level that are made manifest in the image which can give rise to significant intrapersonal and interpersonal change. All of us, like Andy, who work with images in a therapeutic process fully understand this. The problem is how to show it. As someone who embarked on a research project in 1975 with exactly this problem in mind, I know how difficult it is to measure change and the efficacy of any type of treatment modality. In those days Rank Xerox funded research into art therapy and supplied a research grant for one year. The study was to evaluate art therapy with particular interest on creativity and its potential effects in therapy by comparing art therapy groups and verbal psychotherapy groups for psychiatric patients on an acute admission ward. In particular I was looking at measures of change in self-esteem, creativity and anxiety levels. Two papers, published from my thesis (Dalley 1979, 1980), identified changes in individual patients as measured on their own self-reporting rating scale. I also demonstrated how changes in their artwork reflected changes in mental state as reported by them on completion of the image. Although this study produced 'hard evidence', with changes that were statistically significant, I think I was left with more questions than answers. For example, what is being measured – the therapeutic relationship, the art process or the combination of the two. It seems to me that empirical research in dynamically oriented therapies is complicated by the nature of the relationship with the therapist and for this reason lends itself better to a qualitative or descriptive approach. Andy does not align herself to one particular research methodology, but explains in detail and depth the various approaches that are possible and desirable according to the approach of the practitioner. Her overall message, however, is emphatic. Not to engage in this process is not an option.

Following on from this, I found myself thinking about change. Change is the essence of any therapeutic endeavour. Art therapy offers a particular opportunity to engage with making art forms in the context of a therapeutic relationship to work towards some significant change. We work to help understand the meaning of this change. How then is it possible to translate this sensitive and delicate process, which involves internal shifts and unconscious processes, into an external body of evidence? In healthy infant development Winnicott (1971) described how the 'good enough' mother enables the child to move forward in his or her development. The mother's interventions are sometimes experienced as impingements by her infant. These impingements are however necessary for the infant to develop a robust sense of self with an internal world that is integrated and not fragmented. This helps the infant's ego development, helps s/he relate to the external world and all the potential demands that are experienced in becoming independent and a viable person in his/her own right. For me, Andy's encouragement and commanding approach to her subject resonates with this process as we have to develop through the impingements of Evidence-Based Practice to ensure our professional growth to stand on our own. The burgeoning of empirical research into other psychotherapies (e.g. Fonagy et al., 2002) and also in neurobiology (Schore, 1994) is playing a central part in our overall understanding of change and is a world in which we must continue to engage.

Tessa Dalley
June 2006

Introduction

Research has much to offer art therapy. It can generate new knowledge about the discipline, its theories and practices and really progress its recognition as an effective and innovative treatment for clients of all ages across the sectors and settings where art therapists work. Research of all kinds has always seemed to me to be an intrinsically worthwhile and creative process that leads to all manner of interesting findings about all kinds of things. Outcome research has similarly always seemed both possible and desirable and so, when Evidence-based Practice (EBP) first came to my attention in the mid 1990s, my response was understated and pragmatic. Examining one's practice and subjecting it to research and to the quality assurance procedures that EBP requires seemed challenging but potentially hugely helpful. It could demonstrate art therapy's effectiveness and speak to the particularities of clinical work with different client groups. It could not help but improve practice and support the development of services, especially where the profession remains relatively unknown, under-resourced and unavailable to those who would benefit from it. I was concerned that 'our own kinds of evidence' might get lost in a drive towards quantitative research but, generally speaking, thought that EBP could well be 'a good thing'.

As I began work on this book the EBP literature was expanding exponentially and the demands for evidence of the effectiveness of every treatment and practice across the public sector were becoming much more pressing. At the same time services were being eroded and were financially under threat. Treatments that could demonstrate their evidence base were developing and competition for reduced resources was rife. In the midst of these pressures was an acute awareness of the need for 'evidence'. This seemed to elicit various responses from art therapists: often alarm and anxiety; often a pragmatic engagement with an aspect of the EBP process such as audit; sometimes thoughtful engagement with the paradigm and with research; sometimes despondency; sometimes dogged resistance. There also seemed to be a lack of knowledge and understanding about what research and EBP actually were and a sense of being overwhelmed in the face of their uncompromising demands. Perhaps EBP was not quite such a good thing after all.

EBP, as I came to realise, constitutes a paradigm, that is a particular philosophical framework that has its own theories, laws and assumptions. A seminar about the 'audit culture', given by Cris Shore (an anthropologist, at that time working at Goldsmiths, elaborated in Shore and Wright (2000)), heightened my awareness of EBP's political underpinnings and set the book on a new trajectory. It began as a pragmatic book outlining the relatively straightforward methods and processes of research and EBP; what you now have in your hands paints a broader picture of the philosophies, politics and practices that constitute research and EBP and how these interact with art therapy.

My aim is to show that while research and EBP mutually inform one another they comprise significantly different activities, construed in a particular way because of EBP's roots in medicine. EBP's key precepts – that policy and practice should be informed by research and that services should be delivered in the most efficient way – are not in dispute, but the power relations and economic imperatives that have driven its implementation across the public sector have the potential to restrict the development of practices and services that exist outside its value-laden framework. Along with many other non-medical practices in the public sector, art therapy cannot escape being positioned, at present rather unfavourably, within this system. But, rather than acceding to the prerogatives of orthodox EBP, I argue that art therapy should develop a pluralistic evidence base *appropriate to the discipline*, one that challenges the implicit hierarchies and beliefs that underpin EBP and contributes to the paradigm shift that has undoubtedly begun to happen.

There is, however, a tension in the process of art therapy becoming evidence based that lies at the heart of this book, that is, between the discipline and the systems in which it operates. The paradigms of knowledge, practice and research in which art therapy has developed come from the visual arts and from psychotherapy and psychoanalysis. When I was working on the connections and disconnections between these traditions and the new traditions of EBP I attended a conference that illustrated the extent of art therapy's difference from EBP's orthodoxy. The conference (on art-based research methods in education at Queens University, Belfast, 2005) included presentations from a number of researchers who had used various forms of art making to collect and analyse data and had chosen performance, music and visual display to convey their findings. This made the processes and outcomes of their research accessible in wholly different ways than through the written word or statistical tables. This helped me think about how research and the arts can enhance one another and evoke new ways of knowing in an audience who cannot remain disinterested spectators. These innovations and traditions in allied fields sit alongside art therapists' awareness of many clients' social deprivation and a certain 'alternative', not to say subversive streak in the profession that sees mental health care differently from the way it is construed by the psychiatric mainstream. Embedded in art therapy's discourse is ambivalence towards the medical and behavioural models of psychiatry and their conceptualisation of peoples' problems as illnesses that can be treated by medication or the application of psychological techniques. The positivist approach of cause and effect, treatment and outcome, is directly linked with EBP's medically based hierarchies of evidence and research and flourishes within it, but these do not fit comfortably with art therapy's values, theories, practices and research.

The purpose of this book is to make research and EBP more accessible and manageable for practitioners, bringing the construction of an evidence base for art therapy into the realms of possibility and into everyone's everyday practice.

I want to encourage art therapists to take on everything that research and EBP mean, and to stress that much that is required – such as critical reflection – is part of our existing skills set. New skills, however, have to be learnt and developed over time, for example those of research. Making art therapy evidence based entails *work*. New work. Different work. Work to do with research methods, writing, policy, politics and argument. Work on this book has involved all of these and led to moments of exasperation and bewilderment such that I could hardly believe what I had chosen to write about. The arts and therapeutic practice involve relationship and are about individuals and diversity, and research comprises a hugely diverse range of methods and practices. All open up the world. Yet EBP seems to close things down, seeking conformity and reducing everything to universally applicable and ranked formulae that can be micromanaged. This creates a potential for homogenised practice, for the development of prescriptive packages of art therapy linked to diagnosis and setting. It need not be so. Despite the undoubted problematics of bringing art therapy and research together with EBP I remain enthusiastic about its potential to legitimise our work, inform our practice and make art therapy's undoubted benefits explicit in utterly convincing ways, *if* we engage with EBP in strategic and politically informed ways.

As well as giving practitioners practical ideas about how they might go about making their practice evidence based, I hope that this book will help the reader to *think* about EBP. This is especially important when the paradigm as a whole seems to attack thinking and to provoke anxious reactivity rather than reflection and creativity. I want to give practitioners arguments so that when managers and medics say, 'where's your evidence?' art therapists will not react defensively but will instead have a critical take on the question. They will be able to engage with the discourse and say 'what do *you* mean by evidence?' closely followed by, 'this is what *I* mean by evidence' and, critically, 'this is the *range of evidence* that informs my discipline and this is how *we* judge it'. Evidence comes in different forms. It is gathered and assessed as part of the social process of different communities and so evidence from one paradigm cannot and should not be critiqued in terms of another. Evidence is eclectic. It can be interpreted in different ways at different times and different kinds of evidence suit different claims and different discourses. Outcome research is situated within the discourse of efficacy. Within this discourse Randomised Controlled Trials (RCTs) are critical. We need to know about art therapy's efficacy, but we need to research process as well as outcomes, drawing on other methods that are situated within other discourses. I hope that this book enables you, the reader, to challenge the value-laden orthodoxy of EBP and argue for an open and fair system where different kinds of evidence are judged according to the merits and values of their discourse, rather than all being judged by the values of one.

I begin in Chapter 1 with an outline of the origins of EBP in Evidence-based Medicine (EBM), explaining its principles and procedures, and situating the paradigm within the politics of healthcare in recent years. I describe how government policy has influenced the nature and funding of research in mental health care and explore what is meant by 'evidence' and 'proof', situating the medically based paradigm that is EBP within modernist and postmodernist debate. This enables EBP to be seen as a powerful meta-narrative that diminishes the multiplicity of voices that could, and should, inform the evidence base of mental health care in general and art therapy in particular. I also describe the development of frameworks that offer more inclusive systems in which to review different forms of evidence.

Chapter 2 explores a striking metaphor in the literature that seems to me to encapsulate anxieties about what might happen when therapeutic practice has to address questions about its effectiveness – the issue at the heart of EBP. The filmic narratives and socio-cultural contexts of Bambi (representing process-oriented psychotherapy research) and Godzilla (representing clinical and cost-effectiveness research) are unpacked to show how Bambi invites an identification with acute vulnerability in the face of the hugely destructive, alien 'other' that is Godzilla. Bringing an awareness of these characters' stories and the contexts of their production, representation and audiencing in different cultures during times of economic uncertainty and social change conveys an important message about how EBP confronts complacency and the status quo. A counterproductive dialectic of 'us' and 'them' is explored alongside the potentially empowering nature of relationship and related to the strategic initiatives art therapists might take in the construction of the discipline's evidence base.

Chapter 3 shows how art therapists can make an immediate and significant contribution to the discipline's evidence through developing clinical guidelines. These are key because the process requires an immersion in and critical reflection upon evidence from different sources and that direct links be made between evidence and clinical work. I propose that concerns about the potential for prescriptive and uncreative practice embodied in guidelines be tempered by a strategic engagement with the process so that the discipline's existing evidence can be fully articulated and disseminated to practitioners, employers and users. The practical nuts and bolts of the whole procedure are described.

Chapter 4 explores audit in a similarly practical and expedient way, showing how art therapists can sustain a constructive engagement with the different activities that comprise the audit cycle. A series of simple and straightforward tasks are described which, when undertaken in a politically informed way, can make a real contribution to demonstrating the efficiency and effectiveness of art therapy. But once again this, like other parts of the EBP cycle, is situated within the social and political context of public sector services that require new layers of administration which can generate a persecutory, micromanaging gaze. The development of the 'audit culture' is explored and different kinds of art therapy audit are discussed, differentiating audit from research.

Much of the debate within and around EBP focuses on its favourite research method, the Randomised Controlled Trial (RCT). In Chapter 5 I explore the pros and cons of RCTs, situating them as one method within a broader discourse about the relative merits of quantitative and qualitative research. This leads to a description of the processes of research, including the writing of research proposals and grappling with ethics committees, before embarking on a world tour of research methods in Chapters 6 and 7. I explore the possibilities offered by visual research methods, historical and heuristic approaches, collaborative research and ethnography, interviews, surveys and various forms of case study and explain the nature of different kinds of experimental research, offering examples from the British and American art therapy research literatures.

Chapters 8 and 9 take an inclusive approach to an exploration of art therapy's present evidence. This seeks to differentiate between different areas of art therapy theory and practice and describe distinctive 'clusters' of literature that are beginning to demonstrate effectiveness and identify and articulate different approaches to practice with different client populations. This paints, I believe, an optimistic picture. In some areas there is a small body of the 'right' kind of evidence; in others there is sufficient inductive research to embark on the outcome research that EBP orthodoxy requires. All have rich and rigorous descriptions of practice and theory. All need much more. A few have important qualitative research that explore the interior of the art therapy process, often in methodologically interesting ways, and there are important outcome studies that pave the way for art therapy to be able to demonstrate its effectiveness with some client populations. Art therapists in Britain and America work in different ways in very different systems, describing theory and practice and generating research that can seem (on either side of the Atlantic) as if from another discipline entirely. This can make generalising from one to the other problematic, but their juxtaposition brings to light interesting resonances and dissonances that merit further research and transatlantic collaboration.

A few final points. Throughout the book I have used the term 'art therapy' because it remains the most common international descriptor of the profession and all its practices. I have spoken to the development of an evidence base for art therapy in general terms and have not differentiated how this might be achieved in the health and social services, education and justice systems. This is because the EBP paradigm has entered practice and discourse across the public sector and is no longer restricted to healthcare. Practice, research and guidelines will differ from one sector to another, but EBP's underlying principles are generic.

My hope is that this book will enable you, the reader, to become more research aware and better equipped to challenge the canons of scientific research and evidence and, if you have not done so already, to embark on your own research. Either way my primary target – the outcome that I have aimed for – is that art therapists will see how the particular interweaving of research and quality assurance procedures that constitutes EBP could be hugely helpful to the development of art therapy, *if* it is done on our own terms. EBP is a contested paradigm and a social and political phenomenon that should not be engaged with uncritically. We must utilise every kind of research methodology, including those required by orthodox EBP, but engage with them in ways that make them our own. All can then become our own kinds of evidence.

This book has been a long time in the making. Many have contributed to it along the way, knowingly and unknowingly, through conversations about its subject and support in the production of the object. I would like to thank the many art therapists, colleagues, friends and students who have helped me think about art therapy research and all that it means for the discipline to become 'evidence based'. I owe particular thanks to friends and colleagues at Goldsmiths

College for their continuing support and interest, especially the staff group and research students in Art Psychotherapy and particularly to Sally Skaife, Kevin Jones and Jacky Mahony for their comments on chapter drafts. I am grateful to the art therapists and users at Oxleas NHS Trust for learning with me about the development of clinical guidelines, to the members of the guideline group's Expert Panel (Jane Dudley, Helen Greenwood and Roger Wilks) for allowing me to quote their opinions and to those who helped me think about what makes art therapy unique (Joy Schaverien, Sally Skaife, Chris Wood and Diane Waller). I am very grateful indeed to Jane Mace for her generous yet critical editorial eye, her attention to detail and to 'voice' and for helping me stay in the writing bubble through to the end. The Library at Goldsmiths has been a gold mine and I thank its staff for doing their job as well as they do and for acquiring a modest collection of Godzilla films on my behalf. I acknowledge Cris Shore whose seminar on the 'audit culture' sent me into uncharted territory. For her patience alone I thank Alison Poyner and colleagues at SAGE Publications. Lastly, I thank the London and Edinburgh branches of my family and also my friends who have tolerated my absence and preoccupation with the BB for what has seemed like an enormously long time.

1 Evidence-based practice: principles, process, policy and proof

Evidence-based Practice (EBP) is a political and social phenomenon particular to our times, its origin and development being intimately related to government policies in the UK's health, social, justice and educational services. It is characterised by a cycle of activities that seek to guarantee that all interventions are effective and based on rigorous research and to make certain that services are delivered in the most efficient and economic way. Undoubtedly it has the potential to improve practice and ensure the equitable provision of good and effective services across all sectors, including effective but relatively new and innovative practices like art therapy.

All of this seems unquestionably positive but EBP is a contested paradigm and debates about its nature and influence are now embedded in the literatures of healthcare, social welfare, education and the criminal justice system. It has influenced research, practice and provision and, while there is much that could be good, there are fears that some of its effects could be detrimental. This is because EBP's demand for unequivocal evidence of effectiveness and efficiency has created a situation where one research methodology – the Randomised Controlled Trial (RCT) – is privileged above all others. Perhaps this is not surprising in general healthcare, nor in psychiatry where the medical model and its research methods prevail, but the same standards and criteria have extended to research and practice in other sectors. This privileging of findings from a single method can create pervasive feelings of vulnerability and inadequacy in professions where the availability of such research is limited; these are exacerbated by problems with funding for different kinds of research and inadequate resourcing of other potentially evidence-generating activities through quality-assurance procedures. This suggests that, while EBP could be of enormous benefit to every aspect of state-based provision – including art therapy – its values and systems could also inhibit the development of evidence appropriate to different practices, services and settings.

There are real pressures to provide evidence of art therapy's clinical and cost effectiveness in all sectors and, in its absence, a potential for service erosion. Art therapy has a developing evidence base, but not one that fits the orthodox framework of EBP. Why not? In order to answer this question it is important to understand exactly what EBP is, how it has been shaped by social, political and economic forces, why it has become so influential, and exactly what is meant by 'evidence'. In this chapter I describe the paradigm that is EBP and consider its origins and history within the socio-political context of medicine and the effects of government policies on research funding. Situating EBP in a critical context is essential if art therapy's engagement with it is to be constructive, strategic and meaningful to the discipline.

The history of evidence-based medicine

The last few decades have seen enormous changes in Britain's public sector. Services are being provided by new, large and specialised organisations, resources are being pooled and functions transferred in an effort to eradicate the divisions between health and social care. This has gone hand in hand with numerous government initiatives: the move to community care; the monitoring of changes in provision and the cost-effective use of resources; the creation of internal markets and a huge increase in quality-assurance procedures. All of this has been coupled with serious concern about the effectiveness and quality of treatments in the NHS and about the interventions and methods of social care, justice and education.

This sets the scene for the development of Evidence-based Medicine (EBM). It began with a text by Archie Cochrane (1972), a British epidemiologist who commented on the worrying variation in practice and outcomes in medicine and the lack of empirical evidence to support many treatments being offered in the NHS. The structure and process of EBM were developed during the early 1980s in Canada through papers that aimed to guide doctors through the critical appraisal of the immense amount of research at their disposal so that they could update and improve their practice and reduce treatment inequities. The Evidence-based Medicine Working Group (1992) at McMaster University in Ontario, Canada, claimed this as a 'paradigm shift' in the teaching and practice of medicine. EBM rapidly gathered momentum and by the 1990s was common parlance in international healthcare, being described as an 'emerging clinical discipline' that brought 'the best evidence from clinical and health care research to the bedside, to the surgery or clinic, and to the community … a process of life-long, problem-based learning' (EBM Editorial, 1995: 5).

EBM has since become central to British and American government care-related policies and a worldwide social movement, spawning a huge industry with many journals, web pages, books, CD Roms and so on. Central to these are collaborative organisations that collate, review and disseminate up-to-date information about the latest research in medicine, namely the Cochrane Collaboration, the NHS Centre for Reviews and Dissemination and the National Institute for Clinical Excellence (NICE, a special health authority). The Cochrane Collaboration is key, being an international organisation that maintains up-to-date information about various healthcare interventions; this has within it the UK Cochrane Centre and a number of specialist groups who focus on specific issues and client populations.

The principles of evidence-based practice

The origins of EBP are in Evidence-based Medicine (EBM); 'EBP' and 'Evidence-based Health Care' (EBHC) being terms that encompass the transfer of EBM principles to all spheres of work and policy in the public sector. Although EBP is a relatively recent phenomenon it is so significant that it has been described as a 'social movement' (Sturdee, 2001). In essence it is a response to the proliferation and variation of practices and outcomes that are accompanied by a lack of supporting research, exacerbated by the need to provide public services for an increasing population with diminishing resources. EBP in all sectors seeks to demonstrate that 'the procedures adopted by a profession are safe, effective and cost-effective' (Roth and Fonagy, 1996: 1) through ensuring that practitioners are working to the best of their abilities because they constantly review, update and adjust their practices according to the latest research findings. Service provision should follow the same principle so that the general public can be assured that they are receiving what are demonstrably the most effective interventions, delivered in the most efficient way.

According to the EBM Working Group (1992) and Goldner and Bilsker (1995), the first authors to discuss EBP in psychiatry, the implementation of EBM/EBP required a change from a 'Traditional Paradigm' to a new 'Evidence-based Paradigm', a paradigm being a framework or model that encapsulates a set of theories, methods, standards and assumptions about what matters, what happens, what the problems are and how they should be addressed. The new EBP paradigm was said to represent a fundamental change in approach to knowledge, its acquisition and implementation in medicine and psychiatry The 'Traditional Paradigm' placed high value on standard approaches: these were that training, experience and expertise were an acceptable basis on which to make decisions about diagnosis and treatment; costs were not necessarily an issue. Value was afforded to clinical authority or expertise that had been accrued over time and, if a senior colleague could not provide an immediate source of expertise then practitioners could turn to textbooks (Richardson, 2001). This 'traditional' approach was challenged by the four key principles of the new 'evidence-based' paradigm. I think these deserve careful attention so that all therapists can engage with them point by point, and so I first set out each principle in summary form and then offer reflections on how the paradigm is beginning to change.

1. That systematic observations that are reproducible and unbiased can increase confidence in knowledge about practice. The absence of systematic observations must lead to caution about information that is derived from clinical experience and intuition as it may be misleading

This principle suggests that experience and intuition do not ensure continuing best practice. Practice must be based on research that is both replicable and objective. The principle aims to counter difficulties with knowledge that is derived solely from experience; to question decisions made on the basis of intuition; to challenge the 'received wisdom' of those whose expertise comes from authority, charisma and longevity in the field; and to act as 'a healthy corrective to maverick individualism' (Richardson, 2001: 170).

Freshwater and Rolfe (2004) discuss how EBM and EBP are a mass of contradictions: about authority and no authority, conformity and diversity, practitioner and researcher. They explain how EBP's attempt to do away with authority and replace it with an egalitarian focus on research originated from senior medical staff, in effect substituting one authority with another and overriding the expertise of the practitioner with the expertise of the researcher who can generate and identify the 'best' evidence. EBP seems to be egalitarian, but as diverse sources of 'evidence' are welcomed they are also diminished. The language becomes slippery: sometimes 'evidence' includes expert opinion and audit findings but, on closer examination means research, or nothing else but RCTs, everything else being deemed 'weaker' and without meaning. Nonetheless the opinions of experienced practitioners and the consensus of 'Expert Panels' are included in 'levels of evidence', experience being considered as credible and reliable evidence when none other is available. Experience and expertise are also considered key to the accurate interpretation and appropriate application of research.

Where does this leave art therapy? With a mixed message. The discipline does have an evidence base but this is derived from various forms of research, from the knowledge and opinion of experienced practitioners and from those the profession deems as 'experts'. However, for the discipline's 'evidence' to be respected, art therapists from all sectors must challenge the rigidity, authority and power of orthodox EBP. I think this is critical. Why? Because art therapy is a relatively small and new discipline; because we draw on practices and research methods from the arts and social sciences; and because our activities are cross-sectoral and extend beyond the NHS into the social, educational and criminal justice systems. This is not to say that we should abandon RCTs and the other forms of experimental research that EBP requires, rather that art therapy needs to develop a pluralistic evidence base that has meaning for the discipline as a whole.

2. That the study and understanding of disease are necessary, but insufficient, guides for clinical practice

Medicine's 'traditional paradigm' depended on knowing the cause of an illness and its effect, enabling prevention and cure, but the 'new' EBP paradigm requires that treatment outcomes be studied too.

I suggested in an earlier paper (Gilroy, 1996) that discomfort with doubt and ambiguity about treatments in psychiatry relate to its origins in medicine – to the cause and effect approach – and to a desire for certainty about 'what works', for the absolute knowledge that comes from the positivist approach of the physical sciences (physics, chemistry and biology). Positivism assumes that there is an objective reality that can be reliably observed and measured in a linear fashion, but there is significant debate about whether or not a positivist approach can evaluate the outcomes of psychological and other interventions in an entirely causal way and can adequately investigate the complex experiences of people with mental health problems and disabilities. Outcomes are particularly problematic when the treatment being evaluated cannot be broken down into measurable, component parts because it involves human interaction. Brown et al. (2003) point out that this is so in every area of healthcare, giving the example of nursing that involves social relationships, experience, trust and tacit knowledge. These important aspects of care that affect outcome cannot be addressed in the orthodox EBP framework because they cannot be moulded to fit the favoured research method – RCTs.

3. That the understanding of certain 'rules of evidence' is necessary to correctly interpret the literature

This principle is at the heart of EBM/EBP. All clinicians should understand the nature of scientific enquiry in order to discriminate between trustworthy and not so trustworthy research. This refers to the view that only certain kinds of research, that is, certain kinds of knowledge, are admissible as evidence of a treatment's effectiveness. This means only giving credence to research where certain procedures have been followed, that is:

- there is an explicit hypothesis;
- 'reliable measures' have been used;
- subjects have been randomly allocated;
- statistical evaluation has been used;
- there have been large samples;
- blind experimenters have been used;
- the measures have been specific and sensitive to the variable measured.

These procedures are part and parcel of the 'gold standard' of research in medicine, the RCT. In EBM/EBP terms a RCT is the only research method that has sufficient rigour to credibly determine whether or not a treatment is effective.

There is of course a huge debate about whether or not RCTs are indeed a 'gold standard' and about the relative worth of other quantitative methods and qualitative research in medicine, the psychological therapies and interventions in other sectors. Important research questions are not amenable to investigation through RCTs and there are many areas of theory and practice that do not have sufficient inductive research on which to base RCTs. However, within the medically based EBP framework, RCTs are thought to provide stronger evidence than case series research, which in turn are considered stronger than expert and practitioner consensus about what constitutes best practice (Richardson, 2001). Using this hierarchical structure enables some interventions to be described as empirically 'supported', particularly as evidence accrues, but those without such empirical support are considered 'experimental' until strong evidence can be gathered.

According to the orthodox EBP paradigm, art therapy is neither empirically supported nor does it have sufficient inductive research on which to base RCTs, despite the fact that a number of RCTs and important qualitative research have been completed in different areas of art therapy practice in America and Britain (see Chapters 8 and 9). It is acknowledged that the absence of outcome-based research does not equate with an absence of knowledge, nor does it infer the ineffectiveness of an intervention (Parry and Richardson, 1996; Richardson, 2001), and it is worth remembering that the Cochrane ideal was not to determine practice but to inform it, but there is an assumption that there is now enough research-based evidence to determine policy, service and practice decisions, regardless of the fact that this is not the case for many disciplines and interventions. Although there is a less doctrinaire approach to what is and is not sufficiently rigorous research, EBP's 'rules of evidence' still hold significant sway. It is this specific methodological orientation, and the narrowness of debate about what constitutes 'acceptable' evidence, that identifies EBP as a social movement (Sturdee, 2001).

4. That those whose practice is based on an understanding of the underlying evidence will produce superior patient care

This principle aims to ensure that clinicians continually improve their practice through keeping it up to date and in line with the latest research findings according to EBM/EBP's 'rules of evidence', asserting that those who do will be more effective and efficient practitioners.

The explosion of information technology and the increase in research-based literature in medicine make it well-nigh impossible for clinicians to keep up to date, hence the establishment of organisations such as the Cochrane Collaboration that aim to distil the latest research findings and make them easily accessible. But these too are problematic because of the rigid and value-based criteria of systematic reviews that privilege RCTs and quantitative research over qualitative and process-oriented research, excluding an enormous amount of knowledge and creating value-driven care through organisations such as NICE. However, the necessity for change within the present system of synthesis and review is gradually being recognised. This is exemplified through the establishment of the Campbell Collaboration, an international organisation parallel to the Cochrane Collaboration that prepares, maintains and disseminates systematic reviews of the effectiveness of social and behavioural interventions in education, crime and justice, and social welfare. Davies (2004) describes how, when the Campbell Collaboration was established in 2001, a strategic decision was taken to focus on intervention studies, experimental and quasi-experimental research in the same way as Cochrane, but also to include qualitative research when it was part of a quantitative study. He says that qualitative research *per se* was not included because the methodology for evaluating the range of studies was, at that time, under-developed, but that initiatives such as the Quality Framework for Qualitative Research (Cabinet Office, 2003) are developing consensus about what constitutes high quality, qualitative research. Davies adds:

> These developments will put qualitative research on a similar footing to experimental and quasi-experimental methods in terms of having explicit quality frameworks, and will increase the pressure for a wider conception of qualitative research to be included in the Campbell Library of systematic reviews.

> (2004: 31)

Kuhn (1970) discussed how scientific research and thought are defined by a series of paradigms, each operating within a tacitly accepted frame of reference until its limits are exposed, at which point a new paradigm emerges. EBP is a paradigm that has been shaped by medicine. Its structure has spread to non-healthcare sectors but, like all paradigms, will change when its fundamental concepts, problems and questions can no longer be addressed within its existing frameworks. EBP is increasingly subject not only to the social, political and cultural forces within the NHS that challenge the medical canon, but also to those of other sectors with which it interacts. Hopefully the Cochrane Collaboration and NICE will gradually become more inclusive as social and political forces are brought to bear by 'policy-makers, providers and consumers of services whose demands for sound evidence go beyond any particular methodology or research design' (Davies, 2004: 32).

But how does the EBP process work? How does evidence from research accumulate and transfer to the routines of practice? And what exactly do art therapists have to do to engage with the paradigm, now, and demonstrate that what we do is evidence-based?

The EBP process

Parry and Richardson (1996) usefully outline how EBP in the psychological therapies can be developed, offering a structure that can be applied in all settings and sectors. They refer to a spiralling model (Figure 1.1) that shows how practice, theory and research are linked to guidelines, audit and continuing professional development. This shows that EBP comprises a cycle of activities which enable practice to become evidence based and, critically, that primary research is but a part of this cycle. Thus individual practitioners – individual art therapists – do not have to do research in order to become evidence based in their work. What they do have to do is engage with the EBP cycle and demonstrate that their practice is informed by research and other forms of evidence derived from quality assurance procedures.

Parry and Richardson, like Roth et al. (1996), are careful to emphasise that EBP in the psychological therapies comes directly from clinical work, describing how research should develop from practice. Observations of particular phenomena that catch the clinician's eye should be documented and systematically described in case studies and single case experiments. These initial studies, together with the development of associated theory, result in innovative practice; this should be followed by small-scale research projects that develop and explore the approach. Such inductive research should then move on to what has been described as 'the pinch in the hourglass' (Salkovskis, 1995) of 'research that conforms to the most rigorous standards of enquiry' (Roth et al., 1996: 49), that is to RCTs. There follows a broadening of the hourglass into slightly more varied kinds of research activity through further, usually comparative, RCTs in the field that, in this model of research development, enables an orthodox evidence base to be constructed. A body of research like this takes time to accumulate and few psychological therapies have been through the entire research cycle, from first observations to comparative studies. Needless to say art therapy is very much at the beginning of this particular research trajectory, one that lies at the heart of the medically oriented EBP paradigm.

Once research findings have been generated they are put to the specific use that characterises EBP. First, research is critically appraised. It is then systematically

Figure 1.1   The EBP Process

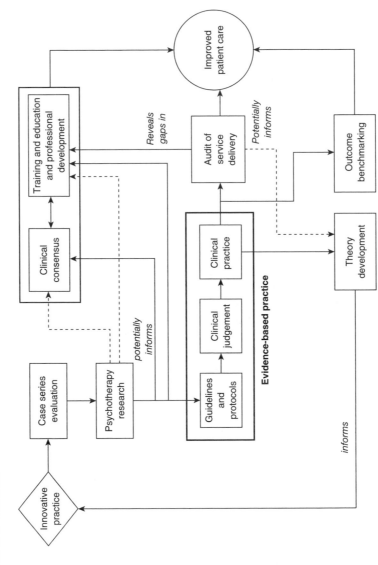

Source: Parry and Richardson (1996) *NHS Psychotherapy Services in England: Review of Strategic Policy.* Reproduced with permission.

reviewed and placed in a hierarchy of 'levels of evidence' that grades different kinds of research. A clear hierarchy of medical evidence has been given by the NHS Centre for Evidence-based Medicine (Box 1.1), but the more detailed version cited by Mace and Moorey (2001) is, they say, fairly typical (Box 1.2). This more complex hierarchy has been adopted, with minor adaptations, not only by psychotherapy (Parry, 2001; see Box 1.3) but also by social care and education (see Smith, 2004; Thomas and Pring, 2004). There is more caution and critique of these hierarchies, and indeed of the medical basis of the whole paradigm, in these sectors but RCTs remain the 'best' evidence. In this orthodox EBP framework experimental studies are graded at lower levels, expert opinion is the lowest level and qualitative research is excluded altogether. Once research has been graded through systematic review it is distilled into recommendations and guidelines that inform practice and from which standards of service delivery can be developed. Audits of practice and delivery are then conducted. It is this formalising of the norms of clinical work and service delivery into guidelines, and their subsequent clarification and monitoring through audit, that typifies this part of the EBP cycle (described in Chapters 3 and 4).

Box 1.1 NHS Executive hierarchy of evidence

A RCTs;

B Other robust experimental or observational studies;

C More limited evidence but the advice relies on expert opinion and has the endorsement of respected authorities.

Source: Mann (1996b: 16).

Box 1.2 Levels of evidence of therapeutic effectiveness

Level 1 Either a systematic review of comparable RCTs, or an individual RCT with a narrow confidence interval, or introduction of the treatment has been associated with survival in a previously fatal condition;

Level 2 Either a systematic review of comparable cohort studies, or an individual cohort study (which may be an RCT with a significant drop-out rate);

Level 3 A systematic case series (or poor quality cohort or case-control studies);

Level 4 A reported case series (or poor quality cohort or case-control studies);

Level 5 Expert opinion based on consensus or inference from 'first principles' in the absence of formal critical appraisal.

Source: adapted from Ball et al. (1998), in Mace and Moorey (2001).

Box 1.3   Psychotherapy levels of evidence

I(a)   Evidence from meta-analyses of RCTs;

I(b)   Evidence from at least one RCT;

II(a)   Evidence from at least one controlled study without randomisation;

II(b)   Evidence from at least one other quasi-experimental study;

III   Evidence from descriptive studies, for example, comparative studies, correlation studies and case-control series;

IV   Evidence from expert committee reports or opinions, or clinical experience of respected authority, or both.

Source: Eccles et al. (1998), cited in Parry, (2001: 18).

The next part of the EBP process is a consequence of audit. Gaps might be recognised in the skills staff need to deliver a service; this indicates their Continuing Professional Development (CPD) requirements. Audit might identify problems such as an absence of the resources necessary for effective service delivery, or demonstrate clients' satisfaction (or not) with the service they have received. Audit and guideline development can also highlight gaps in knowledge and lead to further research and theory development; this completes one EBP cycle and begins the next. Thus, once an evidence base for practice has been developed, the entirety of the EBP cycle should ensure that effective treatments are offered in every service where they are needed.

Becoming demonstrably evidence based is now required of all NHS-based practitioners as part of their routine work and is on the horizon for clinicians working in social services, the penal system and education. It requires all disciplines and every service to engage with the entirety of the EBP cycle. It really is an imperative of our times and art therapists ignore it at our peril. But how has this change come about? As I suggested at the start, thinking about how EBP has been shaped by political, philosophical and economic imperatives is critical to understanding it as a paradigm that, like any other, is subject to influence and to change.

Policy and implementation

Reviewing the trajectory of EBM and EBP shows how the paradigm has been driven by politics and policies. Baker and Kleijnen (2000) plot its development in Britain, focusing on the NHS reforms of the early 1990s. During this time continuing critiques of healthcare research led to a new NHS Research and Development Strategy (Department of Health [hereafter DoH], 1991) and to the major reorganisation of the NHS; together these initiated Evidence-based Health Care (EBHC) as an explicit part of government policy. The White Paper that drove EBP's implementation, *The New NHS* (DoH, 1997a), initiated the National Service Frameworks, basing policy and implementation on the 'best available evidence' about which treatments were clinically and cost effective, and creating 'a monitoring strategy with teeth' (Baker and Kleijnen, 2000: 24). It also instituted a system of clinical governance whose purpose was to ensure that 'Evidence-Based Practice is in day-to-day use with the infrastructure to support it' (DoH, 1989). Clinical governance covers a raft of measures that aim to ensure that standards are met and that quality assurance processes safeguard and facilitate continuing improvements in care. The introduction of such statutory duties for the quality of care was partly prompted by the government's wish to prevent major service failures following various public inquiries, for example into paediatric cardiac surgery at Bristol Children's Hospital.

Government policies implementing EBP in the NHS therefore aim to reduce risk and monitor the provision and delivery of reliable treatments whose effectiveness and efficiency have been demonstrated through research. This, as Pringle (1996) and others have pointed out (e.g. Brown et al., 2003; Freshwater and Rolfe, 2004; Hammersley, 2004; Smith, 2004), has both ideological and pragmatic imperatives. The ideological imperative centres on government reclaiming the policy initiative in the management of healthcare through shifting the balance of power away from professionals and towards managers and policy makers. This has been achieved through a 'good housekeeping' philosophy, the adoption of a business model and an emphasis on 'applied' rather than 'basic' research that has, in turn, influenced its commissioning and funding.

The ideology of the marketplace leads directly to the pragmatic drivers of policy: the familiar need to do more with less. However, there are huge challenges when systems have to initiate and resource change: costs might rise and a lack of resources can inhibit services that the evidence recommends. This has created a paradoxical situation when the policies that drive EBP are 'at least partly based on the belief that evidence-based health care would reduce health care costs' (Baker and Kleijnen, 2000: 15). Robinson (2002) comments on the influence of this pragmatic imperative and the use of targets and standards which, she suggests, does no more than encourage practitioners to devise ways to cope and survive in new systems which attempt to micro-manage services and their delivery. This introduces a climate of fear and a system where judgements are often made solely on an economic basis. This has the potential to distort both 'performance' and 'production':

> because it encourages, indeed to a large extent forces, individual practitioners to adopt an instrumental orientation in which scoring highly on the (performance) indicators becomes more important than doing a good job in terms of their own judgement. (Hammersley, 2004: 144)

Baker and Kleijnen describe this as 'a system for enforcement' (2000: 28), one where the rhetoric of diversity is 'undermined by the constant sense of surveillance' (Freshwater and Rolfe, 2004: 114). This sense of unease supports conformity to EBP's demands that come directly from an ideologically driven (and often reactive) policy focus on health and effective practice that require continual improvements in the quality of care. In such a climate the development of practices and services becomes very difficult, the plethora of government documents, research papers and continuing reform resulting in EBP fatigue and concerns that a system is being created that will only deliver that which can be measured (Robinson, 2002).

Kane, a member of the National Health Service Executive, unpacks the 'often uncomfortable' (2002: 215) relationship between research and policy making. He describes how policy initiatives are driven by short-term political events, policy priorities and resources. Policy making is not a clear, linear process because at all levels – national, regional and local – policies are made in 'turbulent environments' and 'filtered and translated' at each level (2002: 217). Kane identifies five issues that drive policy making and action:

- political, professional and ethical values;
- resources;
- failures and crises;
- canvassed views of selected focus groups;
- representation from pressure groups. (2002: 221)

Note that research is not on the list; it is not a policy driver, despite EBP's rhetoric and Kane's insistence that research *should* guide policy making. Evidence-based policies have, he says, an 'intuitive appeal' (2002: 223), but there is a mismatch between the ideal and reality because values and subjective responses to events, crises and policy initiatives influence the judgements that policy makers make. Policy making is a political, largely reactive and subjective process, and so research has to be 'timely, comprehensible and practical' (2002: 224), that is, it has to be strategic and have a direct bearing on the immediate concerns of policy makers.

Research and science in the healthcare marketplace

Kane's insider perspective helps make sense of the intertwined nature of research, policy making and the development of EBM and EBP, especially in light of the hugely influential NHS Research and Development Strategy (DoH, 1991). Bury (1998) and Baker and Kleijnen (2000) explain how this strategy had significant political support because it recognised the enormous amount of healthcare research available, the frequency of conflicting results and that, consequently, reliable information was often inaccessible to clinicians, policy makers and managers. As described earlier, the Cochrane Collaboration, NICE and the NHS Centre for Reviews and Dissemination were instigated with the express purpose of compiling and distributing research-based evidence to those who needed it. Alongside these a new national research programme (DoH, 1997b) identified key areas for research, supporting and commissioning research that addressed the healthcare needs of the entire population and aiming to ensure that the government's healthcare policies, as well as changes in services and practices, were underpinned by research.

In such a context it is not surprising that research oriented towards service needs has been prioritised over curiosity-driven research. This is reflected in the *National Service Framework for Mental Health* (DoH, 1999) that states that investment will explicitly focus on the knowledge necessary for the implementation of the framework, specifying among its priorities the evaluation of the effectiveness and cost-effectiveness of psychological and psychosocial interventions. Slade and Priebe (2002) say that drug companies routinely fund psychopharmacological research and taxation funds service-oriented research, leaving charities to support the remainder. The DoH (2001a) has identified mental health as one of three research priorities, recognising that spending on mental health research has been significantly less than that on the other two priorities – cancer and heart disease – both of which have substantial charitable funding sources.

The government's, and therefore EBP's, focus on the clinical and cost effectiveness of treatments has accelerated the shift in research attention away from understanding mental health problems and exploring them in a social, cultural and political context, towards positivist approaches to treatment, that is, to outcomes. Indeed the very nature of the EBP cycle and its particular research trajectory supports a prescriptive commissioning of large-scale research projects about treatments where certain kinds of inductive research have been developed or for those whose outcomes look promising, that is, within the 'hourglass' model (Salkovskis, 1995). Research agendas are set by policy makers and funding bodies, commissioned research often being directly linked to policy initiatives and to the interests of researchers involved with large-scale outcome studies. This leaves other stakeholders, practitioners, users and researchers interested in other methodologies with relatively little influence and involvement, both the macro and micro socio-political contexts influencing the commissioning, publishing and uptake of research so that 'only that research which conforms to and reinforces the dominant ideology is conducted and adopted' (Brown et al., 2003: 105). Allard, a user representative, challenges the rhetoric of EBP when he suggests that the government's provision of 'safe, sound and supportive' mental health services (DoH, 1998: 23) is more about protecting the public from mental health users than caring for them. He suggests that the lack of funding for research 'into what really works for people', combined with support for research that supports the medical model of psychiatry, may lead to researchers and mental health workers being at the mercy of political and market forces and 'becoming agents of social control' (Allard, 2002: 209–10).

Inevitably the availability of research funding has knock-on effects on the construction of the evidence base for treatments. Sturdee (2001) and others (e.g. Cape, 2000) argue powerfully that the knowledge-generating process of EBP is dominated by the vested interests of medicine and the pharmacological industry which focus research activity on some issues at the expense of others:

> research into mental health problems is increasingly being weighted towards those problems which offer at least the possibility of profitable marketing opportunities for commercially vested interests. Only certain problems are addressed, only certain questions are asked, only certain results are actively marketed. (Sturdee, 2001: 70)

The vested interests and biases implicit in the way research is funded inevitably lead to many aspects of public sector work remaining without an adequate evidence base, and often without access to the resources necessary to construct it. The funding of research is not a level playing field.

Science and evidence

Sturdee (2001) and Laugharne (2002) agree that the kinds of mental health research that receive funding focus attention on some issues at the expense of others, and that this narrows debate about what constitutes evidence. Both discuss science as a social activity that has particular knowledge-generating processes which are dominated by the vested interests of medicine and the pharmaceutical industries, as well as those of researchers, practitioners and government. Sturdee argues that the advocates of EBP rely on a false ideal of science as an impartial seeker of truth, affording their kind of knowledge acquisition a particular authority. He, like Brown et al. (2003), suggests that the ideal of science as an impartial, disinterested and transparent means of developing knowledge has to be contextualised within the 'research market' that supports the investigations of interventions likely to benefit certain vested interests. This presents conceptual and practical difficulties for EBP when the climate of opinion, coupled with government policy, favours some kinds of research over others that might explore the aetiology and treatment of psychological problems in different ways. Brown et al. go further and say that EBP's 'terrier-like adherence' to RCTs 'reflects a governing value that favours science and medicine and disadvantages allied health care' (2003: 96–7). Sturdee gives the example of research into medication compared with research into non-drug treatments:

> The effect is to create a social movement away from a liberal conception of psychiatric practice (in which science is an adjunct) towards a more oppressive conception of psychiatric practice as being dominated by scientific considerations. (2001: 71)

He suggests that EBP is therefore likely to yield clear winners and losers, specifically because of the centrality of 'disease entities' that conform to the diagnostic criteria of DSM-IV and ICD-10. These, according to Finzen (2002), reflect the socio-cultural values of America, DSM having been constructed by various committees of the American Society of Psychiatry and ICD by the World Health Organisation neither being 'the result of scientific work that matches the criteria for EBM', (2002: 26). Sturdee proposes that diagnostic categories of 'illness' and treatment, such as schizophrenia, and the practices and activities linked with them, are likely to flourish within this model and in the present climate, while other difficulties and practices less amenable to neat categorisation, such as anxiety, and those less amenable to change, such as severe and enduring mental health problems, all of which are difficult to study according to the precepts of EBP, will struggle. He suggests that therapies which challenge the 'disease entities' of DSM-IV or ICD-10 (as does art therapy; see Dudley, 2004) 'will lose credibility and ultimately decline' (Sturdee, 2001: 78) and mental health care become a loose set of disciplines that compete for credibility and status within the EBP framework.

McLeod (2001) argues that the positivist approach to knowledge acquisition dominates research in the psychological therapies, outcome research having been governed by the assumptions of medicine. He says that this will probably continue because RCTs represent 'the core values of modern bureaucratic forms of governance' (McLeod, 1999: 158). RCTs are privileged because their structure fits the homogeneity of bio-behavioural systems of diagnosis and because they give supposedly reliable information about outcomes that is required by managers which are, in turn, intimately linked to government policies. The demand for performance indicators came from the political argument that taxpayers have a right to know how their money is being spent, public accountability of this kind being central to democracy, and from a managerial wish to make different parts of an organisation accountable without direct contact with, or detailed knowledge of, its work (Hammersley, 2004). This political and managerial requirement fits with the single trajectory of quantitative outcome research and, as Silverman (2000) says, quantitative methods reflect the research approach of government agencies.

Modernism and postmodernism

Sturdee (2001) and Laugharne (2002) progress the discussion about the underlying assumptions and pervasive influence of EBP, offering a refreshing critique of its positivist and essentially modernist philosophy. Laugharne argues that the notion of 'scientific evidence' that underpins EBP is a modernist concept and that EBM is an essentially modernist paradigm. Modernism is a philosophical movement that emerged from the Enlightenment which challenged existing world views and social and religious systems in a rational, material and scientific manner. It had hugely beneficial effects: methods of production improved, technology developed, prosperity increased and there were important advances in medicine and healthcare. However, Laugharne describes modernism as seeking universal absolutes that derive from a single narrative trajectory, quoting Lyotard's (1984) view of science as a meta-narrative that assumes its truths are superior to others. He takes up the postmodern rejection of such meta-narratives and of concepts such as universality and objectivity, challenging the 'disinterested' nature of research and the consequences of this kind of knowledge acquisition. Laugharne considers them as both futile and unacceptable and proposes instead that there are many truths that derive from different perspectives – from users, their carers, the differing members of multi-disciplinary teams, managers and policy makers – all of whom cite different kinds of evidence to support their views.

This view of modernism and the espousal of difference implicit in postmodernism may seem to deny the undoubted benefits of the post-Enlightenment world, but for me there is a ring of truth in the critique of medicine's modernist faith in the absolute knowledge science seems to offer and its fit with the basic assumptions of EBP. EBM's roots are in the modernist paradigm and medicine's ideology 'remains relentlessly modernist' (Brown et al., 2003: 278). This is not to say that science and EBP should be rejected wholesale, rather that a postmodern view suggests that the limitations and temporary, provisional nature of knowledge in all its forms should be acknowledged and that some sources of information and knowledge, some kinds of evidence, should not be privileged over others. Different kinds of evidence should co-exist and the multiplicity of viewpoints from medicine, psychopharmacology, users, purchasers, carers and the public should be acknowledged. The use of multiple perspectives, as in nursing and allied health care, 'challenges the grand narrative of the medical profession' (2003: 279) and creates an 'overall narrative of mental health care provision' (Laugharne, 2002: 56). 'Evidence' can be drawn from RCTs, but it can also be drawn from the multiplicity of research methods available across the sectors and disciplines in which practitioners work. This begs an important question: what exactly do we mean by 'evidence'?

What is 'evidence'?

No more than a momentary search reveals that there are differing kinds of evidence: circumstantial, hearsay and indirect, not to mention that which is self-evident. A dictionary definition of 'evidence', taken at random, offers us:

1. a) an outward sign b) something that furnishes proof; specifically something legally submitted to a tribunal to ascertain the truth of a matter;
2. one who bears witness (*Merriam-Webster Online* at www.webster.com).

There are immediate associations with law which, in western culture, is situated within a public demonstration or process that seeks to prove a 'truth', either through showing something that conveys convincing knowledge or by speaking from personal experience. This begs another question: what is meant by 'proof'? Our dictionary source answers:

1. a) the cogency of evidence that compels acceptance by the mind of a truth or fact, b) the process or instance of establishing the validity of a statement especially by derivation from other statements in accordance with principles of reasoning;
2. something that induces certainty or establishes validity. (*Merriam-Webster Online*)

'Proof', then, is about establishing confidence about a fact or a statement. This can be done through statements, revealing another defining feature of 'evidence': that it explicitly involves 'witnesses', people telling their experiences firsthand, proof being something that furnishes 'testimony, a testament, a firsthand authentication of a fact, a solemn declaration usually made by a witness' (*Merriam-Webster Online*). Oral and written statements from witnesses furnish evidence in law, and it is only when such firsthand knowledge is not available that other kinds of evidence are drawn upon. This resonates powerfully with the importance of evidence from the 'firsthand witnesses' of treatment, the clients.

How and by whom is such evidence judged? Jackson (2001) gives a lawyer's view, describing its changing meaning over time and how it is currently viewed. He says that the current, adversarial system of 'free proof' – in which everything relevant is admitted, cross-examined and judged on the merits of the case by common-sense jurors – is critical because it checks an undue deference to experts and to 'scientific evidence', instead requiring the education and understanding of those making the judgement, that is, the jury. Verdicts must be acceptable to all those involved in a case and 'must command respect within the entire community' (2001: p. 15). Public confidence is crucial, especially in terms of the fairness of the process, and is achieved by all parties having a voice in the proceedings and contributing to the outcome, power balances being maintained and everything being open and transparent. However, Jackson adds that evidence is determined in uncertain conditions and, to prevent constant challenges to final decisions, some kinds of evidence are privileged over others. Those that are privileged are those afforded a particular value by the society of the time, for example, battle and ordeal were considered evidence of truth in early Europe, while in the late 17th century official, written records were privileged over oral testimony. In our times 'science may seem the new saviour' (2001: 25) over common-sense reasoning but, as Jackson remarks, 'scientists as much as other witnesses adhere to different interpretations of reality and what is accepted as scientific fact in one context is not necessarily accepted as such in another' (2001: 25). Evidence is socially determined.

Several authors explore what is meant by evidence in psychiatry (Bolton, 2002; James and Burns, 2002; Schmiedeback, 2002 in particular) considering what has constituted evidence about mental health care in Europe since the 17th century. He describes the work of Pinel, one of the first to adopt an empirical approach to knowledge acquisition through observation, description, comparison and classification of his patients' illnesses, a method later developed by Kraepelin and Freud. This approach was oriented towards understanding an illness, its aetiology and diagnosis, and the associated anatomical, physiological and neurological issues, rather than treating it. He goes on to describe how, during the latter half of the 20th century, attention moved from understanding mental health to investigating the effectiveness of treatments. Parallel to this were considerable developments in the statistical methods used in research. These two factors together led to a great increase in the number of RCTs in the late 1950s and changes in the kind of evidence sought. McLeod (2001) adds that the success of experimental research methods and statistics at that time was enhanced by the invention of calculating machines, computers and PCs which led to an understandable fascination with the potential of quantitative research methodologies. He notes too that these methods have been appropriated by powerful political groups, statistics having originated from a need to measure the income and possessions of the state. Priebe and Slade (2002b) draw attention to how different kinds of evidence are sought at different times, remarking on how outdated and amusing texts about mental health care from 100 years ago now seem, few having stood the test of time. They suggest that current beliefs about what constitutes 'evidence' of effective treatments of mental health problems will change too as the social processes of research and knowledge generation develop.

Schmiedeback's (2002) historical analysis usefully identifies three types of evidence in the history of mental health care. The first is based in and explores the social, cultural and political context of the times; the second is based in scientifically oriented methods and concerned with both understanding and treating mental health problems; and the third kind of evidence focuses on treatment alone and addresses neither the nature of a problem nor its context. The ideological and pragmatically driven, medically based paradigm of EBP requires the third kind of evidence alone. Its focus is on treatments and their outcomes, not on furthering the understanding of complex mental health problems, nor their contextual, social and cultural factors. It is this particular focus that has led to the continuing domination of RCTs because, as McLeod says, their legitimacy is 'politically and socially defined' (2001: 7) within and by the EBP framework. Brown et al. concur: 'Research evidence is only deemed to be relevant and acceptable if it reinforces the values and existing ideology of the professional groups involved' (2003: 98).

Such privileging of one kind of evidence does not constitute a fair and open process. The examination of evidence from the range of research methodologies, including that from firsthand witnesses and from other evidence-generating activities within the EBP cycle, and debate about them within a process that commands the respect of the communities it serves – the clients, their families and all those offering the treatments and services – would make for a far more egalitarian, less biased and methodologically robust system.

EBM originally arose from real concern about the quality of clinical practice and service provision in healthcare, but it is now widely accepted that its derivative, EBP, has been supported by a government-driven need to increase individual, professional accountability. Government policies during the 1990s sought to monitor all kinds of interventions and services through the development of internal marketplaces and the implementation of the EBP framework, initiating a period of huge systemic change. This sought to replace practitioners' capacity to make judgements with research-based protocols, effectively undermining the professions. The increased accountability of professionals to managers and funders has led to a shift in power and an increased emphasis on the (supposed) certainty and predictability offered by outcome research, all so that services can be seen to be doing the greatest good for the greatest number of people.

The evidence on which practices and services should now be based has three components: research, preferably from RCTs or other experiments; guidelines and/or standards; and audit. The first delineates practice likely to lead to the best outcomes while the others assure its implementation, its quality and the results of its delivery. All contribute to the cumulative evidence base of a discipline. But resources for generating the primary source of evidence, research, come from government and its agencies, from psychopharmacological companies and from charities. Research agendas, funding and what constitutes the 'best' evidence are directly linked to, and socially constructed by, government policies and systems, and by commercial interests. EBP implicitly supports the bio-behavioural model of care that assumes that superior truths are achieved through a particular form of research – the RCT. This may work within the framework of medicine but it disadvantages disciplines (like art therapy) and research (other than experiments) that operate outside the medical mainstream and in a cross-sectoral way. However, the grand narrative of medicine and its essentially modernist concept of single, unitary and causal truths is challenged in a number of ways: by the development of systems outside medicine that review the nature and quality of different kinds of evidence; by postmodernism's espousal of different kinds of care and 'voice'; and by the consequent inclusion of multiple, inclusive and provisional knowledge that comes from different kinds of primary research. As Slade and Priebe say: 'evidence-based mental health care' does not mean 'RCT-based mental health care' (2002: 229) and as a Minister for Health has remarked' '"Trust me, I'm a patient" should be the guiding principle of the (new) agenda' (Reid, 2003).

I think art therapists have no choice but to engage with EBP but believe that we should do so in full awareness of the principles and policies that situate EBP in the UK's public sector marketplace. Reviewing EBP's underlying assumptions and the systems that continue to drive its implementation enable what constitutes the 'best' evidence to be seen as socially constructed by medicine, management and government, and the paradigm to be understood as a contemporary social movement, as a product of history, as a process. Entering the EBP arena able to challenge and trouble the paradigm, its values, research priorities and blinkered view of 'evidence' will contribute to a shift in the paradigm and enable art therapists to adapt its framework to the discipline – to make it make sense for art therapy. How this might be achieved, and what might be encountered on the way, are the subjects of the next chapter.

2 Anxiety, empowerment and strategy

I have described how concern about widespread differences in practice and outcome in all areas of healthcare was the primary 'driver' of EBP and how, during the 1990s, government policies were developed that required practices in all state-based provision to be research based. Theoretically this has always been the case, the difference nowadays being that employers *require* that practitioners demonstrate, in particular ways, that their practice is based on certain kinds of research that have proved its clinical and cost effectiveness. What was once sufficient to say and show, now not only has to be written but also has to be 'proved' and continually monitored through quality-assurance procedures. In this chapter I explore a particular metaphor in EBP's discourse about 'soft' and 'hard' research that encapsulates some of the anxieties about EBP. I then consider how art therapists might respond, strategically and creatively, to EBP's imperatives.

Art therapists work cross-sectorally with a range of clients and employ a variety of different approaches. This makes for a rich practice that revels in its diversity, but different practitioners have different ideas about what they do, how they go about doing it and what their ultimate aims are. This is problematic because EBP requires a certain uniformity of practice and precision about goals and outcomes specific to different sectors and client populations. Outcome research requires standard, 'manualised' approaches, agreed aims and common means of establishing whether or not they have been achieved, all so that results can be generalised and good, effective practice disseminated and developed. Art therapists resist notions of uniformity, but adding this to the fact that, at the moment, the discipline cannot claim to be 'empirically supported', puts art therapy in an invidious and anxiety-provoking situation. Rustin (2001) described the anxieties that can be generated by the very word 'research': a fear of being 'found out', of being judged in an imaginary court and giving the wrong answer because the wrong research methods have been used, and because there is a paucity of good 'scientific' research. This seems to me to resonate with art therapy's current position. Huxley (2002) reviewed the 'evidence' in social care and established that, while there was a body of knowledge available, it was neither in the required EBP format nor was it widely known and implemented. Similarly, art therapy does have an evidence and knowledge base, it has a body of research, but it too is neither fully known nor articulated within the EBP framework.

However, in 1997 art therapy in the UK was able to demonstrate its 'knowledge base' when it produced evidence for the Council of Professions Supplementary to Medicine (now the Health Professions' Council/HPC) sufficient for it to become a state-regulated profession. This 'evidence' showed that the profession had reached maturity, for example through having an established and recognised governing body, the British Association of Art Therapists (BAAT), which advises government departments; relationships with colleagues in medicine and other professions; university-based, professionally accredited postgraduate trainings; a theoretical base to its practice; and a substantial literature that includes scholarly publications and showed an increasing involvement in research. Since then HPC has contributed to art therapy's evidence base through its *Standards of Proficiency* (2003a) and *Standards of Conduct, Performance and Ethics* (2003b). Recent years have also seen strategic policy documents that have recognised the important role of the arts therapies in the UK's health services (e.g. DoH, 2000). These clearly situate the arts therapies as some of the effective psychological therapies that make a valuable contribution to service provision (DoH, 2004). The DoH has also stated that users consistently place access to psychological services at the top of their list of unmet needs, citing MIND's 'My Choice' campaign that surveyed the extent of user choice in their treatment. Users listed art, music and drama therapy among their top five alternatives to medication, 75 per cent of respondents having found the arts therapies helpful (MIND, 2003).

All of the above have contributed hugely to art therapy's profile but the jury is still out about art therapy's effectiveness because the discipline does not yet have the critical mass of outcome research required by EBP. However, many psychological treatments in the health, social, penal and educational systems, with many more practitioners and longer research histories than art therapy, continue to have large gaps in their research literature. These are thought to be impossible to fill and leave practitioners with much to learn about how best to implement EBP. It has been made clear that the NHS does not intend to develop a list of 'validated', evidence-based therapies but:

> it is unacceptable for the NHS to provide any therapy or service which declines to submit itself to research evaluation. Practitioners and researchers alike must accept the challenge of evidence-based practice, one result of which is that treatments which are shown to be ineffective are discontinued. (Parry and Richardson, 1996: 43)

This rather chilling statement is followed by an acknowledgement that achieving EBP in the psychological therapies, and inferentially in art therapy, is not easy, not only because of an absence of the particular kind of research required but also because it can be difficult to implement research findings. This is because, first, there is often a gap between practice and research; second, because clinicians tend to be pretty entrenched in what they do; and third, because RCTs have their limitations and are only appropriate when a therapy is well developed, and when research exploring that therapy is pretty well on too (Parry, 2000a: 64). Nonetheless time is rolling on and, although the EBP paradigm is the subject of vigorous critique and challenge, the evidence base for all practices across all sectors is being developed. Art therapists cannot afford to fall behind.

The need for targeted, efficient, clinically and cost-effective services was first discussed in relation to psychotherapy in the early 1980s. Parloff (1982) expressed significant concern about psychotherapy research in American mental health care. He suggested a strategic shift in researchers' attention away from the pursuit of knowledge about the processes of psychotherapy and towards the pursuit of evidence on which policy makers could make fiscal decisions, reluctantly concluding that this was a necessity because process-oriented research was unlikely to have any influence on policies whose focus was the containment of costs. He advocated large-scale RCTs investigating which therapy is the most clinically and cost effective for particular patient populations so that healthcare managers and insurance companies had evidence on which to base their economic decisions about what treatments to make available for which patients, an approach now at the heart of EBP. Parloff concluded this was necessary because 'research findings can be expected to exert all the impact of a quixotic Bambi planted firmly in the path of the onrushing Godzilla of cost-containment policies' (1982: 725).

A while later Parry (1995) replied. She urged psychotherapy researchers to resist capitulation to the clinical and cost-effectiveness imperatives of EBP in the NHS, arguing that the fragmented nature of psychotherapy and counselling provision was in part to do with the scepticism of those who believed these services were a luxury the financially strapped NHS could not afford. Parry pointed to the major emphasis on EBP in government policy on mental health during the early 1990s, saying that it was a well-intentioned move to commission research for the benefit of the general public that would lead to well-organised, effective psychological services. She argued for outcome studies, but also for a pluralistic approach to research in the psychotherapies that included descriptive, naturalistic research and case study methods. This required 'psychotherapists from all professions and schools to sink their differences enough to work together with commitment, patience, integrity and knowledge. That can happen, and when it does, it's a power-ful combination. Bambi, hold on in there' (1995: 167).

The picture that Parloff and Parry paint of Bambi meeting Godzilla has often captured my imagination. Both authors use the image to represent a particularly hostile and fearful sense of what might happen when curiosity-driven and/or process-oriented research about the interior of psychotherapy, represented by the vulnerable Bambi, encounters policy-related questions about clinical and cost effectiveness in the form of an omnipotent and destructive Godzilla. Perhaps Parloff's intention was to demonstrate the overwhelming nature of the financial 'drivers' in American mental health care and so stimulate researchers into partic-ular, perhaps defensive, activity. However, Bambi, representing process-oriented psychotherapy research, has a particular cultural resonance in the western world to do with vulnerability, loss and hunting. Parloff makes a direct and powerful connection between this and a representation of economic and pragmatic imperatives – Godzilla – that is likely to be construed not only as omnipotent and violent but also as 'other', originating as it does from a non-western culture. This metaphorical meeting creates a powerfully resonant image of helplessness in the face of an overwhelmingly destructive force. In Parloff's scenario Bambi looks set to take on the alien Godzilla and he stands little chance of success. Indeed, an ani-mated film entitled *Bambi Meets Godzilla* (Newland, 1969) in its 30 seconds of running time shows Bambi happily grazing in the woods until he is completely flattened by an enormous reptilian foot. In neither paper are these two 'actors' explored: they are there to illustrate the danger facing a defenceless creature when it meets a rampaging monster and thus to make a strategic point about the timely use of particular kinds of investigation. These representations need to be related to the whole of their respective stories, their characters and to the impetus behind the films because all is not as it first appears: Godzilla is more than a wantonly destructive freak of nature and Bambi is not quite the pushover he seems. This involves some storytelling, and so I ask you, the reader, to bear with me while we revisit the tales of these two, very different, creatures.

The evolution of Bambi

Everything about Bambi is contained in one seminal film made during the early 1940s by the Walt Disney Studios. The movie begins with everyone in the forest gathering to see the new-born fawn. This is the almost archetypal image of Bambi: newly born, defenceless, and resting in the protective gaze of his mother – a powerful evocation of maternal love. As he begins to grow Bambi is taken to the meadow by his mother. This is an inviting, wide-open space in which to play but, as his mother warns, it is also potentially dangerous because they are unprotected. Here they meet other deer and the stag, his father, 'the great Prince of the Forest'. Bambi also meets Faline, a young female deer, but their play is cut short by the arrival of man in the meadow. In the resulting panic Bambi is separated from his mother but is guided back to the safety of the forest and his mother by the stag. Winter comes and during a thaw Bambi and his mother return to the meadow but man and the hunt return. Bambi and his mother flee; there is the sound of a shot as Bambi runs and runs. He searches in the snow, calling for his mother. The stag appears again and says to Bambi, 'Your mother can't be with you anymore'. This moment of maternal death is doubtless the one we remember (I certainly do; it was hard work watching the film again), and indeed McGreal (1993) describes the terrified cries of children when Bambi's mother is shot. Then the scene changes and it is spring. Bambi is growing up and he meets Faline again. He fights a rival young stag for her but the hunt arrives and Faline is pursued. Bambi saves her but is shot and then trapped by a forest fire. Bambi's father appears once more and together they escape to an island. Bambi, Faline, his father and their friends are safe and the forest soon celebrates the arrival of two young fawns. The last scenes are of Bambi and his father standing on a crag, looking out over the now calm, peaceful forest. The 'great prince' departs, ceding rule of the forest to the adult Bambi. What a seering image of psychotherapy research!

Disney's *Bambi* was made during the early 1940s when America was preparing to enter World War II and was distributed while many fathers were away and mothers were, to all intents and purposes, single parents. Payne (1995) notes the power of the opening sequence of Bambi's birth, the scene created representing the status quo where mothers talk, children play and fathers remain the authority. What is contrasted in Bambi is the idyllic world of animals and the cruel and violent world of humans, paralleled by the stereotypically intimate world of mothers and children and the harsh, wider world of men and fathers. McGreal describes Bambi as 'the highest form of anthropomorphism' (1993: 56) where the heroes are animals, characters culturally associated with children, adding that the film therefore represents an 'overwhelming nostalgia for our own pasts' (1993: 56), for the safe world of our childhoods.

Lutts (1992) discusses the significant influence of Bambi in shaping American attitudes towards woodland life through anthropomorphic representation. He, like Hastings (1996), debates the influence that Bambi has had on the anti-hunting movement in the United States, exploring how the nature represented is far from real. All the woodland creatures are furry and cuddly – no species dominance, predator and prey, nature 'red in tooth and claw' here. The threat in Bambi comes from man, the hunter; he is the only predator who kills, and he does so indiscriminately and unseen. Lutts also explores how elements of reality were retained within the anthropomorphism, for example through the solitary life of Bambi's father, appearing and disappearing without warning which, says Lutts, is key to his survival: 'To be visible is to be vulnerable' (1992: 163) and to be mature is to learn how to survive. Lutts discusses how Bambi is associated with 'something soft and sentimental, even wimpy' (1992: 168). Bambi remains a spotted fawn for three quarters of the film, the anthropomorphism equating the proportions of the fawn with those of a human infant; no wonder most of us immediately picture the cute and vulnerable Bambi rather than the mature stag. Both Lutts and Hastings discuss the moment of Bambi's mother's death as the most traumatic and effective moment of the film and how we are invited, perhaps for the first time, to put ourselves in the position of the hunted.

The use of Bambi to represent process-oriented psychotherapy research associates it with separation and maternal death and the awe-inspiring distance of a great, powerful and absent father. The almost archetypal image of the vulnerable, helpless creature stays in our memory and we forget that Bambi grows up and learns; he enters the wide-open dangerous spaces, encounters loss, and survives a number of life-threatening encounters to take on his rightful mantle of Great Prince of the Forest. Bambi explores the intrinsic difficulties of life that continues despite trauma, but is said to represent nostalgia for the past, for childhood (McGreal, 1993). This makes me wonder if some of the ambivalence about outcome research is associated with nostalgia for times when practice was not so heavily scrutinised and jobs were relatively safe. Relating this to art therapy reminds me of the rather romantic image of the discipline as anti-psychiatry and anti-establishment. The necessary critique of the status quo implicit in this position is an important part of art therapy's discourse but, if associated with a wish to disassociate the discipline from all that it might mean to engage with EBP, I think could leave art therapy dangerously outside contemporary practice and discourse in mental health care. In 1987 Waller suggested that art therapy was in its adolescence. Perhaps everything that orthodox EBP represents requires art therapists to grow up rather fast, like Bambi. Perhaps we too feel hunted by faceless others in the wide-open, dangerous space of the meadow: the managers, the audit teams, the Cochrane Institute and all those who ask, 'does it work?' and 'are you doing it properly?' Perhaps this leaves us longing for the safety and security of our profession's 'childhood' and for the fantasised protective father that can lead us to safety. The deer become vulnerable when they make themselves visible. Might we fear that to be seen, to 'stand up and be counted', literally and metaphorically, in the effectiveness-oriented arena of EBP, could lead to our downfall?

The evolution of Godzilla

The character Godzilla has a 50-year history and many films to his credit. He was first created in 1954 in Japan's Toho Studios and has become a cult figure in Japan, with additional, occasional appearances in the United States. Filmic legend has it that Godzilla is a dinosaur, buried deep in the seabed in the Pacific, who is irradiated by atomic explosions that release him from 100 million years of hibernation in an infinitely more powerful and frightening form than before. Godzilla is a freak, an alien, with huge taloned feet, radioactive breath that burns buildings and a tail that demolishes several skyscrapers with a single swipe. In many Japanese movies he is repeatedly shown as an indestructible force that annihilates everyone and everything in his path (Glut, 1978; Kalat, 1997).

Anisfield (1995) and Noreiga (1987) explore how the whole genre of Godzilla movies developed and the monster evolved. Noreiga describes how, in the first Japanese Godzilla films in the 1950s, the monster was associated with something dark and evil, but that gradually he changed from being a terrifying, dinosaur-like beast to being a rather sympathetic creature, more of a bumbling, gorilla-like person than a monster. As the films evolve, sympathy with Godzilla develops; he begins to have a personality, he has a son, and the Japanese attempt to understand and appease him, even to care for him when wounded in battle. From a monster that threatened and destroyed Japan, Godzilla was transformed into a monster that protected Japan from even worse monsters (Anisfield, 1995). He was no longer killed, blasted off the earth with the same weaponry that created him, but instead chose to leave once the battle was won and return to the sea until Japan needed him again.

Noreiga (1987), Anisfield (1995) and Kalat (1997) agree that the whole genre of Japanese Godzilla films draws a direct equation between the monster and Japan's nuclear history. Noreiga describes the socio-cultural environment in which the first Godzilla films were made in the 1950s, that is, following the dropping of two atomic bombs by the USA on Hiroshima and Nagasaki in 1945, the American occupation of Japan until 1952, and US atomic tests in the Pacific in 1952 and 1954. He argues that the Japanese versions of Godzilla gradually absorb the monster into Japanese culture, embracing the violence in the monster and the violence through which he came into being. In Japan, monsters are not construed as 'other'; they can be friends and heroes, and dragons are befriended rather than slain (as in the European story of St George). Noreiga associates this with the particularities of the Japanese language that merge self and other.

Godzilla in America has a rather different history. His first appearance was in 1954 in a much-edited version of the Toho Studio's first Godzilla movie. Explicit references to Nagasaki were deleted and substantial new footage, American actors and allusions to King Kong were added. This, according to Noreiga (1987), shifted the film's narrative towards an American agenda that addressed a sense of guilt about its nuclear warfare against Japan through the projection of guilt and blame on to the monster. Gradually Godzilla came to be portrayed in American cartoons and comics as a fire-eating dragon rather than a monster with irradiated breath – a more dinosaur-like beast that suggested Godzilla's existence millions of years prior to the splitting of the atom and obscured the nuclear allusions embodied in the Japanese Godzilla (Kalat, 1997: 156). In the American versions of Godzilla the monster and his violence are pushed away, destroying any causal relationship between Godzilla and his creator (Noreiga, 1987; Kalat, 1997). Godzilla remains different: he is other.

Wells (2000) describes these and other 'Creature Feature' movies of 1950s and 1960s America (e.g. King Kong) as addressing the 'Us and Them' dialectic of the post-World War II atomic period. Noreiga suggests that these films represent America's exploration of its support for nuclear weapons and the Cold War. The freaks and monsters that embody 'otherness' are created by atomic testing but then destroyed by nuclear missiles, creating the 'circuitous logic of the arms race . . . The monster created by the bomb requires the bomb to kill the monster' (1987: 67). Sontag (2001) suggests that these movies allow a moral simplicity: the viewer is taken away from everyday life and allowed the fantasy of fighting a 'good war' where international unity against a mutual enemy co-exists with a longing for peace. Here the monster becomes an agent of unity that allows the simultaneous expression of cruel and amoral feelings together with a sense of superiority over the freaks, monsters and alien beings.

The 1997 Hollywood version of Godzilla is a lizard-like monster-come-dinosaur that owes more to *Jurassic Park* and *Alien* than to the Japanese Godzilla films. However, this Godzilla explicitly refers to its atomic origins, associating them with Chernobyl and Mururoa Atoll. Wells (2000) says that this film revisits America's historical anxieties about nuclear power that re-emerged in *Jurassic Park* in 1993, but here the nuclear horror is no longer local (to America and Japan) but global. However, in this Godzilla there is a distinct thread of sympathy for the monster. Godzilla travels 'home' to New York in order to reproduce and meets the sympathetic American hero, the encounter being accompanied by stirring, poignant music and the distinct possibility of a relationship. However, the American military attack and Godzilla retaliates. In the resulting chase Godzilla is represented as a sentient being: there are repeated shots of the eyes as Godzilla looks around and thinks, evades missiles, chases and swats helicopters, even managing to engineer the military's destruction of their own equipment. Other moments build sympathy for the monster. One is when Godzilla finds all the newly hatched baby Godzillas dead: Godzilla howls in maternal anguish and begins to chase the hero who has helped bring about their destruction. The moment of Godzilla's eventual death is poignant as well as triumphant: the hero and Godzilla look at each other again as Godzilla dies – a light, quite literally, goes out in Godzilla's eye. But right at the end one remaining egg cracks and a baby Godzilla emerges, doubtless to fight another day. It all adds up to a very strange image of effectiveness-oriented outcome research.

Knowing and owning the 'other'

The meeting of Bambi and Godzilla is an extraordinarily powerful image of an indestructible, irradiated monster meeting a vulnerable and bereaved fawn. Economic and pragmatic imperatives are equated with an essentially timeless, violent, 'hard' and masculine 'other' that needs containing or destroying lest it kill off the vulnerable, 'soft', female 'self' of process-oriented psychotherapy research. Look at the language: Brophy describes Godzilla as 'energy without control' whose task is 'to plainly destroy' (2000: 41). Parloff (1982: 725) echoes this in his description of the 'onrushing Godzilla' of fiscal realities hurrying to encounter the 'quixotic' Bambi of psychotherapy research, that is: 'an enthusiastic visionary, [a] person who utterly neglects his interests in comparison with honour or devotion' (*Pocket Oxford Dictionary*, 1987: 732).

The language alone begs the question about how the small, all-too-human Bambi – who tends not to look after himself and is rather idealistic – is supposed to fight such an uncontrollable, indiscriminately destructive monster. There can be no doubt that Parloff used this rather alarming metaphorical encounter to demonstrate the necessity for effectiveness-oriented research, but I suggest that it also creates a potentially damaging and fearful resonance with powerlessness and destruction. Even if residual, such a response could exacerbate hostile and paranoid attitudes towards entering the EBP arena and engaging with discourse, research and quality assurance activities in a way that could be both productive and empowering for art therapists. If we are to avoid this it is useful to deconstruct the narratives and characters of these films and place them in their wider historical, political and cultural contexts.

Horror and monster movies have long been correlated with times of recession and war. Hill (1958), Sontag (2001) and Carroll (1981) link such films with economic uncertainty and depression and with the expression of powerlessness and anxiety. Wells calls the history of horror films 'essentially a history of anxiety in the twentieth century' (2000: 3), illustrating the concerns and phobias arising in a society dominated by technological and economic determinism. He describes monsters as central to horror films as they enable exploration of the struggle between good and evil, the monster representing particular threats, fears and contradictions that disrupt and cause the breakdown of the status quo. Wells says that monster movies have 'flourished in periods of social difficulty or collapse' (2000: 22) because the monsters ignore the usual social world and so are constantly challenging and subversive, bringing our worst fears to the fore so that the audience cannot remain complacent or accepting: 'The monster is the anachronism of certain tools and technologies in the wrong hands at the wrong time. The true horror lies in the fact that these things cannot be uninvented, and that their impacts are inevitable' (2000: 48–9). Such is EBP. It too is flourishing in times of economic uncertainty, of immense pressures on resources and widely differing approaches to care. It too is a 'tool and technology' that disrupts the status quo and challenges us so that we cannot be complacent, and it too cannot be uninvented nor its impact denied.

Sontag (2001) explored a related techno-phobic theme. Anxieties of contemporary life are addressed in sci-fi films' 'negative imagination' of an impersonal and emotionless 'it' or 'they' who take over the world. Sontag describes the resultant cool and mechanistic being as 'undead', someone or something that loses its humanity but becomes more efficient: 'the very model of technocratic man, purged of all emotions, volitionless, tranquil' (2001: 222). Reaction to such filmic narrative is ambivalent: on one hand there is horror but on the other there is the attraction of 'the ascendancy of reason over feelings, the idealization of teamwork and the consensus-creating activities of science' (2001: 222). However, she goes on to say that sci-fi films critique neither the society that depersonalises and then projects the depersonalisation on to an alien 'it', nor science as a social activity that is linked with political and social worlds. I wonder if the image of the depersonalised automaton is similarly associated with fears of a prescriptive approach to practice that might develop through EBP, outcomes being related to a narrowly defined 'dose' of art therapy administered in a rigid way that loses the unique encounter between client, therapist and the art process so that an undead practice ensues.

Wells (2000) says that every monster is the promise of death and demise. They embody difference and exemplify the other. They are related to us yet they constantly threaten. Noreiga (1987) considers how the Japanese Godzilla movies enable exploration of the repressed but not destroyed aspects of the Japanese self through projection on to the other. Indeed Brophy (2000) suggests that the playing of Godzilla by an actor in the later Japanese films supports the audience's identification with an other who has the power to be extraordinarily destructive but who chooses to harness the energy and use it constructively. Although exploration of otherness can define the self, it avoids the culture of the other and consideration of the self as other in another culture. Le Guin suggests that when the sci-fi other is construed as different, whether annihilating, lumbering monsters or cool, mechanistic aliens, 'your fear of it may come out as hatred, or as awe – reverence' (1979: 88). Hence there is either absolute opposition and a need to destroy – 'the only good alien is a dead alien' (1979: 88) – or there are wise beings who come to earth to advise and rescue and are placed on a pedestal. Whether the other is hated or deified, either way its reality and equality are denied: 'You have made it into a thing, to which the only possible relationship is a power relationship. And thus you have fatally impoverished your own reality. You have, in fact, alienated yourself' (1979: 89).

For art therapists to view the paradigm that is EBP as other, as something that has nothing to do with the discipline or its practices could, in my view, be extraordinarily counterproductive. Indeed, to believe that art therapy will flourish in the current climate without engagement with the challenges and questions that EBP presents is to have, as Parloff said, 'a dazzling degree of wilful optimism' (1982: 720). While this is not the position most art therapists take, I think that to either fear or revere the other of EBP – as a destructive force or as a potential saviour – and to accept the paradigm and its practices in an unquestioning way, will result in inequality and alienation and the activities, their implementation and the associated power will not belong to art therapists but instead be assigned to others. In my view it is critical that art therapists own EBP. This can be achieved through participation in EBP discourse at grassroots level and through the adjustment of its frameworks to fit the discipline, as other, non-medical sectors have begun to do. Godzilla, as a metaphor for the evaluation of what is and is not efficient, cost-effective and clinically effective practice, may be the bomb in our midst that represents our feared and fantasised destruction in times of uncertainty and change, but effectiveness-oriented inquiry appropriate to the discipline could protect what we know to be sound and effective practice, providing we harness the power of EBP and engage with it critically, on our own terms, no longer considering it as something imposed upon us that is potentially destructive and to be hated and avoided.

Parloff's image is of Bambi and Godzilla encountering each other one-to-one. Maybe this too has some resonance, especially with those art therapists working single-handed, but art therapy is a worldwide practice with international, national and local communities and a developing body of research. We also have a community of colleagues in the arts therapies, the psychological therapies, the Allied Health Professions and the multidisciplinary teams in the different sectors where we work. I think that if art therapists work collectively with each other and with colleagues, then it becomes possible to withstand the demands of EBP, indeed to challenge the 'grand narrative' it represents and, in so doing, preserve the particularities of the discipline. What is important is to engage, neither colluding with an 'us and them' unity against EBP nor acceding to its demands in an uncritical way.

The prevailing image of Godzilla is the terrifyingly powerful, indestructible monster, but Godzilla develops. Initially a wantonly destructive monster, something to be hated and feared, he becomes a beast with a purpose: to protect as well as destroy. In the broader socio-cultural context the role of monsters is to remind us that 'nothing is certain; all the benchmarks of normality and the preservation of the status quo are being interrogated and redefined' (Wells, 2000. 34). This exactly describes the exigencies of the public sector nowadays and the influence of EBP on our work. Bambi preserves a social order where the social system of the authoritative male remains. Godzilla disrupts it, representing a fear of the unknown, of destruction and death, of forces beyond our control that lead to the collapse of the status quo. Monsters appear – in this instance in our literature – at times of economic uncertainty when there is significant change and challenge. But there is more to the representation of Bambi and Godzilla than initially meets the eye. Bambi moves from vulnerability to strength to become the Great Prince of the Forest who has experienced various trauma, grown up and survived. Godzilla becomes the not-always-so-unreasonable, sometimes vulnerable, heroic and helpful Godzilla whose energy and power can be harnessed. Thus the 'self' of process-oriented therapy research might not be quite so helpless and vulnerable as is feared, and the 'other' that inquires about effectiveness and efficiency might well prove to be a powerful ally. A more positive prognosis for EBP in art therapy emerges, albeit one that acknowledges the difficulties of entering a relationship with something initially experienced as 'other' and which requires significant learning, change and challenges to art therapy's, and EBP's, status quo.

Plainly art therapy cannot quickly conjure up the research base that EBP orthodoxy requires. Research of all kinds takes time and funding priorities need to be established and strategies devised. Parry and Richardson (1996), in accordance with the research trajectory of EBP, prioritise the economic evaluation of psychological treatments and attention to clinical effectiveness that includes the development of outcome measures appropriate to psychodynamic change. Single case studies, heuristic studies and an explicit commissioning strategy of services and research into therapeutic needs across the lifespan are also recommended, though perhaps with less urgency. What might art therapy's priorities be, and how might practitioners respond to EBP's imperatives?

Face to face with Godzilla

I think art therapists have to prioritise evidence-generating activities that will capture the attention of key audiences, that is, the policy makers and managers – those whose interest is in effectiveness. The discipline already has a few RCTs and others are under way but these take time and, meanwhile, different kinds of short- to medium-term projects could make a significant contribution to the discipline's evidence base. These need not be entirely outcome-oriented as art therapy urgently needs research that describes the particularities of practice with different client populations. This means case studies that are detailed, specific and systematic which address outcome and include follow-up; these can be narrative and naturalistic studies or single-case experimental designs. Art therapists sometimes get uncomfortable at this point and turn away from the beastly other of empiricism, but single-case experimental research can sit comfortably alongside routine clinical work and is a relatively speedy route to establishing a baseline of effectiveness. Such studies need not conform to the standard format that reports no more than before and after measures and rarely describes the intervention itself; they could include narrative description, images and display, and the client's voice too so that the interiority of art therapy is documented as well as its results, combining quantitative and qualitative methods in a way that fits the discipline's values and norms. This, in EBP's research trajectory, can lead to case series that document process and outcome in similar ways that can then inform subsequent cohort studies and, eventually, RCTs.

I think art therapy outcome research can utilise the well established routines of outcome evaluation in allied disciplines and agree with art therapists who say that there is much to learn from positivist approaches (Gantt, 1997; Juillard, 1998; Carolan, 2001; Dubowski, 2001; Kaplan, 2001). Single-case experimental designs are well within the capacities of art therapists and are relatively easy to do especially when, as in some services, evaluation routinely occurs alongside clinical work. Research like this and modest cohort evaluations can draw on the expertise of colleagues familiar with standard psychological, social and educational tests that measure change and development. Some might protest that these are crude and inappropriate instruments that do not capture the outcomes of art therapy, but do we not seek to alleviate our clients' symptoms and enable change?

Measures of behaviour, social adaptation and educational attainment might seek to 'normalise' behaviour and development but does this mean that we do not work towards improvements in clients' capacity to function in their world? I think that the development of art therapy-specific methods and outcome measures are issues for the longer term. In the meantime symptom inventories and standard psychological, behavioural, educational and social measures have already been used to good effect in art therapy outcome research (e.g. Tibbets and Stone, 1990; Rosal, 1993; Rosal et al., 1997; Sheppard et al., 1998; Richardson et al., forthcoming) and I see no reason why this should not continue.

A note of caution needs to be added, however, as outcome research, which by its nature often requires interdisciplinary work, needs careful negotiation so that the values and practices of art therapy are not compromised. Indeed Dubowski (2001) has suggested that it may be unreasonable to expect arts therapists to research their own effectiveness. He, like Karkou (2002), does not entirely sub-scribe to the notion of a practitioner/researcher. I have mixed views about this; the majority of British art therapy research has been qualitative, conducted by lone researchers who are also practitioners, although initiatives such as Clinical Outcome Routine Evaluation (CORE System Group, 1998) and the Art Therapy Practice Research Network (ATPRN) enable practitioners to take part in research through gathering and pooling data on a scale beyond the capacities of solo researchers or research groups. In my view these do not preclude individual prac-titioners from conducting simple outcome studies and documenting the nature and extent of art therapy service provision.

It is all about language, all about audience. Art therapists have to think, act and write with a political purpose in mind. This is critical because, at the moment, our primary audience – the policy makers and managers – are outside art therapy. This requires the use of unfamiliar voices and methods and curious, unpoetic lan-guage to describe practice. It can be done, and it can be done our way, as a few American and British art therapy researchers have shown. American art therapists have engaged with outcome studies much more than British art therapists and developed an inclusive and eclectic approach to research. Some prioritise outcome investigation and, interestingly, argue that normative baselines of artistic ability and development across the lifespan and between different cultural groups must be established if this kind of research is going to relate meaningfully to art therapy (Gantt, 1998; Carolan, 2001; Kaplan, 2001). Art therapists in the UK have not developed a parallel interest in experimental, outcome research and art-based measurements, having been more interested in qualitative, process-oriented research that explores practice and develops theory. It was just this kind of psy-chotherapy research that Parloff critiqued in his call for strategic investigations of psychotherapy's clinical and cost effectiveness. A parallel shift in art therapy research might be what Males (1980) termed a 'defensive assessment', but out-come studies do not preclude research about the interior of art therapy practice that use more familiar methods and language. I think art therapy needs to develop a multi-voiced evidence base, one that includes an outcomes dialect. This does not mean that the discipline should privilege this effectiveness-oriented art ther-apy voice, although others outside the profession might, nor that the theory and practice of art therapy are eroded or compromised; rather it recognises that the sceptical world outside the discipline needs convincing in its own terms, in its own language. Getting to know Godzilla, getting to grips with a new language, even enjoying the process as we establish the effectiveness of what we do and ensuring that this is not alienated from the discipline's existing discourses, then becomes both possible and eminently worthwhile. We can continue developing our own kinds of evidence and gather it in creative and imaginative ways, but we can make 'other' kinds of evidence our own too.

And now for something completely different

One day, after an afternoon immersed in reading about systematic reviews, single-case experimental designs and critiques of RCTs, I longed to leave the world of evidence and therapy. I felt stuffed full of rhetoric, bored, dispirited, my capacity for thought deadened by the apparent logic and remorseless tunnel vision of everything to do with EBP. I enjoy research, would go so far as to say I love it actu-ally, but orthodox EBP can be so rigid, so hidebound by political and professional rhetoric, such a bandwagon. Pragmatically I don't think art therapists have a choice but to engage with EBP – it's a simple matter of survival – and it could, eventually, be enormously helpful to the profession, but the struggle sometimes gets the better of me. In such a mood I rummaged through my video backlog and found a programme I'd forgotten to watch: *20 Years of the Turner Prize* by Matthew Collings. What a relief it was. How interesting to listen to Nicholas Serota describing a taxi driver dropping him off at the Tate Modern, switching his lights on and off and saying, 'Is that the Turner Prize winner this year?' How stimulating to wonder about beds and painting and videos and excrement and photographs pinned on a wall and rooms just full of stuff all of which seemed delightfully familiar to me, and doubtless would to other art therapists who think about these and other such things in their clinical practice, and here it was as part of the postmodern debate about the contemporary art world.

The Turner Prize was known and enjoyable territory for me that was somehow connected to what makes art therapy what it is: a unique intervention that engages people with making and looking and thinking about art, about the mate-rial stuff that is made in the context of a therapeutic relationship but which exists within the *visual* culture, the social, political and cultural context that is Britain. It made me wonder all over again how on earth can this core activity, this funda-mental premise of the whole enterprise that is the profession of art therapy – ART – enter into a dialogue with EBP? Aren't they fundamentally at odds? Never mind the debate about Bambi, Godzilla and RCTs: this puts that in the shade.

Collings unpacked how the Turner Prize has enabled contemporary art to enter the public imagination, how art has become inclusive rather than exclusive through creating controversy and getting publicity. He describes art as 'dissing' traditions and hierarchies, poking at the edges of taboos and beliefs in a society that has increasing difficulty with authority. Art challenges old traditions and creates new ones, painting being one of many media competing alongside video, photography and film in contemporary art. Collings suggested that the Turner Prize gives the public a 'superficial gloss' about art, but wondered if this is so bad because it makes people curious and then they become involved. He described himself as an 'apologist' or explainer of art, but he also said that art is inexplicable. This, according to Collings, is a good thing because art is profound; it is a belief system, not entertainment, one that enables the world to be seen differently.

So how do we evidence that the entry into art that occurs in art therapy is a worthwhile and effective treatment? How do we show that art therapy also enables the world to be seen differently? That in its challenges to beliefs, taboos and authority, it can bring about change? Can an enterprise like art therapy, one that is often sceptical about the goals, values, procedures and terminology of diagnosis and treatment, find a creative synergy with a government-sponsored movement that is driven by the dominant paradigm of medicine, that supports the rise of policy makers and managers and seeks to micro-manage the professions and their practices? Art 'disses' traditions and hierarchies, and art therapists like to diss the traditions of psychiatric orthodoxy, yet here we are (or rather, here I am) trying to engage with a paradigm-cum-social movement that seeks conformity, that challenges old traditions but quickly replaces them with new ones and definitely places everything and everyone in hierarchies. How on earth can we cope with this tension, this pressure to buckle under and come up with the evidence that proves our worth, while our (or rather my) impulse is to challenge, nay rebel against such orthodoxies and conformities? Are we still the adolescents that Waller (1987) wrote about? Is this what it means to grow up? How do we ensure that the evidence we generate is meaningful and relevant to a clinical practice based in the making of art?

I found the work of Mulhall (1998) helped me think about this. She suggests that before identifying what evidence is needed a profession needs to define exactly what it (the profession) is, to establish what makes it unique. Only then can significant research questions be identified and the means of addressing them be determined. Juxtaposing this with Parry and Richardson's (1996) recommendation – that psychological services should differentiate between various types of therapy and services – made me think about what it is that makes art therapy unique and ask a few friends and colleagues what they thought too. Here is a summary of what we came up with:

- art and art therapy move between worlds; between interior and exterior spaces; between the painted world and the spoken world;
- art therapy rooms and studios offer particular kinds of physical space in which to be and to make art that encourages reverie, a mindful thoughtlessness that enables thoughtfulness;
- the sensory and sensual nature of art materials accesses somatic memory and therefore preverbal, presymbolic material; it can also help memory retention and enable a continuity of experience;
- art materials provoke a somatic and behavioural response that can be witnessed by the art therapist and so become able to be known;

- art is evidence of an act. This gives art therapy a unique, physical and tangible form whose artefacts survive, are touchable, visible and available for review. Art makes an interior monologue visible, creating the potential for dialogue (with self and/or another/others);
- art 'subverts' the conscious mind and reveals previously unconscious psychological relationships;
- making art within a therapeutic relationship gives clients a unique engagement with, and sense of agency in, the management of their psychological well being;
- art therapy engages and maintains clients not usually deemed to be 'psychologically minded' in a dynamically oriented therapy. Based in the public sector, it also works with clients from a wider class spectrum than other insight-oriented therapies;
- art therapy has a cumulative culture. Its theory and philosophy of practice are unique and come from a particular interweaving of art with social psychiatry and psychoanalysis;
- art therapists' primary discipline is usually outside health and social care, giving us a unique and particular 'take' on mental health issues.

What emerged is (of course) that the role and function of art are pivotal, but so too are the social backgrounds of many of art therapy's clients and the visual arts and humanities background of most art therapists that contrast with the science backgrounds of many of our colleagues. It is art therapy's 'alternativeness', its *difference* from the mainstreams of care that makes it unique and especially helpful for those who find it hard to engage with routine services. This makes it all the more important that we argue vigorously for, and continue to actively pursue, research that enables us to investigate art therapy's unique properties and distinctive applications. Edwards (1999) suggests that this can be achieved through closely observed case studies, though the visual and oral story telling that form the essence of clinical practice. He recommends that art therapists use a style or 'voice' that is comfortable, eschewing a 'scientific' approach if it is not appropriate for the topic. I entirely agree. Social and experientially based research that looks and listens, observes and documents what happens in art therapy is essential, but I would add that using visual research methods to collect, analyse and even present our research, inviting clients into the heart of the research process and privileging user voices, will also enable us to convey the particular sensibilities, properties and underlying culture of our practice that differentiates it from the mainstream of care, and from other psychological therapies. Such research would be opportune, especially given NICE's prioritising of research into an 'orphan' condition, treatment, patient group, setting or aspect of care that does not have evidence readily available (2003: 32).

This is all very well but many art therapists are encountering real pressures to provide evidence, now, of art therapy's effectiveness. Given the impossibility of generating the required research at speed, art therapists need strategies to manage this onrushing Godzilla. Clinical governance is key, that is to say, the secondary sequence of evidence-generating activities within the EBP cycle where practitioners can demonstrate that the primary evidence from research and other forms of knowledge *are* informing practice. Full, and public, engagement with the cycle will enable art therapists to say that they have conformed to the criteria for evidence-based disciplines because they will have:

- *Adopted* clinical guidelines for standard practice;
- *Ensured* that guidelines are informed by research and service evaluation;
- *Specified* the patient groups for which the service is appropriate;
- *Monitored* the outcomes of innovative treatments;
- *Audited* the key elements of standard practice (Parry and Richardson, 1996: 47, emphasis added)

Groups of art therapists can develop standards and clinical guidelines for local use (see Chapter 3), immersing themselves in art therapy's evidence base through the processes of critical appraisal and systematic review. Modest audits can demonstrate service-level effectiveness (see Chapter 4). A few accounts of art therapists' clinical governance activities have been published but I am aware, anecdotally, that much more is happening than is entering the public domain. Publishing art therapy audits and clinical guidelines could make a significant contribution to the discipline's evidence base and offer other art therapists useful models to follow.

Another, perhaps key, strategic response that could be accomplished relatively quickly would be to synthesise art therapy's evidence base through systematic reviews, much in the manner of Roth and Fonagy (1996) and Fonagy et al. (2002) but within a framework appropriate to the discipline. The aim would be to articulate exactly what art therapy's 'best evidence' – its research, academically rigorous literature and expert, practitioner and user opinions – says about different approaches with different client populations, according to explicit criteria and evidential levels devised by the profession. Cape and Parry (2000) speak about differing kinds or levels of evidence, saying that what constitutes valid evidence will vary according to the kind of knowledge being sought and the volume, quality and nature of the evidence available in differing healthcare disciplines. Gilbody and Sowden (2000) and Richardson (2001) agree, saying that disciplines will therefore have to define their own evidential standards, deciding what constitutes 'good' and 'poor' evidence, which levels of evidence are appropriate to their discipline's research profile and what each discipline means by the 'best available evidence'. Assigning art therapy's evidence to a hierarchy of levels therefore requires a structure that enables meaningful distinctions to be drawn within the literature that we have. This, as Andrews describes with regard to systematic reviews in education, is an important 'navigational decision' (2004: 68) when the dominant scientific paradigm of EBP does not allow other paradigms – where research may be largely qualitative – and different kinds of evidence come into play. The Art Therapy Levels of Evidence (see Box 2.1) were devised in consultation with the art therapists at Oxleas NHS Trust as part of a guideline development process. These are an adaptation of Eccles et al.'s (1998) model used by Parry (2001), described in Chapter 1. A measure of political expediency keeps these within the broad parameters of EBP but they nonetheless afford significant value to qualitative research, to expert opinion, to user views and to local practice, and in so doing recognise art therapy's present research and knowledge base.

Box 2.1   Art therapy levels of evidence

I(a)   Evidence from at least one RCT, or evidence from at least one controlled, experimental or quasi-experimental study;

I(b)   Evidence from other research, for example, case studies, phenomenological, ethnographic, anthropological, art-based and collaborative studies;

II   Evidence from other academically rigorous texts;

III   Evidence from expert committee reports or opinions, or clinical experience of respected authority, or both;

IV   Evidence from local clinical consensus or from user representatives.

Source: Brooker et al. (2005).

The views of experts and the clinical consensus of experienced practitioners could be accessed through standard consensus procedures and focus groups, for example at specially convened conferences. The findings from these different sources of evidence could be combined to produce overall statements that summarise our knowledge about a topic, leading to national standards and guidelines that could be presented in the public domain and made available to clinicians, clients and employers. The findings embedded in art therapy's literature and the views of expert and experienced clinicians will then have been gathered, distilled, judged and articulated within the EBP framework, according to criteria deemed appropriate to the discipline, by the discipline. Goss and Rose (2002), Andrews (2004) and Sebba (2004) emphasise that this is critical, saying that there should be no collusion with the implicit methodological bias in standard evidence hierarchies.

The point about inclusion, about drawing on the different discourses within art therapy is key. The evidence base of art therapy is, and should continue to be, eclectic. A healthy discipline, according to Freshwater and Rolfe (2004) embraces diversity in a way that allows a community of discourses to co-exist and not be overridden by a dominant paradigm. They, like Brown et al. (2003), cite nursing as an example of a discipline that has a history of different ways of knowing that comprise knowledge from ethical, personal, aesthetic and socio-political dimensions, as well as the empirical. Here notions such as 'bricolage' and 'differance' come into play, terms that are derived from French cultural usage. McLeod (2001), for example, speaks of the researcher as a 'bricoleur' who uses whatever methods seem appropriate to the task in hand; and Freshwater and Rolfe (2004) draw on Derrida's (1982) concept of 'differance' that allows conflicting discourses to co-exist without coming into dispute and so 'defer(s) indefinitely any attempt to chose between them' (Freshwater and Rolfe, 2004: 113). Evidence can and should be drawn from multiple sources that go beyond the edges of EBP's habitual territory.

Art therapists also need to show, quite unequivocally, that we offer all the types of therapy that Parry and Richardson (1996) identified in a cross-sectoral way. Such a process has begun in the UK through the ATPRN's development of an audit tool that will capture an overall picture of art therapists' caseloads (BAAT, 2005), but other research projects are also needed that map and interrogate the detail of art therapy provision, such as Mahony's (1994, 1999) and Karkou and Sanderson's (1997) surveys of art therapy in alcohol services. Hartley's (2005) project offers an interesting example of service mapping of children's health services in England that aims to provide demographic data about provision across the health, social and educational systems and to document their development over time. These represent a timely shift of attention from documenting art therapists' areas of employment to identifying the presence and absence of art therapy services in different sectors serving different client populations.

Art therapists need to review the evidence we have, articulate it within the framework of EBP in a way that is appropriate to the discipline, and then identify the kind of evidence we need to develop. This implies three over-arching strategies for the short, medium and long term:

1. In the *short term* develop processes, locally and nationally, that synthesise and articulate art therapy's research, knowledge and experience as represented in the literature and embodied in practice, that is, narrative syntheses and guidelines that can be published, implemented and audited;
2. In the *medium term* conduct single-case experimental research as part of routine clinical work, working with colleagues to measure sector-specific outcomes, for example, symptoms, educational attainment, recidivism and so on, while continuing to narrativise the work in textual and visual forms;
3. In the *long term* collaborate with colleagues to develop qualitative and quantitative outcome research that involve/collaborates with users and draws on visual research methods.

Art therapists will be familiar with holding several different strategies and possibilities in mind. We know how to move between painted and spoken worlds and between the intimacy of clinical work and the exigencies of organisations, but we also need to pay attention to the pragmatic imperatives of our EBP-driven systems. Entering the EBP arena – facing Godzilla – means engaging with challenging questions, different discourses and many new and unfamiliar practices. It is to these that we now turn.

3   Developing art therapy guidelines

Guidelines are at the heart of EBP. They are one of the primary means through which practitioners can engage with art therapy's differing forms of evidence and demonstrate, on the discipline's terms, the evidence base of practice. Guidelines are situated at the beginning of a practice becoming evidence based, being fed by research, clinical consensus and CPD. They inform clinical work. Guidelines are therefore not only a strategically important means of drawing on art therapy's existing literature to articulate the evidence base in the short term but are also an intrinsically helpful process that enables art therapists to become research aware and develop skills in the critical appraisal and systematic review of evidence. In this chapter I describe guidelines and how they can be developed in a practical and politically informed way.

What are guidelines?

The term 'clinical practice guideline' is usually shortened to 'clinical guideline' or 'guideline'. Their aim is to assist the identification of the best process that will lead to optimum outcomes. There is an emphasis on being systematic, on the specificity of the problem or illness or circumstance, and on guidelines being for practitioners and users, their development often being a cross-discipline procedure.

Guidelines act as an *aide memoire* to 'normal expected practice' and state 'the right thing to do', but there are concerns that they could become homogenised and prescriptive delineations of practice. The literature repeatedly emphasises that guidelines should describe what would *usually* constitute best practice in a particular situation, and that their use is discretionary. They do not delineate exactly what should happen, neither do they 'replace individual clinical judgement, but provide the means for a better-informed judgement' (Parry, 2000b: 276). Cape (1998) explicitly states that guidelines are neither management nor commissioning tools for the definition or purchase of services and the NHS Executive has said that clinical guidelines cannot be used to 'mandate, authorise or outlaw treatment options' (Mann, 1996b, quoted in Parry, 2000b: 280). In fact, Roth et al. (1996) say that if guidelines are not fundamentally informed by an amalgam of practice, training and experience they are likely to be narrow and unhelpful and will not lead to the development of an evidence base for practice. Instead of constricting practice and stifling innovation, guidelines are supposed to be a springboard for new approaches and techniques.

So what makes a good guideline? Descriptions from the Department of Health (Mann, 1996b) and the Effective Health Care Bulletin (1994, cited in Cape and Parry 2000), say that they should:

- *Address an important topic*, one where decisions have a real impact on patient care and outcomes, for example, because the intervention is frequent or 'resource intensive', or where there is wide variation in practice;
- *Cover specific circumstances*, the client population and setting being clearly defined so that both practitioners and clients are clear about when and with whom to use the guideline;
- *Be both systematic and representative in the process of development*, the process being structured and clearly described in the final document. Cape and Parry (2000) suggest that guidelines should be developed by a multi-professional group that, when appropriate, includes user representatives;
- *Be truly evidence based*, the evidence used for each recommendation being clearly specified;
- *Be user friendly*, the language being clear, unambiguous and easy to follow for both practitioners and, where appropriate, service users.

The most common type of guidelines developed in medicine and mental health are *prospective*, that is to say, they guide practice and are either:

- *Condition based*, that is, to do with particular issues with specific client populations. For example, the guideline on treatment choice in psychological therapies lists a wide range of disorders to which the guideline applies, but is equally explicit about what it excludes (Parry, 2001);
- *Problem based*, that is, they address how to deal with particular situations. Cape and Parry (2000: 172) give the example of the management of violence in clinical settings.

They go on to say that guidelines in psychotherapy can be further divided into:

- *Assessment/triage decisions*, addressing patient suitability for different therapies and what form they might take;
- *Treatment decisions*, those made by the therapist about the treatment itself once clinical work has begun.

As well as acting as a guide to good practice, guidelines can lead directly to the development of audit criteria that are *retrospective*, providing feedback on practice (Cape and Parry, 2000).

A published guideline may vary in length from a paragraph, to a page, to a book. Usually there are succinct desktop versions and longer versions that give a summary of and cite the evidence, and sometimes user versions are produced too. Guidelines are usually developed by professional bodies, but Cape (1998), Cape and Parry (2000) and Parry (2000b) emphasise that local development makes guidelines more likely to be implemented and to have a positive impact on outcomes than nationally produced ones, although national guidelines are more likely to be valid.

This begs the question why, if guidelines may be neither valid nor followed, should art therapists expend time and energy developing them? The imperative of developing art therapy's evidence base in the short term is reason alone, but Cape and Parry (2000) suggest that the significant differences in theory and practice between schools of psychotherapy, various trainings, differing backgrounds of practitioners and therapists' allegiance are all important reasons too. Also expert views are often inconsistent and at variance with systematic reviews of the evidence, practitioners are often sceptical about research, and Cape (1998: 185) suggests that practice is often found to be out of date and substandard. These matters can be directly addressed through the development and implementation of guidelines. Good guidelines should also reflect the views and values of users, giving information that enables them to influence and choose the services they receive.

All of the above applies to art therapy too. There may not be so many trainings and quite the radical divergences in theory and practice as in psychotherapy, but nonetheless they do exist. I am not suggesting that this is bad nor, by implication, am I advocating a standardisation of practice through the development of guidelines. Rather I want to argue that different approaches to art therapy, whether they be due to culture, local custom and practice, individual preference, institutional or personal history – 'I've always done it this way and it seems to work OK' – vary in their suitability and effectiveness. Guidelines make implicit processes explicit. In so doing they identify the strengths and potential weaknesses of different approaches and are a means of addressing inconsistencies in the literature and in practice. The precise description of practice that guidelines require helps to distinguish what approach suits which clients and does so in a way that feeds, and is fed by, research. The narrative syntheses of evidence from different sources within guidelines will, in themselves, make a significant contribution to art therapy's evidence base.

Who might use art therapy guidelines? There are numerous points at national, regional and local levels at which decisions about resources and treatment are made, making guidelines potentially useful in the development of art therapy services and practices in all sectors. How, then, might we set about drawing up guidelines in art therapy? The procedure is straightforward:

- *Decide* the topic and form a Guideline Development Group;
- *Define* the exact parameters of the guideline;
- *Search* for art therapy literature that directly addresses the topic;
- *Critically appraise* the literature;
- *Systematically review* the literature, assigning it to 'levels of evidence';
- *Consult* widely, considering the results of the systematic review in the light of clinical consensus, 'expert' opinion and, if appropriate, the views of service users;
- *Link* the evidence from the systematic review and wider consultation to the final recommendations;
- *Write* the guideline.

It looks like a clear-cut procedure, which it is; it also looks simple and undemanding, which it is not. It demands time and resources for which art therapists should not hesitate to seek support from their employers. Figure 3.1 provides a map of the overall process.

While teaching about EBP in art therapy I have developed an active learning strategy that demonstrates the procedure, albeit in much abbreviated form. We begin with brainstorming the art therapy literature on a given topic, for example working with children who have been sexually abused. This usually results in a creditable list of papers, books and authors that art therapists already know. This

Figure 3.1   Process map: developing a clinical guideline

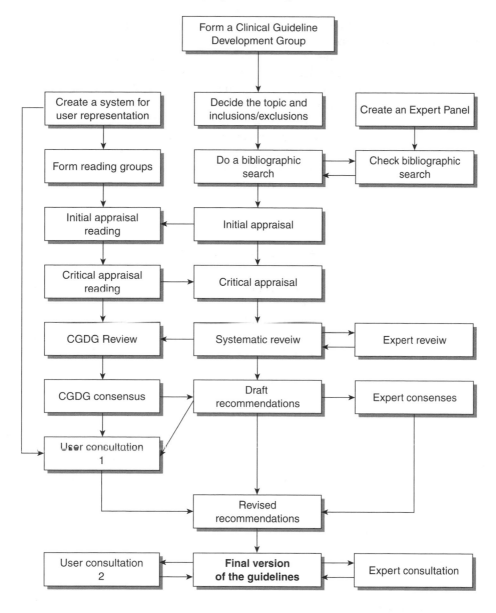

is supplemented with a hand search of edited books and journals going back to 1990 which always reveals a few chapters or articles that participants have forgotten or did not know existed. Each participant then reads and appraises a different, single text using a very brief checklist that addresses whether or not the piece is research based, academically rigorous, is credible and applicable to the appraiser's experience; s/he is also asked to identify the key findings in their text. Everyone then spends 20 minutes reading together in silence – a pleasurable experience in itself. Then the group goes through each text, everyone giving their immediate impressions of their text and its relative merits according to the checklist. This process gives snapshots of texts that offer research-based or other rigorous 'evidence' and enables comparison with less rigorous texts. It also enables participants to see how key issues or findings can recur and become distilled into recommendations. For example, one of the key issues that repeatedly emerges in the British literature on art therapy with sexually abused children is the mess that is part of the art-making process and resulting artwork. This indicates potential guidelines (and auditable criteria) about art materials and studio-based resources with appropriate flooring and storage facilities. The whole process of guideline development can be both interesting and informative, contributing to art therapists CPD and with an outcome likely to be useful for clients, colleagues and employers. What follows is a more detailed description of the whole process of guideline development.

Forming a Guideline Development Group

Prior to getting a Guideline Development Group together the initiator/s of the whole process will have an idea about the topic and the kind of guideline to be developed. This is likely to be broad but it infers who should be part of the group, for example, if the guideline is to address clinical practice then art therapists would comprise the group, but if the guideline is about the referral process to art therapy then the group might include colleagues. Similarly, if the guideline is about local custom and practice it follows that local art therapists and colleagues would get together, but if the aim is to develop a guideline for wider use then regional or national professional organisations should be represented. BAAT would be key to the consultation, as would the professional associations of other disciplines involved. The group that developed the national guideline on *Treatment Choice in Psychological Therapies* (Parry, 2001) involved a multidisciplinary group of 11 people, nominated by several professional organisations. A more local model in art therapy is a clinical guideline being developed about *The Use of Art Work in Art Psychotherapy with People prone to Psychotic States* by the Art Psychotherapy Service at Oxleas NHS Trust. This has been funded both directly and in-kind (in terms of time) by the Trust, the group comprising 12 art therapists and myself as external consultant/Chair (Brooker et al., forthcoming).

User representation

For both local and national guidelines user representation and/or consultation should be sought. This can include current users, past users, or elected representatives from local user groups, Community Health Councils or from national organisations such as MIND. It may be that thinking about user involvement is part of the initiator/s preliminary work or it may be one of the first tasks of the group; this depends on the extent of user involvement. Duff et al. (1996) say that users in all areas of healthcare can be involved at every stage of guideline development, from identifying the topic and being continually involved to only commenting on the final recommendations. It is important to avoid tokenism through inclusion of more than one user/user representative and that users be thoroughly prepared, for example, about the procedures of guideline development and differing kinds of evidence, although the amount of information will depend on how involved users are. Duff et al. emphasise the importance of continuing dialogue between users and practitioners, and recommend that user participation is ensured through working in small groups with a neutral group facilitator who can address the power dynamics, understand the role of all the participants, enable plain and open speaking, ensure clarity of purpose, and protect the boundaries of all involved. User involvement in the development of clinical guidelines in mental health care is an important collaboration that can be a mutually beneficial encounter.

It is interesting to note that the group that devised the guideline on treatment choice in the psychological therapies set up a separate User Panel that was consulted at key points in the procedure (Parry, 2001). The group at Oxleas are consulting, via the local User Council, with ex and current users of art therapy services (ongoing at the time of writing). Parry (2000b) states elsewhere that the best methods for ensuring a clinical guideline is actually of value to users has not yet been established and that another, user-led guideline on psychological treatment choice is planned.

The expert panel

Another early task of the initiator or the Guideline Development Group is the creation of an 'Expert Panel'. This is a small group of five or six people who are involved at key points in the procedure. Parry (2001) recommends that members of the panel should be nominated or elected by the professional organisation/s associated with the guideline topic and according to explicit criteria. They should:

- be recognised by peers as having expertise in the topic;
- have experience in the sector;
- have service management experience;
- all should wish to achieve consensus on best practice.

How the Expert Panel are involved and the amount of work they do will, like user participation, vary according to the nature of the guideline being developed. The Panel may, for example, exist only virtually, never meeting either each other or those developing the guideline and communicating individually, by post, with the group; on the other hand they may meet each other and the group on several occasions. Their tasks are to:

- *check* that all the relevant literature has been consulted and included in the bibliography;
- *review* the research evidence/literature once it has been appraised;

- *assist* in the development of recommendations that arise from the literature;
- *assist* in the development of recommendations where literature is either absent or differs from the group's view;
- *confirm* the clinical appropriateness of the final recommendations.

BAAT Council nominated five art therapists to be members of an Expert Panel who have been consulted by the group at Oxleas. At the time of writing they have commented upon two drafts of the guideline and will be sent a third and final draft at the same time as the user consultation group, that is, as user consultation is completed.

Defining the exact parameters of the guideline

The first task of a Guideline Development Group is to define the topic of the guideline and make a formal statement that describes its scope, that is, the client population and the setting. Parry's *Treatment Choice in Psychological Therapies and Counselling* (2001) specified the range of clients including, among others, those with depression, PTSD and chronic fatigue, and those excluded, for example, children and adolescents, those with learning disabilities and substance misusers. The professional practices involved were also defined (and did not include the arts therapies). The Oxleas group is addressing art psychotherapy with clients who are prone to psychotic states. We have excluded children, adolescents and families and all other client populations, for instance those with eating disorders, who are depressed, have substance abuse problems, learning disabilities and so on. A guideline needs to be similarly specific about the circumstances to which it refers. In broad terms this means whether the setting is in the NHS, education or the penal system, and in an acute ward, day hospital or pupil referral or young offenders' unit. If the guideline is to address a particular clinical intervention then the exact nature of the intervention or procedure needs to be described as well.

Searching the literature

The next task is to locate and identify the relevant literature. The process of bibliographic searching involves members of the group asking two questions:

1. What books, chapters in edited books, journal articles, conference papers and authors do we already know on the topic?
2. Where else might we search for relevant literature?

The topic is usually one of significant interest to those involved so it is likely that the first question will generate the majority of the relevant literature. However, the second can identify literature outside the group's knowledge, for example, in the 'grey' unpublished literature in theses and literature from other countries. Excluding overseas literature may make the literature less than culturally representative, but the practicalities of language, translation and time exclude some texts, and issues of context and culture need consideration in terms of their relevance to practice in the UK. It may be that the search identifies a large amount of literature, in which case it needs limiting. For example, Parry's (2001) national guideline included all the relevant international literature post-1990, and the art therapy guideline being developed at Oxleas limited its appraisal to the entirety of the relevant art therapy literature published in Britain.

The literature on developing clinical guidelines in psychotherapy suggests searching extensively for material on databases such as Psychinfo and Medline and for Cochrane-registered reviews. The search is for RCTs and meta-analyses of RCTs – the familiar gold standard of EBP. Roth and Fonagy's (1996) review drew on these, as did Parry's guideline on *Treatment Choice in Psychological Therapies* but, because there are relatively few RCTs of psychotherapy, Parry's guideline also referred to other 'high-quality published reviews' (2001: 11). Meta-analyses of RCTs in art therapy are clearly a non-starter at the moment, but a more broadly based review of research and academically rigorous texts is, in my view, entirely appropriate. Such a review reflects and respects the evidence that is both appropriate and available to the discipline. The validity of any review, and of a subsequent guideline, depends not only on what is reviewed but also on the rigour and transparency of the review method and an equality of methodological approach appropriate to the topic.

It is easy for a guideline group to miss relevant and recent literature and so it is at this point that the Expert Panel has its first task – to check the group's bibliography to ensure that all the relevant and most up-to-date texts are included. Then the appraisal can begin.

Appraising the literature

Appraising literature for a guideline is a slightly different process to a literature review for an essay or a research project because it is explicitly systematic and involves a group of people working together. How to appraise a text is a skill that can be learnt, usually assisted by the use of a checklist (Bury and Jerosch-Herold, 1998). Clinical guidelines usually have one appraisal process, but the interrogation of a literature has to fit what is available. A real difficulty for art therapy is the limited size of the research literature. I think this necessitates the appraisal of *all* the art therapy literature relevant to a topic, and I have found it helpful to have two discrete appraisal processes: a first, very brief initial appraisal which limits the amount of detailed reading to be done in a second, in-depth appraisal. In my experience it is also helpful to form small reading groups of three to four people where the collective part of the appraisal process occurs.

Reading groups

A guideline group of 8 to 12 people would have two or three small reading groups who regularly feedback their findings to the group as a whole. How often a reading group meets varies, but regular and relatively frequent meetings seem to work well, for example, once a month. Leadership of the group is important, preferably by someone who has experience of critical appraisal or research, but this can be rotated as participants gain confidence in the procedure. Each group should be randomly assigned texts to read so that everything in the bibliography is appraised. Individuals then read independently, scoring texts on the Initial Appraisal Checklist and taking this to their reading group for discussion and consensus, bringing rigour and validity to the process. Reading for the initial appraisal may be relatively fast as research-based and academically rigorous papers can quickly be identified and set aside for later critical appraisal, and the questions asked of other texts are few. Reading for the critical appraisal requires in-depth consideration of each text with the same small- and whole-group processes continuing throughout. Rigour can be increased if the initial and critical appraisal of each text is done by different reading groups.

The appraisal process is time consuming, but it enables practitioners to gain a thorough knowledge of current thinking about the topic of the guideline that may not otherwise have been acquired, that is, to become research aware. This, after all, is the key aim of EBP; new books are not read immediately they are published nor is the latest edition of the professional journal the minute it lands on the doormat! What makes this part of the process particularly engaging is the discussion of each piece in a reading group, using the checklists to guide discussion and appraisal. This ensures that individual reading is active and focused and that the material is thoroughly absorbed; it also assists the effective use of limited time. Group discussion can explore conflicting findings and compare the literature with local practices, taking the first steps towards consensus about any changes that may be appearing on the horizon.

Initial appraisal

An initial appraisal of art therapy literature uses a short checklist (see Appendix 1) to enquire about the research base and academic rigour of a text. If a text is research based and relevant to the guideline topic then no more needs doing other than marking it for inclusion in the critical appraisal that follows. The remainder of the initial appraisal helps to decide which non-research texts should be critically appraised, assessing whether a text has been situated in a critical context within an existing literature – crucial to its rigour and validity – and enquiring about its intelligibility, credibility and resonance with the reader's experience and its potential application to practice.

Critical appraisal

The purpose of critical appraisal is not to demolish a text but to assess its rigour, truthfulness, relevance and applicability. Bury (1998) says that the basic premise should be that there is no such thing as a perfect piece of writing or research as there will always be flaws of some kind, but the issue is whether these flaws are sufficiently serious to call the conclusions of the paper into question. It is important, however, to be open to new ideas and challenges that the literature offers and to appraise it in an unbiased way, even if this implies that well established practices not supported by the literature have to change. Like the initial appraisal, critical appraisal reviews the validity and applicability of a text, but in more detail. It considers the structure of a text and the presentation of research, based on a model described by Bury and Jerosch-Herold (1998), and explores visual material in general and case studies in particular, that is, it attempts to evaluate issues that are particular to the critical appraisal of the art therapy literature.

The Art Therapy Critical Appraisal Checklist (see Appendix 2) begins with a series of questions checking the research basis of a text and ascertaining its quality. Research texts should describe a clear aim or research question and research methods should be appropriate to the aim or question. The transparency of the research process should enable the tracing of the researcher's thoughts and actions, the processes of data collection and analysis should be clear and the reader should be able to understand how the findings relate to the literature and how the whole research process led to the eventual conclusions. Transparency and critical reflexivity should extend to the researcher's motivations, interactions and role with the participants. The reader therefore has to have some knowledge of research methods, and indeed these are sometimes acquired during the appraisal process. For example, does the paper describe a single case study? Is it an ABA design or a narrative description? Is it a piece of action research in an organisation? Is it an ethnographic study, an archive-based piece of historical research, or a survey-based project using both quantitative measures and open-ended questions? This first series of questions explores both the form and the content of the research and interrogates the scrupulousness with which researchers have justified their approach and substantiated their findings.

The critical appraisal goes on to explore the academic rigour of those texts that are not research based, the next two series of questions interrogating a text in terms of its clarity and critical context. Given that most of the art therapy literature is not research based, these are important issues. Academic rigour will be reflected in the clarity of the author's aims and approach to their writing. For example, does the text focus on an unambiguous and precisely articulated topic, presenting theories, ideas and different kinds of information that are properly sourced, or is it generalised, vague and anecdotal, presenting familiar concepts as if for the first time, without situating the text in a context? Is the literature relevant to the topic and does it include the most recent national and international publications? Does it give an overview of the whole subject and critique contrasting views, or is the author's position individualistic and reliant on only one or two sources?

Much of the art therapy literature on both sides of the Atlantic is case study based. The checklist takes account of this by addressing the quality and thoroughness of case studies, including illustrations. Case studies can sometimes be more like case vignettes used to illustrate a theoretical point. This does not necessarily diminish the quality of the text, but the brevity of casework description can make it hard to gain a comprehensive picture of the client, the context, and the process and content of the therapy; this can call its validity into question. Similarly, a fully described piece of clinical work that is without a theoretical framework and is not situated within a critical context lacks a necessary thoroughness, although it may be a 'thick description' of casework that is both credible and applicable. The discussion of ethical issues, as well as those relating to consent and confidentiality, is not always explicit in art therapy case studies, the assumption being that the usual professional practices have been observed, but consent and anonymity have to be explicit in research studies of all kinds. Illustrations of a client's artwork are not always included in a case study; they may be of good quality and in colour or they may be poor quality and in black and white; the artwork may or may not be adequately discussed and the author's commentary on the illustrations may or may not make sense to the reader. Such questions allow a critique of the author's visual and verbal representations of their practice.

The final part of critical appraisal requires the reader to articulate the key findings of a research project or the main points made in non-research texts, and then to assess their credibility and applicability. The reader should be able to identify the results of research with relative ease; these may be presented in a discrete section, followed by discussion in relation to the literature. Non-research-based texts that are academically rigorous should also have the main arguments clearly articulated and situated within a discourse. For research and non-research texts there should be sufficient description of the material to satisfy the reader of its truthfulness and the adequacy of the author's interpretation. Finally, does the text relate to the reader's knowledge and experience and improve their understanding of clinical work? In other words, are the results of a research project or the key points of a text transferable to similar situations? This last series of questions become particularly significant when moving from consideration of the literature to articulating the recommendations that make up the guideline.

By the end of the whole appraisal process the group will find themselves with a pile of completed checklists about the literature that then has to undergo another round of review and assessment.

Systematic review

Once the literature had been critically appraised it has to be graded within a hierarchy of evidence. This is what is meant by systematic review. The system has been devised in order to make accessible the disparate, often replicated but variable quality of research literature in a way that is as transparent and as free from bias as possible. Systematic review therefore infers thoroughness, completeness and reproducibility. It requires the gathering together and collation of every text on a topic, assigning them to different levels of quality that meet specific criteria that have been set so as to aggregate the findings of the appraisal process and make judgements about the validity of the evidence overall.

Rather than using the DoH's or psychotherapy's levels of evidence that reflect the dominant paradigm of medicine, I suggest that practitioners use the 'Art therapy levels of evidence' (see Box 2.1, p. 42). This positions qualitative research alongside quantitative research and affords significant value to art therapy's current knowledge base, to the opinions of experts and respected authorities in the discipline and to the views of practitioners and users. The levels of evidence position research in terms of type, not quality, and of course research of all kinds, as well as other literature, varies in quality. The scrutiny of each source of evidence should be on its own terms, and its quality should be addressed during the critical appraisal process and described in the guideline's narrative.

Cape and Parry (2000) say that when research evidence is limited there will be more than usual use of 'consensual evidence'. For many disciplines, and for art therapy, the consensus opinion of experts, experienced practitioners and users is critical to the construction of a useful, valid and truly representative evidence base. This is the second point at which an Expert Panel can be involved when, for example, they may be asked to come to an independent consensus about a set of predefined issues or to comment on the consensus agreements of other, perhaps local, practitioners. This is helpful when there is variation in practice and/or a mismatch between local practice and the research evidence, and may involve the Panel in clinical consensus procedures. The Oxleas guideline, for example, required the creation of a fourth level of evidence derived from local clinical consensus and user consultation so that aspects of local practice, not represented in the literature, could be included in the guideline. These were amplified and verified by our two expert panels: of experienced practitioners and local users.

Clinical consensus

Clinical consensus is a process through which a group arrives at agreement on a topic or clinical intervention, 'agreement' ranging from unanimity to a generally acceptable opinion on a topic. It is all about custom and practice, that is, the routines of clinical work. This kind of evidence does not represent new knowledge (although in art therapy it may) but current views of what constitutes best practice. Its inclusion is critical when an approach is new or under-researched.

Clinical consensus can be achieved through using an explicit, usually structured procedure. Olsen (1995) and Murphy et al. (1998) describe three methods:

1. The *Quasi-judicial approach*: involving an impartial group hearing the 'evidence' before establishing a consensus view;
2. The *'Delphi' approach*: so named because it asks experts to forecast opinion. Individuals record their views and then vote on them anonymously, the process being repeated several times. The experts do not meet;
3. The *nominal group process*: each member of a group, of practitioners or an expert panel, receives a copy of the literature review together with draft recommendations and is invited to rate them. They then discuss their views in a structured meeting with a facilitator, followed by another cycle of rating and discussion until consensus of 85 per cent

is achieved. It is important to eliminate the views of 'outliers' (those with extreme opinions) and to have broad, inclusive definitions (Scott and Black, 1991).

The last two are the methods most frequently used by expert panels to gain consensus-based evidence for guidelines (as per Parry, 2001). A modified version can be adopted for achieving local clinical consensus, for instance, when a group of art therapists wish to define their practice, either in the absence of a literature on an aspect of a topic, as has been the case at Oxleas, or so that local practice may be compared to evidence derived from the literature. Murphy et al. (1998) suggest that giving participants in clinical consensus procedures a literature review before discussion enhances their reliance on the research evidence, especially if it has been presented in a synthesised way, for example, in a table format.

This points to a final task prior to writing the draft recommendations: creating a synthesis of the critical appraisal and systematic review of the literature. This can either be a narrative account or the statistical pooling of a meta-analysis, ideally both. The narrative allows qualitative material to be explored while the meta-analysis aggregates and averages statistical material. Some (e.g. Andrews, 2004; Sebba, 2004) argue that literary syntheses are implicitly more useful and less biased than statistical reductions because they allow the inclusion of evidence from a variety of sources, not just from RCTs. For art therapy narrative syntheses, detailing the purpose, methods, findings and implications from the range of evidence, are clearly the way to go.

Drafting recommendations

Finally a guideline development group gets to the point where they are able to draw on the enormous amount of work they have done to draft the recommendations that make the clinical guideline. The systematic review will have assigned each text to a level of evidence, enabling the group to decide which texts and key findings have the greatest validity. They will then be able to distil draft recommendations from the evidence, explicitly linking each recommendation to the evidence supporting it, the hierarchy of levels guiding how strong and valid each recommendation can be. Thus, a text assigned to Level 1(a) will have the greatest strength of evidence and the draft recommendation arising from it should be the most closely attended to, and so on down the hierarchy, the evidence base of each recommendation being explicitly stated and sourced.

Wider consultation

Once the narrative synthesis and recommendations have been drafted they should be disseminated for comment to the Expert Panel and to users and, if relevant, to colleagues in the multidisciplinary team. Amendments are made on the basis of feedback and revisions and are circulated again before producing the final guideline.

The national guideline that Parry's team developed involved a final critical appraisal of the entire process conducted by eight external scientific reviewers who had not been previously been involved, plus comments from 30 national service-user organisations. Local guideline development groups should work reflexively.

The amount of time and work involved in developing a guideline should not be underestimated. Of course there is a difference of scale between the development of national and local guidelines but, if local guidelines are to have any credibility, or be used as the trailblazers for funding applications to develop national guidelines, as Parry (2000b) suggests, they should be no less rigorous.

Problems, dissemination and implementation

It is unfortunate that, after such a huge amount of work, clinical guidelines are, like research in general, notorious for their lack of impact on therapists' behaviour (Parry, 2000b). Their potential desuetude is likely to be associated with a fear that a guideline will become a protocol, part of a cookbook practice that will determine the use of increasingly scarce resources and whose use or misuse might lead to litigation (Mead, 1998; Needham, 2000; Parry, 2000b). In this context it is important to recall once again that the original intention of Cochrane was to inform, not determine, practice, and that the NHS Executive has explicitly stated that guidelines must not be used to 'mandate, authorise or outlaw treatment options' (cited in Parry, 2000b: 280). Nonetheless it can still be said that the EBP paradigm tries to force change, and change is not an easy process, especially when a guideline conflicts with long-held beliefs and experience, does not seem to apply to the clients in question, and when practitioners cannot see how change will be beneficial. Andrews (2004) says that practitioners will only engage with evidence if they believe it will make a real difference to their practice and its outcomes, the utilisation of research and guidelines being highly context and person specific. Practitioners have a highly skilled to job to do when it comes to relating and implementing the evidence distilled in guidelines to their particular circumstances and clients, and so understandable reservations about relevance, appropriateness and indeed beliefs concerning 'what works' can lead to guideline development becoming a wasteful expenditure of time and energy. It is therefore all the more important to take active steps to ensure the appropriate implementation of guidelines in a collegial and inclusive way.

It is a good idea to use several strategies. Ensuring ownership, varying the methods of communication, working with resistances and giving feedback are effective means of dissemination (Mead, 1998; Needham, 2000). Indeed, at the outset of guideline development it is critical to ensure that the topic is one that needs to be addressed and that the guideline is developed and owned by the community for whom it is intended. Creating a shared vision depends upon the creation of a broad basis of support for any change at the outset of guideline development. Once the process is complete the information should be communicated to practitioners, colleagues and users in as accessible a form as possible, for example through active educational initiatives such as local workshops, in-service training, educational outreach and professional networking by members of the group. This can occur at local, regional and national levels, perhaps through the professional association, using local opinion leaders that can include members of the Expert Panel. These strategies help practitioners to engage with change in a way that more passive dissemination (for example, through a mailing) does not.

Implementation of clinical guidelines is another matter again. It is inevitable that there will be some resistance because of disbelief, disagreement, anxiety and a lack of incentive to change, and so it is important to anticipate obstacles and demonstrate (through educational initiatives) the positive likely outcomes of following a guideline that are part of self-directed inquiry and lifelong learning. In essence, change should be managed locally, sensitively, and with full consultation with those concerned. Needham (2000) states that change, a subtle social process that is not necessarily amenable to deliberate planning, is more likely to come about when it corresponds with what practitioners already think, or are beginning to think, assisted by an ownership of the entire process.

The development of guidelines establishes a direct relationship between research-based and other forms of evidence and clinical work, fulfilling the primary *raison d'être* of EBP. Their development in art therapy will result in syntheses of the best evidence available, enabling clinicians to learn about research and improve their practice. Guidelines differ from literature reviews that lay the foundations for research because they offer an interpretation of the evidence that is directly translated into recommendations, and because they take account of the views of service users, experts in the field and the realities of clinicians' experience and working practices. They are especially important in areas of work where there is significant variation in practice and indications that some approaches are more effective than others. Guidelines, and the syntheses of evidence within them, are one of the lynchpins through which art therapy can develop and demonstrate its evidence base, a means whereby art therapy can legitimise its practice. I think it critical that art therapists work within an evidential system that uses appraisal criteria and levels of evidence that value the evidence that is both available and appropriate to the discipline. The process requires a verbal and conceptual clarity that will be useful in the articulation of art therapy's processes and practices, but practitioners must take care that both the development and implementation of guidelines does not so delineate practice and delivery that they are reduced to no more than prescriptive, tick-box procedures.

Feedback about a guideline comes from audit (Parry, 2000b). Guidelines 'state the right thing to do' and audit checks 'whether the right thing has been done' and 'whether it has been done right'. Guidelines are not designed to lead directly to audit; rather a guideline's recommendations lead to standards that can be audited (Cape and Parry, 2000). Their purpose is different: guidelines are prospective and guide, whereas audit is retrospective and gives feedback. The following chapter describes the audit process, but argues once again that this aspect of the EBP cycle should also be engaged within a politically reflexive and strategic way that keeps a weather eye on the establishment of art therapy's evidence base.

4 Art therapy audit: culture and process

Audit is a contradictory beast. It is a key part of EBP, being a practical procedure that monitors standards of service delivery and care, one that the NHS Executive intends should become part of every health practitioner's routine practice. Indeed HPC (2003a, 2003b) situates audit within registrants' CPD as 'work-based learning' and it is embedded in the NHS's *Agenda for Change* profiles. Yet audit is critiqued as a phenomenon of the late 20th century and Britain is described as an 'audit society' (Power, 1997: 1). Audit procedures can typify the regulatory mood of centralised control and accountability, inducing fear of government intrusion and the micromanagement of professional practices and essentially operating as a highly critical, persecutory superego. It is therefore hardly surprising to find that almost every author on the topic not only describes the advantages but also the disadvantages of audit, recounting the anxieties and defences that arise from new forms of scrutiny operant within an 'audit culture' where the obligation to audit comes from sources external to and 'above' practitioners themselves. In such a climate it can be hard for art therapists to maintain a constructive attitude to the scrutiny of services and practice that are often solely in terms of financial imperatives, despite the fact that audit has the potential to make a major contribution to the development of art therapy's evidence base. Audit can be a useful tool through which services and their practices can be described and particular aspects of their effectiveness be demonstrated, particularly as it conveys information to purchasers and managers in accessible ways, but for it to be a positive force for change and real improvement it has to be perceived as an intrinsically worthwhile part of reflexive practice rather than as a necessary evil imposed by management.

In this chapter I describe how art therapists can audit their services and practices in simple, straightforward ways. I also explore audit as a socio-political phenomenon, it being, like every other aspect of EBP, an activity that should not be undertaken uncritically and without awareness of its socio-political context.

Definitions

Audit means different things to different people. It is a series of quality-assurance activities that aim to ensure that practices and services, based on the best available evidence, are monitored and continually improved in a cyclic, multi-stepped procedure. Audit seeks to measure the quality of care, changing and improving that which is demonstrably lacking and following up any changes to ensure their implementation and a service's continued improved functioning. In healthcare audit is often described as a problem-solving procedure that reviews services and identifies deficiencies so that improvements can be made – a process that is retrospective in practice and prospective in view. At best it encapsulates an ongoing process of critical self-reflection by clinicians and managers, their collegial audit activities being characterised by curiosity and a wish to learn and improve practice and hence care in a way that enhances intraprofessional and inter-professional trust, improves staff morale and individual self-esteem. The role of audit is thus to formalise a continuing round of dialogue and reflection about publicly funded services and practices by those who offer them.

Such descriptions focus on monitoring the quality of services and practices, their improvement and the continuing professional development of staff. This contrasts with the DoH's definition of medical audit as:

> the systematic critical analysis of the quality of medical care, including the procedures used for diagnosis and treatment, the use of resources and the resulting outcome for the patient. (1989: 1)

Here the economics of delivery are brought into direct relationship with the specifics of practice and outcomes. Effective use of resources and the 'cause and effect' paradigm of medicine and EBP become part of the audit equation where what is sought is:

> a new kind of knowledge of publicly funded practices, one which enables managers to be more transparent to users of those services, more conscious of their resource implications and more oriented to the improvement of what they produce. (Power, 1998: 24)

In such definitions fiscal issues, accountability, transparency, management concerns and practice itself are intertwined. Others describe audit as measuring 'how what is happening matches with what should be happening' (Dolan and Norton, 1998: 112), assuming that what should be happening is well established. Crombie et al. (1993) usefully focus on the problem-solving purpose of audit and show how it can have a direct impact on services and care. Variation in quality can be identified, limited resources and obvious deficiencies in a service can be recognized and the continuing professional development of staff can be supported. However, the NHS Executive's definition has become common currency; this shifts the emphasis away from problem solving to continuing review and improvement:

> Clinical audit is a clinically led initiative which seeks to improve the quality and outcome of patient care through structured peer review whereby clinicians examine their practices and results against agreed standards and modify their practice where indicated. (Mann, 1996a: 6)

In this definition audits of practice (as distinct from service delivery) focus on ensuring that practice really is based on the best available evidence that comes from the whole picture created by research, guidelines, clinical expertise and users' preferences and experiences.

These subtly different and expanding definitions show how the meaning of 'audit' has changed. This has occurred because the politics of the public sector have interwoven economics with the effectiveness of practice and the efficiency of services with identifying and solving problems. This merits some consideration before going on to consider the practicalities of the audit process in art therapy.

The audit culture

There is no doubt that audit in the health, social and education services is a direct consequence of the social, political and economic changes in the UK across the public sector, even though quality assurance and quality control have long been familiar practices in industry and management. It is interesting to read Crombie et al.'s (1993) account of early examples of audit that came about in response to emerging disasters: from the mortality rates of soldiers in the Crimea during the 1850s which changed due to the observations and interventions of Florence Nightingale, to the establishment of the Health Advisory Service which followed investigations of psychiatric hospitals in the late 1960s. The subsequent huge expansion of audit came with the first Thatcher government in 1979 which saw models of quality control in the private sector being transferred to the public sector. Much informal quality assurance activity in the NHS changed following the 1989 reforms when the DoH required doctors to audit their practice; in 1990 the requirement was extended to all clinical professions and in 1991 to non-medical professions. Professional groups have reacted differently to this requirement. Medicine has embraced the new managerialism, initiating medical audit and the language of accountancy to enhance doctors' professional status and clinical autonomy (Walby and Greenwell, 1994) but in so doing is said to have introduced new power hierarchies and lost a sense of collegiality (Exworthy and Halford, 1999). Social workers are reported to have experienced an erosion of their professional values and status (Jones, 1999) and teachers' response has been ambivalent, some embracing the new norms but others feeling professionally compromised (Menther and Muschamp, 1999).

Shore and Wright (2000) explore the changing definitions and responses to audit in relation to its migration from its origins in financial management to virtually every sphere of working life. 'Audit' comes from the Latin 'audire', meaning 'to hear' or 'hearing' and implies scrutiny, examination and judgement in a public event, a process Power (1997) describes as 'a ritual of verification'. As audit activity has increased so its meaning has changed from an association solely with fiscal matters to include other forms of arms'-length accountability. This shift in meaning is associated with the creation of the Audit Commission in 1983; its tasks were to monitor performance, identify best practice, improve value for money (efficiency) and ensure the effectiveness of management systems, directly linking performance, management, effectiveness and economics. This has led to the reinvention of state-funded institutions as financial bodies, these changes being 'symptomatic of a new rationality of government' (Shore and Wright, 2000: 61). This resonates with descriptions of audit in mental health care as: 'a wish and, at times, quite omnipotent hope for a rational, understandable, logical standardization of process and outcome, offering predictability and constant and continued improvement within the human services' (Davenhill and Patrick, 1998: 1). Thus a somewhat depersonalised delivery of care is continually scrutinised by an inhibiting external presence for whom services are never quite good enough. Such an audit culture becomes persecutory, due to the tension between managers and practitioners who are driven by economic imperatives that act against freedom of thought, reflexive practice and learning.

Shore and Wright (2000) develop the discussion about the relationship between auditor and auditee, arguing that the discourse associated with audit has altered the way people relate to their work, to management, to each other and to themselves. The language of audit emphasises empowerment, peer review and self-enhancement judged by standards set by practitioners themselves, suggesting that audit is a democratic and open process. However, the associations between audit, effectiveness and value for money disguise the former's hierarchical and paternalistic roots and plays down its coercive and punitive implications. Terms like 'accountability' and 'transparency' seem relatively benign until the question 'accountable to whom?' is asked. The rhetoric has it that accountability is to the public, the consumer, but the reality is that accountability is to organisations and their representatives that act as intermediaries for government. Thus what initially appears as a democratic procedure couched in benevolent language, becomes reframed as a 'visibility' that is policed through differing kinds of inspection that are enacted in artificial 'staged events', for example OFSTED inspections. This model of accountability damages professional autonomy and erodes trust between management and practitioners. It also changes the way professionals view themselves: 'The audited subject is recast as a depersonalised unit of economic resource whose productivity and performance must constantly be measured and enhanced' (Shore and Wright, 2000: 62).

Power (1994, 1997, 1998) writes interestingly of the differing drives for the reform of state-funded public services, of the familiar financial and political imperatives consequent upon limited resources and unending demands. Within such a socio-political context audit procedures become 'attractive instruments of control' (1998: 25) that seek to maintain and improve services while they are contracting. Audit is a focus of managerial interest associated with the increased regulation and control of professional practices and a consequent conflict between managers and practitioners about who decides what should be audited. For management audit is a tool of accountability that gives outcomes and performance indicators of staff activity, while for practitioners it is part of reflexive practice about the quality of a service, its delivery and effectiveness. Power suggests that audit is therefore about control and power as practitioners become publicly accountable and practice becomes more defined. This has led to concerns about audit as a means of managerial encroachment, an instrument of blame and a means of standardising practice. Interprofessional tensions and conflict between managers and practitioners can be exacerbated by audit, particularly if audit becomes less a locally initiated procedure and more a national, standardised process, one that 'necessarily weakens professional autonomy' (1998: 32). In this view audit is both hierarchical and paternalistic, and the relationship one of power between the observer and the observed. Power states that there should therefore be a clear distinction drawn between managerial scrutiny and financial transparency on one hand, and the routine, reflexive monitoring of practices and services on the other.

The work of Shore and Wright and Power bring into awareness once again the importance of art therapists' political reflexivity concerning the culture of EBP. We need to be acutely conscious of the influence of the changing norms of practice, care and service delivery; of the new normative gaze, the panopticon of standardisation and accountability that is introduced into our view of ourselves as professionals. Shore and Wright's rather depressing account of the audit gaze defies the rhetoric that describes audit as enhancing professional practices and their delivery, replacing it with a mood of compliance, conformity, intense competition for reduced resources and a sense of powerlessness in practitioners' ability to control their conditions of work and the particularities of practice. They liken audit to Foucault's (1977) description of modern forms of power that introduce anxiety and have an effect on both the individual and on entire organisations when everyone is scrutinised and ranked in a way that reshapes organisations and practices so that they may be audited. The structures, bureaucracy and new layers of administration – the endless paper trails – associated with audit make its influence hard to evade and the fiscal imperatives that underpin it inevitably constitute a threat. Audit comprises a series of practices and events that, as Power argues, are introduced when trust has broken down, yet they contribute to that same distrust. Despite audit's much lauded aim of improving care it is debatable whether this is achieved or whether audit is, as Crombie et al. suggest, 'another illustration of a common failing: the confusion of activity with progress' (1993: 2).

Audit in psychological services

Given the debate about the purpose and nature of audit it is perhaps not surprising that healthcare professions have developed different approaches towards it. For example, the Royal College of Speech and Language Therapists (1996) collects audit data about client groups, admissions, discharges and waiting times as well as outcomes, satisfaction surveys and complaints procedures, while physiotherapists specifically exclude questions of outcome and patient satisfaction and assign these instead to research (Bury, 1998; Buttery, 1998). Descriptions of audit in psychotherapy include medical audit, service audit, quality assurance (QA) and total quality management (TQM), service evaluation and operational research (Fonagy and Higgitt, 1989; Parry, 1992, 1996). Although authors differentiate between the audit and evaluation of services and clinical audits of practice, the distinctions become increasingly confused: between audit that is problem solving or which demonstrates effectiveness, and between audit and research. Accounts of psychotherapy audits illustrate the range of activity: there is the complex statistical analysis of Baruch et al.'s (1998) outcome evaluation of a community-based psychotherapy service for young people; McDonald and Blizard's (1998) outcome evaluation of eight years of behavioural treatment administered by nurse therapists; Dolan and Norton's (1998) audits of referrer satisfaction and cost effectiveness at the Henderson Hospital; Margison et al.'s (1998) audit of psychotherapy services and their assessment processes; Target's (1998) retrospective outcome assessment of 763 cases treated at the Anna Freud Centre since 1952; and audits that emphasise the role of self-reflection on the part of clinicians (e.g. Dolan and Norton, 1998; Feldman and Pugh, 1998). This muddying of the audit and research waters comes, I think, from three sources: one is the changing use of the term 'audit'; another because both are about inquiry and some audits utilise simple research methods; but the main reason seems to me to be because many psychological therapists adhere to the research orthodoxy of mainstream EBP. All other forms of qualitative and quantitative evaluation are assigned to audit. This, to my mind, introduces an overly elaborate and unnecessarily intimidating view of audit into what is, essentially, a relatively straightforward procedure.

It is helpful that a clearer picture has emerged limiting audit in psychological services to an expedient and manageable 'review and remedy' (Aveline and Watson, 2001: 200) of service delivery and practice, akin to Crombie et al.'s (1993) problem-solving approach. Contrasted with these are audits that demonstrate a service's efficiency and effectiveness, an approach that has been elaborated by the DoH (2004) with regard to the organisation and delivery of all psychological services. This recommends:

- *Service audit* that monitors whether standards have been met;
- *Service benchmarking* that benchmarks accessibility, equity, diversity and efficiency against other comparable services;
- *Routine outcome measurement* that includes quality of life and user satisfaction;
- *Cost effectiveness* of treatments.

Audit in art therapy

How have art therapists responded to this new audit culture? There is useful, practical guidance about modest, manageable and strategic audits which can be undertaken (Ansdell et al., 2004; Springham and Huet, 2004). These focus not on the problem-solving approach but on how audit can contribute to the demonstration of effectiveness, for example, through demographic information that illustrates the extent and nature of provision in the context of service review. There are a few full accounts of art therapy audit in the public domain, although reports of audit and service evaluation have been given to the ATPRN symposia (Hawtin, 2003; Seth-Smith, 2003). Some accounts reveal a similar slippage between audit and research to that in psychotherapy. For example, Whitaker and Middleton's (2003) engaging account of their struggle with implementing the CORE system describes their practical difficulties with its administration and their resistance to analysing the data, and eventual delight when they did. One-third of their clients were found to be achieving 'clinically reliable and significant change' and the remainder were not significantly deteriorating. The data was reanalysed by a colleague and found to have statistical significance, whereupon they began to enter the muddy audit/research waters. Dubowski's (2001) ambitious audit travelled a similar trajectory. His aim was to develop a tool for routine data collection that could be incorporated into the case notes of severely disabled, preverbal and non-verbal clients in a way that would make statistical and other forms of analysis possible on a national and international level, like CORE. Dubowski describes auditing the archives of arts therapy services in three hospitals for people with learning disabilities, the initial purpose being to see what the archives contained and, having established their content, to examine them for evidence of clinical effectiveness. The audit revealed an astonishing poverty in the case notes: only 261 of 1283 records were complete enough to enable analysis, the audit revealing significant problems with record keeping that clearly needed remedying. The next stage of the project investigated the records to see if, for example, certain client characteristics were associated with outcome and looking at multidisciplinary notes for corroborating evidence. Dubowski's project thus moved from audit into the realms of historical and outcome research, and from 'review and remedy' to effectiveness.

A different example of the blurring between research and audit is Turnbull and O'May's (2002) 'qualitative audit' of art therapy in primary care. This involved questionnaires and interviews with clients, and interviews with GPs on topics such as referral criteria and perceptions of art therapy's effectiveness. Turnbull and O'May found, in contrast to Wilson's (2002) descriptive commentary about the clinical work that was the subject of the audit, that referral criteria varied and that, although the GPs thought people had benefited, they did not understand what art therapy was, how it differed from other interventions, nor why it had helped. The clients and the art therapist reported that art therapy had been effective, but Turnbull and O'May say that effectiveness was not demonstrated because the study lacked a control group. This belies the modest processes and structures of audit and confuses it with outcome research.

Another example of qualitative audit is Huet's (1997) evaluation of an art therapy service for clients with severe and enduring problems. Through semi-structured interviews with staff and clients Huet was able to audit factors influencing the service, for example, the debilitating effects of the work on the therapists and a 'culture clash' between them and care staff that caused communication problems. This has aspects of the 'review and remedy' approach but alongside this is Huet's identification of the 'staying power' of art therapists and the importance of support and supervision that ensures that clients' needs are met. She also noted a flexibility of practice where art therapists attended to practicalities within a quasi-social, 'nurturing' relationship. Huet also remarks on how 'clients became noticeably animated and lively when discussing art' (1997: 19) and how keen they were to learn art techniques and have drop-in sessions. Clearly there was synergy between art therapists' adaptability and the relevance and acceptability of the service to the clients' needs, but interesting information emerged about how they wished to engage. This points to research questions about the role and function of art in art therapy service provision for these clients, illustrating how the EBP process links practice to audit and research.

These accounts show how useful audit can be for the identification of problems and for simple demonstrations of the efficiency and effectiveness of art therapy services, but the effectiveness orientation of some audits and the fluid boundaries between audit and research creates a potential for undue complexity. Ansdell et al.

(2004) suggest that practitioners need only engage with evidence-generating activities appropriate to immediate, local needs, for instance, doing a service review rather than outcome research. So what exactly are the differences between audit and research?

The difference between audit and research

Although there is a relationship between research and audit they are different pursuits (see Table 4.1). Audit usually focuses on services and the documentation of their efficient operation and outcome. Buttery (1998) suggests that audit is often described by active verbs such as 'improve' and 'change'; research has more exploratory sounding verbs such as 'identify' and 'discover'. Audit utilises fairly simple number crunching and qualitative feedback procedures and sometimes borrows simple research methods, but research draws on the entire range of methodologies. Dolan and Norton (1998) suggest that audit is not as methodologically robust as research but, significantly, that the information obtained from it is more convincing to purchasers because the information is often couched in economic terms, referring back to the origins of audit in fiscal accounting.

Audit's focus is on the routine checking of the daily realities of practice and service provision, the monitoring of change and the follow-up of improvements. Research, however, seeks 'truths' and insights, looking for findings that are representative and generalisable which, although this assumes EBP's research orthodoxy, serves to differentiate audit's purpose from that of research. Audit seeks neither to be replicable nor generalisable or, usually, to enter the public arena through publication. Audit does not ask the 'how?' and 'why?' discovery questions of research because its aim is to check that what is said to happen does actually happen, and whether what is happening is doing so in the best possible way. Audit does not look beyond the immediate context as it is always based in the realities of local service provision and is usually driven by the interests and requirements of purchasers, managers and the 'new categories of experts' (Shore and Wright, 2000: 62) created by the regulatory mechanisms of audit itself. Researchers have different 'drivers', asking different questions to those asked by managers, policy makers and auditors. Research is concerned with the multiplicity of topics that surround and inform practice and service delivery that, Parry suggests, is rarely of direct use to purchasers and managers in their day-to-day decision making. However, it is the intention of audit to give planners – be they policy makers, managers and/or practitioners – the information needed to 'improve clinical practice and services, to monitor and justify the use of resources, and to inform decision making' (1996: 423).

The audit cycle

Audit critically and systematically reviews the quality of a service and the care it provides. For audit to become a relatively simple but nonetheless politically informed

Table 4.1 The differences between audit and research

	Audit	Research
Verbs	Improve Enhance Ensure Rectify	Identify Determine Explore Discover
Drivers	Purchasers Managers Clinicians	Research councils Researchers Clinicians

Foci	Monitoring of services and
	    their delivery
	Improvement of services
	Best use of limited resources
	Does not develop new interventions
	Inform decision making about
	    policy and planning
	Ensuring effective use of
	    existing knowledge
		Theory construction
		
		Improve understanding of the
		    processes and outcomes of therapy
		Generating new knowledge
		May develop new interventions

Methods	Simple quantitative and
	    qualitative measures
	Usually done in the short term
		Entire range of research
		    methodologies
		Often done in medium/long term

Context	Local	General and varied

part of art therapists' everyday work, clarity of purpose and approach is critical. The cycle should be short and focus on a relatively small aspect of a service or an intervention so that the audit cycle can be completed quickly and be followed by another cycle that monitors the effects of any changes that have been implemented. Several authors have offered structures in which to think about audit (Crombie et al., 1993; Spender and Cooper, 1995; Parry, 1996; Feldman and Pugh, 1998; Healey, 1998) that can be summarised in a cycle that has six stages (see Figure 4.1):

1. *Construction* of a supportive audit environment;
2. *Selection* of an audit topic;
3. *Development* of service/practice standards;
4. *Collection* and analysis of information to compare what is happening with the standards that have been defined;
5. *Implementation* of changes/improvements to meet standards;
6. *Monitoring* the effects of change.

Construction of a supportive audit environment

Audit aims to create an engaged, curious and supportive environment within a service, staffed by reflexive practitioners who are able to learn about and monitor

Figure 4.1   Process map: the audit cycle

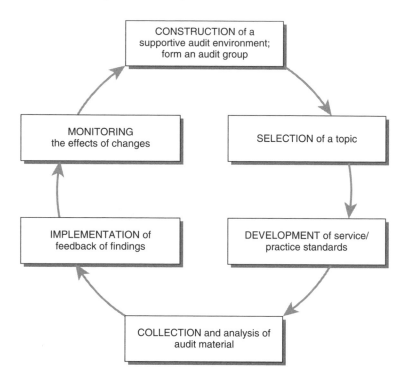

what they do. It is important therefore to ensure that, although the accountability implicit in audit is still to the managers, purchasers and consumers of services, the audit process remains autonomous and practitioner led so that art therapists are able maintain an open mind, be reflexive and learn.

This is all very well but, given that audit is essentially 'a critical scrutiny of what is taking place' (Healey, 1998: 49) involving transparency, accountability and the possibility of change, audit can become a process that gives rise to defensive feelings and conflict as the equilibrium of static patterns of work and relationship are challenged and disturbed. Healey (1998) identifies five levels at which conflict in the audit process can occur – national, institutional, departmental, interpersonal and personal – any one of which may give rise to hostility, anxiety and resistance. Tensions can arise in the relationship between managers and practitioners, auditor and auditee, not only because of the transparency and accountability (practice is seen and known by others) but also because audit can fundamentally challenge individual practitioners and their service's, and their institution's, status quo. The standard-setting part of the audit procedure appears to be based on logic and rational thinking but, if policy at national level does not sit comfortably with practice at local level, then it can lead to a sense of standards being imposed on practitioners who neither own nor are responsible for them. Audit therefore requires systems where it is perceived as helpful rather than a threat, and where colleagues are able to work together to implement any necessary changes.

Several authors have suggested ways in which anxieties and resistance to audit might be addressed and alleviated (Crombie et al., 1993; Feldman and Pugh, 1998; Margison et al., 1998), for example, the collaborative nature of audit should be emphasised and the process remain confidential to those involved. The group, service or individual doing the audit can then remain in control of the process and work without fear of censure or judgement from managers. Audit should be 'carried out by the group for the benefit of the group' (Crombie et al., 1993: 49). Feldman and Pugh advise a focus on 'ineffective systems rather than ineffective people' (1998: 61) and speak of the importance of regular group discussion about clinical matters that informs and enriches what might otherwise be rather dry and routine audit processes. Crombie et al. make the important point that managers are responsible for facilitating audit through allowing the staff involved the necessary time and resources. They summarise the principles of good audit as being:

- *confidential* to those involved;
- *educational* in spirit so that a supportive learning environment can identify educational need rather than making judgements;
- *parsimonious* so that only essential information is gathered in short, simple audits;
- *focused* on aspects of care that really can improve services and practices;
- *flexible* so that audit processes can evolve as issues are identified;
- *collaborative* and actively inclusive of all staff throughout;
- *resourced* so there is adequate time for every stage of the process;
- *tactful* with regard to the implementation of change.

The emphasis on the collegial processes of audit suggests that group-based art therapy audits – of local areas and services – could have much to offer.

Selecting an audit topic

The process of choosing what to audit is critical to a project's eventual success. Art therapists do not have time to waste on audits that are irrelevant and impractical and so should take time to think carefully, and strategically, about the kind of audit that would best serve the interests of a service, discriminating between the demonstration of the effectiveness and efficiency of a service or identifying and addressing a problem. Springham and Huet (2004) suggest simple effectiveness audits that link what art therapists actually do directly with government and local targets. Audit topics are usually interesting to the group or individual but, while this is entirely as it should be, some issues could be neglected because the area of work is unpopular, problematic or hedged with uncertainty and difficulty. It is likely that these are the very topics that would benefit most from 'review and remedy' audits.

It is important to distinguish between different kinds of audit topics. There are those that address the way clients enter a service ('input', 'structure' or 'facilities'), receive treatment ('process') and the extent to which they benefited from and were satisfied with the care they received ('output', 'outcomes' or 'results') (Donabedian, 1980; Parry, 1996). Audits of all kinds can demonstrate effectiveness and address problems. Maxwell (1984) usefully describes six criteria by which a successful service can be judged in terms of its relevance, equity, accessibility, acceptability, effectiveness and efficiency:

1. *Relevance:* a service is relevant if it meets the particular needs of its clients. Criteria for referral and exclusion from a service (e.g. age, actively psychotic) can be audited by looking at client populations by geographical area and matching this to the referrals a service receives;

2. *Equity:* a service is inequitous if people are excluded because of their age, ethnicity and socio-economic status. This can occur when particular referral and assessment patterns have developed without staff awareness and can be monitored through comparison of anticipated referral patterns with actual referrals;

3. *Accessibility:* services that are inaccessible are often so because of their geographical location, waiting lists and the practices of the 'gatekeepers'. Once again, these can be monitored through attention to clients' locations and to referral patterns;

4. *Acceptability:* this directly addresses the needs and views of clients about services and their delivery. The acceptability of a service can be related to user expectations; these in turn can be related to information received and consideration of client preferences and ability to make choices. This is one of the assessments psychological services are recommended to undertake (DoH, 2004). However, satisfaction differs significantly from outcome: one can be satisfied with a service but no better;

5. *Effectiveness:* in theory a service may do well on all the criteria above but may not provide effective treatment. Parry states quite unequivocally that, without the routine monitoring of outcomes, practitioners will not receive the objective feedback needed to ensure effective practice (1996: 438). The DoH (2004) recommends routine measurement of effectiveness, specifically 'quality of life' and user satisfaction, and the use of report cards to monitor deterioration or no change. It is, however, critical not to confuse effectiveness-oriented audits with outcome research;

6. *Efficiency:* there are two aspects to audits of the efficiency of a service: the competence of its procedures and its costs. Parry summarises this with chilling neatness: 'Efficiency maximises service output for a given input: improving efficiency increases therapeutic output for the same costs or maintains throughput at a lower cost' (1996: 441). The competence of a service can easily be audited through time-related measures, for example, between referral and assessment, assessment and the beginning of treatment, length of treatment and so on, and indeed the DoH recommends attention to waiting lists. Anecdotally I am aware that many art therapists undertake just such simple audits.

Audits that measure the cost efficiency of a service get into more troubled waters. Cost-effectiveness audits aim to ensure economic efficiency, for example, improving results for the same costs, or maintaining results for lower costs – based on the assumption that there are resolvable inefficiencies or problems that will either lower costs or improve a service without increasing costs. Quite how services are costed will vary according to local custom and practice and may present technical problems but, when undertaken with appropriately skilled colleagues, can provide useful information about art therapy's cost-effectiveness. Dolan and Norton (1998) give a good example of how a cost-effectiveness audit can work. They describe audits at the Henderson Hospital that compared the costs of clients' use of NHS services before and after treatment. These showed the considerable costs of the Henderson but enabled them to be compared with the huge drop in clients' subsequent use of their local mental health services and consequent savings to the NHS. These audits enabled the Henderson to significantly develop its services.

I think it is important to keep in mind the distinction between audit and research and between audits that identify and solve problems and those that indicate effectiveness. Rather than drawing on the battery of outcome measures that Parry suggests, I suggest that audits, for example of a service's 'results', focus on indirect but straightforward demographic information, as per Dolan and Norton's (1998) audit of clients' subsequent use (or not) of services. Focusing on uncomplicated and well-established demographics and brief client and staff satisfaction questionnaires or interviews means that art therapists can undertake modest endpoint audits to demonstrate effectiveness, leaving complex outcome studies for research. It is important, however, that art therapists do not become obsessed with number crunching – tempting though that might be – because qualitative service evaluations also have a significant role to play.

Crombie et al. (1993) and Parry (1996) both drew on Maxwell's six criteria to articulate three tiers of audit in medicine and psychotherapy that can address problems and effectiveness which I, in turn, have adapted for art therapy. To avoid clouding audits of effectiveness with outcome research I have adopted the term 'results' to describe audits that address the endpoint of art therapy when clients leave a service. Three tiers of art therapy audit can therefore be described:

- *Structure:* physical and personnel resources, equipment;
- *Process:* demographics, referrals, treatments, communication;
- *Results:* patient and referrer satisfaction, demographics.

This structure enables a list of worthwhile art therapy audit topics to be drawn up (see Box 4.1). Users' views are another source of ideas as they are best placed to say what is important, helpful and problematic in service delivery.

Box 4.1   Art therapy audit topics

Structure

- *Premises*: studio space, office space, waiting space, storage space, toilets;
- *Furniture*: tables, chairs, easels, plan chests, drying racks, sinks;
- *Staffing*: number of ATs, training, CPD, specialisms, experience;
- *Equipment*: art materials, kiln, PC, video, camera;
- *Support*: supervision, access to secretarial and technical assistance;
- *Information*: for referrers, for patients, demographics of local population and need for services.

(Continued)

Box 4.1   (Continued)

Process

- *Referral:* accessibility of service, referrers, appropriateness of referral, who is/is not referring, waiting times between referral and appointment, length of waiting list, numbers of and reasons for DNAs;
- *Demographics:* profile of patient population in terms of diagnosis, ethnicity, gender, age, service equity and relevance;
- *Assessment:* who is doing assessments, therapist training and experience, depth and quality, assessment protocols, procedures for risk assessment, matching patient to therapist;
- *Treatment:* what is offered, by whom, timeliness, appropriateness, care pathways, care protocols, therapist caseloads;
- *Documentation:* quality of case notes (clarity of case history, process description, progress), original artworks, photographic records, letters (referrers, family, discharge);
- *Communication:* between ATs, to md team, to referrers, to GPs;
- *Discharge:* protocols, reasons for discharge, information to referrers and md team, follow-up appointments, contact with family/social services.

Results

- *Patient status:* drop-outs, improvement, deterioration, suicide;
- *Symptom control:* levels of medication;
- *Patient satisfaction:* service accessibility, service acceptability, appropriateness and choice of treatments, waiting list/times, outreach services;
- *Referrer satisfaction:* with service availability, information and communication (ongoing and on discharge);
- *Indirect measures:* admission/readmission, frequency of GP/outpatient contact.

Source: adapted from Crombie et al. (1993).

Active and strategic methods of identifying worthwhile audit topics can also help to identify issues that are of immediate significance to a service. Again, it is as well to bear in mind the two types of audit: the problem-solving approach focusing on the identification and remedy of matters of concern, and performance factors that contribute to the success and/or effectiveness of services and practice. Both begin with practitioners brainstorming possible topics.

It is worth separating brainstorming from the process of actually choosing what to do. Different kinds of nominal group techniques can be used (described in Chapter 3). Buttery (1998) usefully describes 'Quality Impact Analysis' (Healthcare Quality Quest, 1997), a process that identifies four areas of auditable practice:

- where there is new research or development;
- where there are known to be problems or concerns;
- areas known to carry high risk;
- areas that are high volume.

Table 4.2   Art therapy quality impact analysis

Area of work	Problems	Risk	Frequency	TOTAL
New research/development				
1. AT groups with dementia patients	3	1	1	5
2. Studio space for psychotic patients	3	3	3	9
Known problems/concerns				
1. Waiting lists	1	2	1	4
2. Inappropriate referrals	3	1	3	7
High risk if incorrect				
1. Assessment protocol	1	3	1	5
2. Discharge protocol	2	3	1	6
Most frequent				
1. Communication with md team	3	3	3	9
2. Documentation in case notes	1	2	3	6

Source: adapted from Buttery (1998) and Healthcare Quality Quest (1997).

Audit topics are scored on a scale of 1 (low) to 3 (high) on criteria that address the extent of the problems, the degree of risk involved and the frequency with which the issue is encountered. The scores are then added together to give a total score for each topic, enabling priorities to be identified (see Table 4.2). The practicalities of auditing any topic remain a paramount consideration. Can standards for the activity be set and the activity measured? Is the problem a real one, and if so, can it be changed? Given that only a few projects will be possible each year a key question is, 'will this audit be worth the effort?' Closely followed by 'is everyone OK with it?' Ideally those conducting the audit should be enthusiastic and not view the project as potentially disruptive but as likely to enhance their work. A final question is whether staff have the expertise to do an audit, and if not, can help be accessed?

Developing standards

The monitoring of services and practices requires that they be measured against something: a standard. Standards define the aims of a service. There are several types: those that are required externally, for example, by government and the HPC; those that are negotiated locally and internally; those that are to do with the efficient operation and management of a service; and those that monitor the effectiveness of specific interventions. None of these standards is without problems. There are concerns about the development of an unhealthy uniformity, regulation and control of practices as they are benchmarked and developed into standards that can be audited. Shore and Wright (2000) suggest that this requires organisations and disciplines to reorganise themselves and to act more collectively than they otherwise would, bringing people, organisations and political objectives into alignment and under 'arm's-length control'. It is therefore important to differentiate between, and to be clear and transparent about, the origins of differing kinds of standards and about how, why and by whom they have been developed. Anything less calls them into question. While locally negotiated standards of a service and care are likely to be owned by a staff or audit group, those from out-with an organisation or a service may be resisted as aspects of the new manageri-alism 'which render political subjects governable' (2000: 71), that is to say, unless they match, or can be modified to match, local circumstances.

The development of local service and practice standards is a significant task in and of itself. One way of defining auditable standards is to draw on guidelines. The DoH (2004) draws on Margison's *Framework for Best Practice in Psychological Therapy Services* that rates services on a scale of 1 to 5 according to criteria (or standards) that correlate with policy recommendations. These include services that target users with greatest need; have single-entry points that emphasise assessment and use referral protocols; have tiered primary, secondary and specialist services; and that manage waiting lists effectively (see DoH, 2004, Annex C). Crombie et al. (1993) suggest drawing on reviews of the literature to develop standards and on audit reports from similar ser-vices. Direct comparison and discussion with other services are other possibilities. Discussion and consensus conferences with local clinicians that draw on best judge-ment, experience, observation and reflection on whether a service is doing as well as it might are also ways in which standards can be defined.

Setting targets that assess the extent to which practice complies with the standards is the next part of the process. Targets are usually measured in percent-ages and should be achievable. Thus, if a target of 100 per cent is set, the standard will address an aspect of care or an event that is always expected to occur, for example, 'Every patient referred to the art therapy service will be assessed by an art therapist'. Although such a target might seem overly prescriptive, the peer review of reasons for non-compliance can provide useful information and enable problem areas to be identified; in this example non-compliance might be because of staff shortages, skills deficits and CPD needs. A target less than 100 per cent is set when the event's occurrence is dependent on other variables, such as the avail-ability of transport for community-based clients.

The collection and analysis of audit material

The gathering of information for audit can be retrospective, from existing documents for instance, or it may be concurrent, such as in the case of new mate-rial collected specifically for the purpose of audit. Retrospective audit can draw on material such as referral forms, case notes or admission/discharge records, but this can be limiting because auditing procedures are partial and only ever as good as the quality and nature of the available records (as Dubowski (2001) discovered). Indeed it may be that the first audit a service does is of its record-keeping proce-dures. Notwithstanding the inevitable flaws, existing documents enable audits of practice, for example, of assessment protocols, of adverse events and sub-optimal care, liaison in a team, follow-ups of non-attenders and so on.

Concurrent audit material will usually require staff cooperation in the recording of new or additional data. This can take several forms. Data can be collected through structured record forms; these can become part of case notes, ensuring that data is collected in a systematised way, especially through computerised systems. However, Crombie et al. (1993) question their use, saying that they work only for short periods of time and for specific purposes because, when used for routine record keeping, there tends to be high levels of missing data. Data for audit topics addressing matters such as client and referrer satisfaction will involve questionnaires and maybe interviews. It is as well to keep these as simple and unambiguous as possible, collecting only essential data using mostly closed questions (that invite only a 'yes' or 'no' answer), ranked responses (assessing an item on a scale of 1 to 5) and a simple coding system, although satisfaction surveys require more open-ended questions. Here the boundaries between audit and research begin to blur, so it is best to keep a tight focus and only collect limited data on a small number of clients.

Springham and Huet (2004) compare the closed questions of audit about art therapists' behaviour – 'do you or don't you do x?' – with the more open-ended questions of therapy, comparing audit topics to the interactive and intrapersonal processes of art therapy that cannot be audited. Whatever data collection method is chosen it will need piloting, but the data analysis should require no more than a simple software package that has database and spreadsheet capability, or a pen, paper and calculator.

Who collects and analyses audit material varies according to time and other resources, although generally speaking a sense of ownership is maintained if the auditees are also the auditors. However, it is often helpful if a member of the local clinical audit team or administrative staff are involved, part of whose task it is to provide practitioners with training and support; advice can also be sought from the National Audit Office. Art therapists can draw on these resources but, once again, must be careful to do so in a politically informed way.

Audit methods that use forms and numbers are perhaps the simplest but might lack a certain spark that ignites the real interest and curiosity of practitioners. It is therefore worth attending to other approaches that draw on the resources of a staff group. Observational methods using video, role play and group discussion can be used, as in Feldman and Pugh's (1998) audits at the Maudsley where the routine collection of text-based data by support staff was augmented by regular discussion of it by clinicians. They give the example of an audit that investigated why more patients were being referred to individual than group therapy; this had led to long waiting times for group-therapy trainees to start work and long waiting lists for individual therapy. The audit led to the staff group's exploration of the countertransference responses of assessors and a review of the referral criteria for group and individual therapy.

Findings, improvement, and the implementation of change

Buttery (1998) usefully distinguishes between audit findings and audit results: audit findings refer to the degree of compliance with standards; audit results are the improvements and the implementation of change that follow on from the findings. This part of the process has to be sensitively negotiated but can be accomplished if all staff have been fully involved as there is likely to be a desire not to waste all the hard work. The key to any change therefore comes from a genuine consensus about the *need* for change. She also emphasises the importance of feedback from audit, particularly on improvements, so that it does not become a punitive exercise. Feedback can be given in written and verbal forms, usually in a meeting at which all those involved have the opportunity to discuss the findings, the initial report, any changes and how they might be implemented, plus the plans for reaudit. After the feedback meeting a final report can be drafted, following the template below:

- *Background* to the audit project, including description of the audit group and the topic;
- *Aims and objectives* of the audit project;
- *Standards*, and how they have been developed;
- *Collection and analysis* of audit material;
- *Findings*;
- *Feedback* process and plans for implementation;
- *Anticipated changes*, for completion after feedback meeting;
- *Plans for reaudit*, for completion after feedback meeting

(adapted from Buttery, 1998: 201–2).

The inclusion of visual material in the form of graphs and pie charts to illustrate findings can make information quickly and easily accessible. Ansdell et al. (2004), and Springham and Huet (2004) give examples and remind art therapists to think strategically about who should be privy to audit findings.

The distribution of an audit report will vary, for example, if the audit was of a service then it will be appropriate to make it available to practitioners, managers and service users, but if the audit was clinical then, according to Buttery (1998: 202) it will usually remain confidential to individual practitioners so that issues of performance can be resolved in a supportive, non-persecutory way.

When it comes to implementing change it is as well to remember that the topic is likely to have been chosen for strategic reasons. Reconnecting with the original motivation can assist with identifying possible solutions and hence implementing change. Crombie et al. (1993) suggest that there are three overarching causes of auditable problems within the 'review and remedy' framework: to do with the individual practitioner, the organisation, or 'external' matters, that is, to do with clients. Problems in each sphere have their associated solutions: difficulties with individual staff, such as a lack of knowledge or experience, defensive practice or entrenched views, can all be addressed through CPD; organisational problems such as a lack of resources, long waiting lists and communication failures should be addressed with managers and through reorganisation of systems; and client issues like non-attendance should be addressed through explanation and review of information. These authors suggest that it is best to implement change incrementally and, crucially, also speak to having adequate resources with which to do so, stating unequivocally that audit can be used to present powerful arguments for increased resources that will directly improve service provision.

Crombie et al. criticise many audit projects because they are no more than surveys of current practice and do not have a built-in intention to implement change. However, their orientation is towards problem-solving audits, and many audits do simply seek to document what a service offers (e.g. Margison et al., 1998) and identify where the gaps are (e.g. Ansdell et al., 2004: 21–6). Following through from findings to results and being active in appropriate dissemination is key to ensuring that services and practices are evidence based.

Monitoring the effects of change

The last stage of the audit cycle is to monitor the results of an audit project in a repeat of the cycle. As ever, time and resources limit art therapists' capacity for reauditing topics and so an expedient approach is necessary to achieve a balance between undertaking a second cycle and beginning new audit projects. Limiting reaudit to topics where non-compliance with agreed standards and targets, or where particular deficits have been identified, can make the task more manageable.

Audit is a mixed blessing. It provides a means of demonstrating effectiveness, of ensuring that the best available evidence is put into practice, of addressing problems with service delivery and making sure that practice is properly documented, modified where necessary and maintained according to standards that have been defined and monitored by art therapists themselves. It can generate change. Audit supports and demonstrates – it evidences – good practice and efficient service delivery and enables the identification of CPD needs when performance is below par. It can be a means through which practitioners really seize the agenda for effectiveness and efficiency in the delivery of art therapy services. This is because audit conveys a particular kind of information to a particular audience (managers and policy makers) and does so in their language, that is, in pragmatic and economic terms, in a way that research cannot.

However, audit is also a self-referential and self-reinforcing system, one that is hard to control and impossible to avoid, becoming so naturalised and pervasive that it goes increasingly unchallenged. This is not to say that accountability is bad, rather that it is important to recall that it is a direct consequence of the authoritarian and financially driven model of the internal markets that were introduced into the public sector during the 1980s. These have become an aspect of the EBP paradigm that seeks to micromanage and implicitly undermines the authority and experience of professionals. It is driven by the new managerialism and represents a wish for a standardised, not to say depersonalised, system of treatments and service delivery that is continually scrutinised in what can become a demoralising and destructive process. Ideally, however, audit is an arena where a particular kind of evidence is considered in a local, public 'hearing', conducted by peers for peers. Within such a frame audit can be a constructive and politically useful procedure.

It is therefore critical that art therapists engage with audit in a politically reflexive way that ensures respect for our professional autonomy, reflects the values of the discipline and operates strategically within systems that can impose their own forms of governance and power. We must be explicit about our professional culture and values, using standards and guidelines that we have developed so that we are able to move between worlds and deal with the political and economic forces that threaten. This can be accomplished by creating our own meanings for the terms and procedures used by those that seek to regulate from above and outside art therapy which acquire their legitimacy through our compliance with them. Foucault (1977) showed how dull and bureaucratic procedures can have a profound effect on how we think about ourselves and on what we do. Art therapists need to keep this in mind and stay involved with every stage of the audit process, asserting our own definitions of quality and accountability that make sense in terms of the profession's values and practices and in terms of local custom and practice, no matter their divergence from those imposed upon us. Only then can audit become a practitioner-led tool for creative and reflexive practice in art therapy, rather than a management-led device that enables economic scrutiny and the external micromanagement of professional practices.

5   The methodological debate

I have described how medicine and its evidence hierarchies dominate the values and structures of EBP, but what constitutes the best evidence is vigorously contested in the psychological therapies, in education (Thomas and Pring, 2004), in social care (Smith, 2004) and sometimes in medicine too (Brown et al., 2003). Psychotherapists, psychologists, counsellors and psychiatrists have taken different epistemological positions about which kind of research provides the best evidence in the psychological therapies. Some argue against a focus on outcome and for methodological pluralism (Parry and Richardson, 1996) and others debate the relative merits of different research methods while promoting how *they* gather relevant, robust and truthful evidence: examples are Wesseley (2001) on RCTs (randomised controlled trials) Barkham and Mellor-Clark (2000) on CORE and PRNs (practice research networks) and McLeod (2001) on qualitative approaches to outcome research.

A parallel pattern of pluralism and personal preference can be seen in art therapy, authors agreeing that both quantitative and qualitative research contribute to art therapy's evidence base, but prioritising narrative case studies (Edwards, 1999), 'normative' studies of artistic development (Gantt, 1998), experimental case studies (Julliard, 1998) and surveys (Wood, 1999b). In order to progress this discussion I think it helpful to describe exactly what 'research' is and to explore the methodological debates that both inform and challenge the paradigm that is EBP before giving a brief overview of the research process.

What is research?

The best evidence in the orthodox EBP paradigm comes from just one kind of research – the RCT – but research comprises a range of approaches to the collection and analysis of data. Definitions of research describe much that will be familiar to the curious clinician. A brief search reveals that it derives from the French *recherché*, which means to investigate thoroughly. It is a:

1. careful or diligent search;
2. studious inquiry or examination; especially: investigation or experimentation aimed at the discovery and interpretation of facts, revision of accepted theories or laws in the light of new facts, or practical application of such new or revised theories or laws;
3. the collecting of information about a particular subject. (*Merriam-Webster Online* at www.webster.com)

It means to be specific, to discover, to be critical, to inquire, to question and to investigate, all in the search for new knowledge. It is a process where existing information is reviewed – *re*-viewed, *re*-interrogated – and placed in a contemporary context alongside newly discovered material. Research is not related to a single approach to investigation and discovery, nor to an ideology. Sometimes the words science and empirical come into play, suggesting certain methods. But dig a bit further and discover that science means:

1. the state of knowing: knowledge as distinguished from ignorance or misunderstanding
2. (a) a department of systematized knowledge as an object of study ...
   (b) something – that may be studied or learned like systematized knowledge. (*Merriam-Webster Online*)

Science becomes knowing, knowledge being 'the fact or condition of knowing something with familiarity gained through experience or association' (*Merriam-Webster Online*). A third meaning of science, taken from the same source however, specifically describes a knowledge focus and how it is obtained:

3. (a) knowledge or a system of knowledge covering general truths or the operation of general laws especially as obtained and tested through scientific method
   (b) such knowledge or a system of knowledge concerned with the physical world and its phenomena.

This speaks to generalisation, to tests and to a certain kind of knowledge of the physical world that has been discovered in a certain way. Allied to this is empirical, meaning:

1. originating in or based on/relying on observation and experience alone, often without due regard for systems and theory
2. capable of being verified or disproved by observation or experiment. (*Merriam-Webster Online*)

This implies close attention to specifics that can be evidenced through careful looking and trying something out in repeatable ways. Note, however, that neither science nor empiricism refer to RCTs, these being situated among several other key descriptors of research like careful, systematic, discovery and interpretation that indicate logic and being methodical in the generation and ordering of understanding and knowing. Research can therefore be understood as learning and scholarship about something new, a means of acquiring and organising information in a focused and critical way; the new learning is then made public. Viewed within this framework, different approaches to research become different ways of finding out different things, and research 'a systematic process of critical inquiry leading to valid propositions and conclusions that are communicated to interested others' (McLeod, 1994: 4).

Such an open-ended definition does not conform to the medical research orthodoxy implicit within EBP's rules of evidence that require an answer to just one question: 'does it work?' Critical inquiry infers more questions, not unequivocal answers, and opens up the field for pluralistic research-based evidence. Nonetheless debate continues about the relative worth of quantitative and qualitative methods. Within EBP debate can be polarised, differing stakeholders arguing their corner passionately. What are they arguing about?

The quantitative/qualitative debate

Quantitative researchers consider their approach to be better because it is value-free; qualitative researchers believe their methods are superior because they enable deeper understanding. In EBP terms, and outside the social sciences and humanities in general, only quantitative models are considered acceptable, qualitative methods being described as unscientific. This is because quantitative researchers tend to regard knowledge as absolute and obtainable only through standardised procedures. Quantitative research is based in positivist traditions whose language comes from the natural sciences, that is, from physics, chemistry and biology that assume there are patterns and regularities, causes and effects that can always be observed, given the same conditions. Qualitative researchers critique the positivist approach, and by implication the whole EBP paradigm, because the differences between the natural world and the social and cultural world are not addressed, neither are the socially constructed activities of defining outcomes and measuring them. The qualitative researcher's view is reflexive, the world being viewed as an individual's own creation that differs from one person to the next and from culture to culture. Qualitative research draws on phenomenological and ethnographic research traditions that enable a reflexive, heuristic approach in naturalistic settings. This draws fire from quantitative researchers because subjectivity and bias are assumed to be a consequence of a qualitative researcher's immersion in the field, making the evidence fatally flawed. This is why qualitative studies are, in EBP terms, deemed suitable only for exploratory and descriptive research, that is, the stages before the counting begins, before the pinch in the RCT hourglass.

Several authors describe the differences between quantitative and qualitative research. Higgins (1996) explores them in terms of left-brain (quantitative) and right-brain (qualitative) activities. Silverman (2000) offers the features of qualitative and quantitative research (see Table 5.1) which are paralleled by McLeod's (1999) research traditions of qualitative and quantitative research (see Table 5.2). These articulate the dissimilarities at their most stark. Quantitative methods consider the *amount* of things. Some quantitative researchers prefer surveys and experiments that collect precise measurements from representative samples of specified populations in order to test hypotheses, while others prefer structured observations, analysis of predetermined categories and the review, or meta-analysis, of large datasets of previously collected material. This, of course, is the framework of EBP. Qualitative methods investigate the *nature* of things. There is no agreed, underlying doctrine but instead lots of 'isms' – feminism, interactionism and postmodernism – and many ways to map, explore and think about the world, for example, through

Table 5.1   Features of qualitative and quantitative research

Qualitative	Quantitative
Soft	Hard
Flexible	Fixed
Subjective	Objective
Political	Value-free
Case study	Survey
Speculative	Hypothesis testing
Grounded	Abstract

Source: Silverman (2000: 2).

Table 5.2   The research traditions of qualitative and quantitative research

Qualitative	Quantitative
Holistic	Reductionist
Elucidates meaning	Measures variables
Sensitive, accurate description	Statistical techniques
Seeks categories used by people	Imposes researcher's categories
Inductive	Deductive
Heuristic	Theory testing
Seeks authenticity	Seeks validity and reliability
Seeks to minimise illusion	Seeks to minimise error
Reflexive	Other directed
Researcher as tool	Techniques as tools
Co-informants/collaborators	Research 'subjects'
Negotiation of outcomes	Researcher decides outcomes
Research design evolves	Rigid initial research design
Methods: interviews, open-ended questionnaires	Methods: experiments, questionnaires, coding schemes
Research genres: qualitative, grounded theory, narrative, human inquiry, phenomenological, feminist	Research genres: quantitative, outcome and process studies, surveys

Source: McLeod (1999: 27).

grounded theory, content analysis, discourse analysis, participant observation, ethnography and phenomenology, working from the premise that there are different ways of defining and understanding reality. Pluralism, uncertainty, co-construction and deconstruction of the world are intrinsic to qualitative research, the notion of the single, unitary, consolidating and legitimising approach inherent to EBP being considered as both privileged and suspect.

However, it is not that quantitative researchers use statistics and qualitative researchers do not, and that qualitative approaches address the social and cultural construction of variables while quantitative approaches correlate them. The difference is one of emphasis between schools who have within them differences and preferences: for the analysis of words and images rather than numbers; for the observation of naturally occurring data rather than experiment; for unstructured rather than structured interviews; for meaning that attempts 'to document the world from the point of view of the people studied' rather than measuring behaviour or symptoms (Hammersley, 1992: 165); and for inductive, hypothesis-generating research rather than deductive, hypothesis testing. These preferences make qualitative research strong on descriptive narrative, but its basic premise – that knowledge is temporary and there is no one objective truth – makes it vulnerable to criticism in services dominated by the positivist orientation of EBP. Within the EBP paradigm the debate moves from the generalities of methodology to how best to address just one research question: 'what works?' This is reduced further to arguments for and against RCTs.

Arguments for and against RCTs

Wesseley (2001) argues fervently for the use of RCTs in the evaluation of psychotherapy, saying that they are the only way to identify when a treatment is doing more harm than good. He describes situations where clinicians, with the best of intentions and who thought they knew best, continued a treatment in the belief that it was effective and because there were good patient satisfaction reports, that is until an RCT showed otherwise. He gives the examples of the cessation of radical mastectomies in favour of lumpectomies and of routine stress debriefing of disaster victims that were shown to increase rather than reduce the incidence of PTSD. Richardson (2001), and Bower and King (2000) also argue in favour of RCTs to study the effectiveness of psychotherapy. Richardson says that RCTs enable generalisation in a way that case studies and matched case series do not. They allow pre- and post-treatment measures; enable the documentation of change across patient groups through randomisation of patients to treatment and non-treatment groups; and they eliminate sample bias and reduce the likelihood of chance differences. This allows greater confidence in an inferred causal relationship between an individual, independent variable (the treatment) and a dependent variable (the outcome) than can be had from other research designs. Authors agree that randomisation – when patients are randomly assigned to a treatment group or to a non-treatment control group – is the only way to address confounding in research, that is, when an outcome is influenced by something else happening at the same time as the treatment being tested, for instance, other treatments or improvements over time.

However, RCTs are regularly critiqued because, fundamentally, they require the transfer of a research paradigm devised for one domain (medicine) to another. They have significant limitations in terms of their appropriateness, relevance and practical application across the public sector and in psychological services, particularly in the dynamically oriented therapies. RCTs also take a long time to prepare, recruit, operate and analyse and are complex, expensive and difficult to run. They require large numbers of patients (a minimum of 170) who are willing to participate, either as a patient or as a control. Richardson (2001) suggests that those who do consent to being part of a trial may not be representative of an entire patient population and that randomisation may have a psychological impact on the treatment received. There are also problems with the measures used to document change. McLeod (2000) critiques the standard psychometric self-evaluation questionnaires, saying that different measures give different results. Roth (2002) also remarks on the instruments used in RCTs and the absence of direct exploration of social factors – of social exclusion and material deprivation – saying that most clients in RCTs are white.

Slade and Priebe (2002), like several others (e.g. Roth and Fonagy, 1996; Margison, 2001; Richardson, 2001; Sturdee, 2001), comment on EBP's and RCTs' dependence on diagnostic criteria and their implicit trajectory of illness and treatment, cause and effect. They argue that grouping clients according to diagnosis assumes that diagnosis determines treatment, reducing the complexity of individuals and their difficulties to a single classification, to a core condition that ignores the dynamic, narrative-based formulations that reveal underlying patterns of relationship in dynamically based therapy. This fundamental (and medically based) assumption can, as Richardson points out with regard to psychotherapy (and Dudley (2004) with regard to art therapy assessment), fail to take account not only of a discipline's language and values but also of the heterogeneity and difference among clients, for example with regard to socio-demographic factors, age, gender, ethnicity, psychiatric history, symptom severity and the treatment setting. This creates further problems with systematic reviews and meta-analyses of RCTs that also cluster around the bio-behavioural system of ICD and DSM-IV. All of these factors call into question the relevance and reliability of EBP's best evidence.

RCTs are undoubtedly problematic, their gold standard somewhat tarnished when applied to the psychological therapies. Their methodological framework rests on assumptions that are best suited to biological, behavioural and cognitive treatments; there are difficulties with generalising from the particularities of rigorously controlled trial conditions to the routines of everyday care in settings in differing geographical locations with local services and delivery structures; they need long-term follow-up study; they require large-scale funding; and the intervention or treatment being investigated must be standardised, all of which limits their application outside a controlled research setting and in diverse socio-cultural contexts with clinicians whose practice is eclectic. RCTs do not address how or why an intervention or treatment works, they simply investigate whether or not, under strictly controlled circumstances, it does. This is not to say that RCTs should not or cannot be done in art therapy; rather that they are not, as orthodox EBP would have it, the yellow brick road to the ultimate evidence.

The processes of psychological and social intervention differ fundamentally from medical intervention and require different means of investigation. Slade and Priebe (2002) suggest that mental health problems can only be measured by proxy because they are not always directly and independently observable but are observed through interactions with others. Mental health problems are individually and socially based and require treatments that are social and interactive, delivered in a social context. This necessitates the explanatory research methods of the social sciences.

The acquisition of evidence from qualitative research

Qualitative approaches have been significantly undervalued in EBP although, as described in Chapter 1, the necessity of diverse approaches to the acquisition of evidence is slowly gaining recognition (e.g., Dixon-Woods et al., 2001; Dixon-Woods and Fitzpatrick, 2001). McLeod (2000) emphasises the potential contribution qualitative methods might make to outcome research, exploring this in the context of research that has demonstrated that it is the qualities of the therapeutic relationship or of the therapist him/herself that influences outcome rather than the model of therapy. Ignoring these active ingredients is, he suggests, missing the point, so to address them means the inclusion of individual or focus group interviews with clients and therapists, transcripts of therapy sessions and ethnographic participant observation that enable 'collaborative and dialogical forms of meaning-making' (2001: 8) and the development of user-based outcomes (2000: 117). He argues that qualitative methods like these allow informants' views – our key witnesses – to be paramount, and for direct links to be made between clients' experiences of treatment and their outcome. This kind of research-based evidence is generated and socially constructed by users and their carers, and by practitioners too, through the privileging of oral and written statements over numbers.

In the orthodox EBP framework of medicine, qualitative research is thought to have significant weaknesses because the circumstances of its production have all the unpredictability and complexities of routine practice that call its validity into question. However, its strengths are in the foregrounding of the meanings, concerns and attitudes of users, the inclusion of practitioner views and locating research in the real world of practice, all of which allows the establishment of rather different criteria through which outcomes, services and their delivery can be evaluated. This is not to say that validity is not an issue in qualitative research; rather that, as McLeod says, it has different criteria and techniques to establish the rigour and validity of a study. Quantitative researchers establish validity through 'comparing sets of scores', but qualitative researchers 'can only compare sets of words' (2001: 182), ensuring validity through descriptive detail of the research and its context and the transparency of the researcher about their personal engagement and heuristic process so that trustworthiness, integrity and credibility is established (McLeod, 1999).

An equal hearing

At present EBP orthodoxy assigns qualitative research a supporting role only, usually as part of inductive research when, for example, a new approach is being developed. Despite acknowledgement of the evidence that qualitative research can provide it is still considered a step, albeit an important one, on the way to RCTs. It is important to state unequivocally that this research trajectory is particular to the positivist model that underpins EBM that has been transferred wholesale to EBP in psychological services, to work in other sectors and could, if there is no resistance, be applied to art therapy too. Choosing a research method to explore any research question, whether or not it is designed to investigate a treatment and its outcomes, does not involve deciding between numbers and words, precise and imprecise data. The choice of method is usually made according to the nature of the project and its fit with the research question, not on the basis of an 'ideological commitment to one methodological paradigm or another' (Hammersley, 1992: 163, quoted in Silverman, 2000: 12). Every approach has its flaws, and no single method can investigate every aspect of a research question or provide irrefutable, absolute evidence of the effectiveness of an intervention.

In my view evidence from the range of quantitative and qualitative methods should have an equal hearing within an EBP framework adjusted to fit the discipline of art therapy. Slade and Priebe (2002), like many other authors (e.g. Parry and Richardson, 1996; McLeod ,1999, 2001; Parry, 2000; Reynolds, 2000; Priebe and Slade, 2002a; Finzen, 2002) argue for an egalitarian, pluralistic attitude towards research-based evidence. 'What works' is but one question among many that can be asked about an intervention, but in the present climate it remains key because throughout the public sector there is a particular task: to legitimise practice through demonstrating effectiveness. What has yet to be fully acknowledged is that this can be accomplished in many ways, and that differing kinds of research make equally valid contributions to the knowledge base about care. What gets lost in EBP orthodoxy is the system of free proof that gives the opportunity to engage in a free and open, if adversarial, process of judgement which ensures that, whatever the nature of the evidence presented, it will be judged on its merits and have the respect of the entire community it serves.

Richardson may be right when he suggests that, while 'certain core principles' could be applied to the evaluation of all treatments, 'each field of enquiry will have – to some extent – its own unique evidential standards' (2001: 159). Art therapists must argue forcefully that the research trajectory of EBP is not a series of research stages or a hierarchy of ever-more rigorous and therefore reliable evidence that is appropriate to our discipline. This is not to say that art therapists should resist participation in quantitative research in general and RCTs in particular. Despite their undoubted difficulties they can, and already have, produced worthwhile and interesting findings. To turn our back on RCTs would, in my view, be extremely foolhardy. The point is that qualitative methodologies, including the all important visual methods so central to the construction of art therapy's evidence base, can and do deliver equally important findings and allow room for user and practitioner voices to be heard, to be represented, in the evidential process. The form art therapy's evidence takes should be determined by the profession and the differing perspectives of all those it serves, and the judgements about it should command the public confidence that Jackson (2001) recommends.

Nonetheless, art therapy is inextricably linked to wider systems and vested interests that attempt to impose their research and evidential criteria on the discipline, despite EBP's inclusive, pluralistic rhetoric. If and when this occurs it must be vigorously contested. Art therapy has to tread a delicate path. We must not bow down before the demands of EBP orthodoxy, but this does not mean that we should refuse to engage with unfamiliar and initially uncomfortable research methods that will make a significant contribution to the evidence base of the discipline.

Whatever its methodology, research is always a methodical and systematic activity. Methods differ according to the research question but there is sequence of activities – a generic process – that applies to most projects that I will now describe.

The research process

Research begins with choosing a topic, although there is usually rather more passion in the process than this suggests. Whatever the topic is, it simply has to be done; you have little choice in the matter because your autobiography will have led you to it. It is important that the researcher is seriously curious about his or her topic, that there is a real 'bee in the bonnet', an itch that has to be scratched which sustains the researcher through some of the mind-numbing moments of data collection and analysis. However, such motivation, although desirable, may not always drive research in these EBP-dominated times; necessity, expediency and simple survival are strong motivators too, but whatever the primary driver the characteristic clarity and precision of research need to be brought to the entirety of the process. Thus research always:

- *Begins with a clear, unambiguous research question*, often about why, what, how and when a particular thing happens;
- *Has a clear goal*, a clear statement of the aims and objectives of the project;
- *Entails a specific programme of work*: much of the process is practical, task oriented and requires planning from beginning to end, including periods of information gathering, reflection, collation, digestion and presentation;
- *Aims to increase understanding* through the interpretation of information that enables conclusions to be drawn;
- *Requires reasoned argument* that supports the conclusions. The researcher has to present a clear and logical argument and an ordered sequence of ideas;
- *Involves an iterative process*, meaning that new knowledge is contextualised and/or based upon previous knowledge, giving rise to further questions and projects (adapted from Walliman, 2001).

Research usually begins with writing a research proposal and ends with public presentation and dissemination. Below is a brief outline of the process overall.

Writing a research proposal

Proposals include a provisional title and sketch out the study overall. They outline the aims and objectives or a hypothesis, state the initial research question/s and give an indication of the literature to be consulted and possible methods of data collection and analysis, and sometimes a timetable for the entire project that includes deadlines for the differing stages. Proposals are by no means definitive documents but a way of getting started and bringing structure to a project. Getting together, writing and, for funded projects, costing a research proposal is in itself a significant piece of work that takes time and energy. Proposals vary in length and style according to their purpose and audience, for example, funding applications usually address the dissemination of findings as well as costs, but most are fairly brief and address five issues:

1. *Background to the investigation*: the area to be researched, including a brief review of the relevant literature;
2. *Aims and objectives*: the purpose of the study and the research question/s;
3. *Proposed method*: how the data will be collected and analysed, including pilot studies;
4. *Anticipated outcomes*: the expected findings and likely answers to the research question/s;
5. *Likely areas of reflection*: potential problems in the research and possible future studies.

Bibliographic searching

This is the first task of most research that situates the research in a critical context. It begins with the identification of relevant books, chapters, papers and authors already known, and perusal of bibliographies for further reading and follow-up of particular authors. It involves checking through edited texts and searching through back copies of art therapy and other relevant journals. CD roms, the 'grey literature' (unpublished material) to be found in theses, the Internet and databases such as Psychinfo and Medline should be searched too. All this material can then be skim-read for relevance and to identify those needing in-depth attention. This can reduce the literature to manageable levels, but sometimes its volume can need limiting further, for instance to just the British art therapy literature or texts published after a certain date. On the other hand relevant literature may be sparse, in which case the search has to be broadened to allied areas.

Reviewing the literature

This involves the appraisal of all the relevant texts, taking special note of the research literature and differentiating between it and other, non-research-based literature (see Chapter 3 on critical appraisal). Significant issues, texts and key authors are identified as the research question is refined and contextualised and gaps in the literature – which the research will address – are clarified. Research-based literature is often particularly helpful as the methods may provide a model for the new project. Literature reviews often involve a concertina-like process where the field contracts and expands as new ideas, authors and models are discovered, and the research question/s, project outlines and proposed methods are modified.

Data collection and analysis

How data is collected and analysed defines the nature of a research project. Broadly speaking, research is usually driven either by hypotheses or by objectives:

- *Hypotheses* are postulated (claimed to be so) and tested in a highly structured way;
- They usually arise from existing research;
- Are essentially a continuation of existing research;
- Usually employ quantitative methodologies;
- Are often described as hypothetico-deductive research.

This is the approach privileged by EBP.

- *Objectives* are simply stated and then explored in an evolutionary way;
- They usually begin with an aim (to find out more, or study x);
- May or may not be based in existing research;
- Usually employ qualitative methodologies;
- Are often described as *heuristic* (discovery) or *hermeneutic* (interpretive) research.

Either the nature of the research and the hypothesis it poses predetermines the study's structure (hypothetico-deductive), or the research is exploratory and the structure evolves as the study proceeds (heuristic or hermeneutic). Once the data have been gathered and analysed the findings can be identified and explored in the context of the literature review, together with any other literature that informs discussion about the data.

Writing-up and dissemination

Again, the differing methodological approaches determine the structure of the final presentation. Hypothetico-deductive research in the positivist tradition begins with contextualising the research within a review of the literature, following this with sections that describe the methodology and the findings, discussing these in the context of literature and finishing with a conclusion and indications for future research. Heuristic and hermeneutic studies often have a narrative structure where the story of the research and the researcher unfolds as methodology, literature, reflections and findings are interwoven. But whatever the approach and whatever the findings it is critical that the researcher's process is transparent and explicit so that, theoretically, it is possible for another to tread the same research path and reach the same destination, that is to say, the research is replicable. Dissemination usually occurs through conference papers and publication but performance or exhibition-based presentations offer other possibilities (see Bagley and Cancienne, 2002).

Art making can help identify the focus of a project early on in its life and assist the articulation and shaping of experience and understanding as it continues. Using art in this way is part of art therapists' critical reflexivity that can usefully be brought to bear on research. As we know, thoughts and ideas accessed and articulated through art differ from those described orally and in text. Moving between visual reverie and data, art making and writing can help transform inchoate understandings into a coherent, thought-through piece of research, the resulting artefacts perhaps becoming part of the project's presentation in the public domain.

Research ethics

Research ethics address matters such as the protection of research participants, the nature of the researcher or researcher/clinician's role, where the data comes from and what happens to it and to the findings after the research has ended. Consideration of ethical issues in the conduct of all research, whether or not the research is clinically based, is an important part of the research process and a matter of increasingly rigorous regulation and legislative change. Research with all human and animal subjects requires approval from the host organisation's management and often involves necessary but time-consuming applications to research ethics committees. The DoH has addressed this through its *Research Governance Framework for Health and Social Care* (RGF) (2001b) and the establishment of NHS Research Ethics Committees (RECs) and the Central Office for Research Ethics Committees (COREC). The RGF established the standards, codes of conduct and responsibilities of all those involved in any aspect of research in health and social care, addressing the dignity, rights, safety and well-being of participants. It requires that every project is independently reviewed, informed consent from participants is obtained, confidentiality is maintained and difference respected, and it ensures the freedom of information about the project and its findings. It also supports, wherever possible, participants' involvement in all aspects of research. COREC coordinates local and multi-centre RECs and offers information and guidance about applications for ethical review.

A progress report on the RGF's implementation in social care (DoH, 2003) highlighted some necessary adjustments to the rather burdensome processes of RECs. This followed consultation with social care communities and service users and criticism of the process as frustrating and time consuming (Tinker, 2001). There were also, interestingly, complaints about a 'focus on research methods rather than ethical issues' that identified a lack of expertise in RECs about social science research methods (DoH, 2003: 8) and the dominance of the medically oriented, positivist approach to research. This has resulted in plans for a parallel system of RECs for the ethical review of social care research under the auspices of COREC; this may expand to parallel systems in universities for student projects (see Doyal, 2004) and Councils with Social Service Responsibilities (CCSRs). Research proposals will only go to one such committee, although Research and Development management permission is required in the NHS for each site where research will be conducted before a project can begin; this can be applied for at the same time as an application is made to RECs. To date these regulatory requirements do not seem to have extended to research in education, ethical review and approval usually being under the remit of local management (Directors of Education, Head Teachers etc.)

Research that actively involves and collaborates with clients needs particular care, for example, in terms of informed consent and accessible information, time, training, support and costs. Psychologists' *Ethical Principles for Conducting Research* (BPS, 1990) and 'Involve' (www.invo.org.uk, formerly 'Consumers in NHS Research') offer useful guidance, and Eby (2000) gives a good overview of the principles and human rights issues involved. There is also commentary about the client-centred nature of practice and the relative lack of client-centred research, that is, research that focuses on client perspectives and priorities about care and service delivery, including user involvement in the development of outcome measures that reflects users' values, priorities, perceptions and preoccupations (Hammell, 2001). Guidance on conducting client/user-led or survivor research with regard to its underlying principles and conduct is provided by Faulkner's (2004) guideline, this being the result of a research project carried out by mental health service users and survivors.

The DoH's (2003) progress review of the implementation of its new research governance procedures acknowledges that social research asks different questions and answers them in different ways to those of medicine's research mainstream, and the Campbell Collaboration's inclusion of qualitative research reflects the nature of the available research within its cross-sectoral, non-medical remit. This bodes well for an acceptance that the privileging of RCTs in the one-fits-all approach of orthodox EBP is inappropriate and untenable for disciplines that are cross-sectoral and draw on different research traditions. Research methods that fall outside the routines of orthodox EBP have to be respected and colleagues have to be educated about unfamiliar forms of evidence presented to them. This is not to say that art therapists should avoid addressing questions about effectiveness within the dominant research paradigm of the organisations that employ them – we have to meet halfway – rather that exclusive use of either positivist or qualitative research models will limit the kind of knowledge we gain. Art therapy needs to adopt a pluralistic approach that includes the visual and practice-based methods that are inherently sympathetic to the art at the heart of the discipline and must not be constrained by the vested interests and research norms of other disciplines. There are many ways of generating evidence through research and all will contribute to the cumulative and eclectic evidence base of art therapy, as the following chapters will show.

6 Generating the evidence through qualitative research

Some years ago I wrote about art therapists' ambivalence towards research (Gilroy, 1992a), describing it as sometimes amounting to resistance and suggesting that this was due mainly to a simple lack of knowledge about what research actually involved. Research was often characterised as inherently unsympathetic to a discipline which embraced the practices of art and the processes of human interaction, being seen as scientific and reductive and, if nothing else, likely to be disruptive to the art therapy process. Since then it seems to me that the tensions have eased. Practitioners are much more open to an involvement with research, indicated by the number of research-based publications, the steady increase in the numbers of art therapists with research experience gained through higher degrees and the membership of the ATPRN. Perhaps research is just more familiar and therefore less frightening, but maybe the anxieties generated by EBP, coupled with the research and EBP-oriented demands of the new national profiles for art therapists within the NHS's *Agenda for Change*, have pushed practitioners towards an involvement with research with greater speed than might otherwise have been the case. Whatever the reason, it bodes well for the profession.

But where do we look for models and methods? So far it seems to me that art therapists in the UK have looked to research in psychotherapy and psychoanalysis, philosophy and sociology and, while colleagues in the USA have done the same, they have drawn much more on positivist approaches. Neither have given a parallel degree of attention to visual research methods. In this and the following chapter I describe the range of methodological possibilities – quantitative, qualitative, numerical, textual and art-based – that could generate relevant, robust and rich research that retains the integrity of our own kind of evidence *and* satisfies EBP orthodoxy. I begin in this chapter with qualitative and visual methodologies and discuss quantitative methods in Chapter 7.

Visual research methods

Images and visual research methods, as Prosser (1998) remarks, are often marginalised by qualitative research's emphasis on text. Images are considered as mere illustrations and are neither a proper research method nor a source of primary data. In some fields, notably anthropology, ethnography and sociology, and of course art history and the visual arts, this simply is not the case; neither should it be so for art therapy. The principal way of looking at and thinking about art in art therapy has been mainly within the narrative chronology of case studies, but I think there is potential to widen art therapy's scopic regime through foregrounding visual data and using rigorous visual methods that will enable us to investigate the hands-on, visual practices that are central to what we do.

Visual research methods come from several disciplines: visual art, art history/ visual culture and film studies as well as anthropology, ethnography, sociology and psychology. These can be loosely organised into four approaches to research in art therapy:

1. case study;
2. art history/visual culture;
3. social research;
4. art based.

Case studies and some art historical methods can be linked as they explore developmental processes over time and require detailed documentation and investigation of making and meaning. Such practice-based research sits comfortably with the routines of clinical work. Later on I describe the various options for case study based research, but here I want to indicate how art therapy researchers can, and already are, directly and indirectly drawing on four art historical methods:

1. *Theoretical/academic*: this includes the historical, theoretical, thinking about, looking at and analysis of art works. Art therapists use a parallel approach to phenomenological, philosophical and case study based research (e.g. Schaverien, 1992; Skaife, 2001).
2. *Hands-on, artist-based*: this involves active, collaborative engagement with live artists using interviews, photographs and videos, a method that has been drawn on by art therapists in collaborative and/or video-based research with clients (e.g. Eldredge and Carrigan, 1992; Hosea, forthcoming; McClelland, 1992, 1993).
3. *Curatorial*: the gathering together and documentation of works, including the establishment of authenticity (the provenance), and the organisation and juxtaposition of works in exhibitions. The potential application to art therapy research is through the collection and different kinds of 'display' of clients' artworks in order to see what new meanings emerge, not in a public exhibition but in private, gallery-like spaces that enable the exploration of different modes of audiencing invited by the displays (Mahony, 2001, forthcoming). There is also the interrogation of the social, historical and political context of collections such as those of Prinzhorn and Adamson; investigations of art therapy departmental archives; and examination of the curatorial and archivist activities that are part of art therapists' everyday practice;
4. *Science of looking after objects*: the preservation and restoration of objects. This refers to various kinds of archival work necessary to the preservation of objects in art therapy and relevant to collections such as the Bethlem Archive, the Jung Collection and the Prinzhorn Collection.

Schaverien (1992, 1993) offers a useful model that interweaves case study and art historical method. She says that clients' artwork is data from the heart of practice and is both a record of their experience and an *aide memoire* for the art therapist. She suggests that analysis of such visual data can include:

- a systematic analysis of marks, form and colour;
- a documentation of changes in the imagery;
- a record of the therapeutic process;
- a comparison of the patient's and the art therapist's experiences.

Alongside these categories for deconstructing the objects in art therapy, Schaverien explores the evolution of the retrospective review of clients' artworks, comparing it to retrospective exhibitions of artists' work. This visually describes the sequences and parallels between artworks and an artist's life, allowing a juxtaposition of biography and image that gives rise to new meanings. The link between an artist and their work and the use of pictures or sculptures as data is an established art historical tradition which, Schaverien suggests, art therapists draw on all the time, writing in a similar way to art historians.

This method emphasises chronology and draws on a classical art historical tradition, that of *ekphrasis*, the verbal recreation of a visual artwork or a verbal evocation of something seen for others who cannot see it. The *ekphrasis* involves a translation from one language to another, from the visual to the verbal, and enables the discovery, articulation and intellectual understanding of meaning. A well-known *ekphrasic* or artwriting structure, one that moves from description to analysis and interpretation, can be found in the work of the art historian Erwin Panofsky (1972). He outlined a process of iconographical analysis that involved the identification and description of the features in an artwork, followed by an analysis in terms of the features' cultural meaning as follows:

1. *A natural, pre-iconographic narrative description* of the image comes first: the *ekphrasis*;
2. *A narrow iconographical analysis* comes next, requiring knowledge of the contemporary cultural context and how things are likely to be depicted. The author knows what these marks represent because s/he recognises them, being situated in the same historical and cultural context as the artist;
3. *A deep iconographical interpretation* enquires why the marks have been made, both consciously and unconsciously, and offers an interpretation.

It seems to me that art therapists naturally, and perhaps unknowingly, draw on this well-established method of pictorial analysis (e.g. Schaverien, 1992), but locating it within the research framework of art history and extending to include interrogation of differently curated visual displays, construes this as a rigorous methodological tool for researching visual data.

Until recently *ekphrasis* was considered a relatively neutral part of the necessary, value-free identification of what an artwork actually is, but this traditional, essentially modernist approach has led art historians to pay significant attention to the influence artwriting has on the subsequent analysis and meaning of art works (e.g. Carrier, 1991; Elkins, 2000). Art history has changed, sometimes reconfiguring itself as 'visual culture', and very different approaches to looking at and writing about art have developed over the last 50 years of art history's history. Nowadays artworks are discussed in terms of their social, cultural and political contexts, in terms of feminist and postcolonial theory, philosophy, structuralism and semiotics. Essentially the concern is with how various artefacts make a visual and material culture – everything from paintings and architecture to cartoons, videos, advertising, media representations, fashion and monumental masonry. Artworks are *interrogated,* not only about where, how, why and by whom they are made, but also about how and why some artists and artworks are discussed and others are not. It is about the meanings artworks have and about discussion of them at particular times and in particular places; how audiences' responses are aroused and how these too differ according to time and place; about how works are arranged, collected, documented and conserved, and how temporary and permanent exhibitions give precedence to some cultural forms over others.

To my mind practitioners have, so far, followed a particular artwriting tradition, that of the single narrative trajectory of an art therapy canon in case studies that seek developmental improvement in the form and content of art. Byrne (1995) suggests, and I agree, that this is an essentially modernist, nay positivist approach to art therapy that involves a narrative of cause and effect. This is not to devalue chronology and development – change is after all at the heart of each therapeutic endeavour and effectiveness is at the heart of orthodox EBP inquiry – but to suggest that there are alternative models, other ways of looking and seeing that could be developed in art therapy research which move away from chronology and position art therapists alongside their clients as co-creators of art and meaning in the social, political and cultural contexts of making and looking. This enables interesting questions to be asked about the very nature of art therapy, such as 'for whom was the artwork made?', 'why was it made in that particular way?' and 'how is it displayed to its audience?', situating practice and interrogating artworks in an interesting sociological field. Such research would move away from consideration of art as pictorial symptoms and towards an intersubjective approach that interweaves analytic, aesthetic, social, sensual and material considerations with creative and imaginative writing and art making about artworks.

Rose (2001) offers a useful structure for this kind of inquiry, describing sites, modalities and methods for interpreting visual works that consider an artwork in terms of 'production', the 'image itself' and 'audiencing', that is, how something is made, what it looks like and how it is seen. She suggests that these sites can be explored through three modalities – the 'technological', the 'compositional' and the 'social': through the tools and equipment used to make and display the work; the visual construction, qualities and how a work is received; and the social, political and institutional practices and relations that produce and interpret an image. This structure enables investigation of different ways of seeing the world, how images articulate social difference and how different visions have social effects. What art shows, how it is looked at and how it invites the viewer to respond are all important considerations that may influence the effectiveness of art therapy, meriting research that goes way beyond the norms of EBP. Such research could explore the social construction of art in art therapy in different organisations and settings, each with their own discourses in terms of practices, economies, rules, group dynamics, gender relations, postcolonial issues and cultural exchange.

Methods that explore different visualities in this way come largely from cultural studies, sociology and visual anthropology, drawing on methods of visual content analysis, structuralism and semiotics to investigate everything about any culture that is visual (see Prosser, 1998; van Leeuwen and Jewitt, 2001). How we live and interact with our environment determines the visual culture, set as it is within the context of the social practices that influence the makers and viewers of images such as photographs, the layout of adverts, oil paintings, videos, web pages, packaging, TV, film and so on. Banks (1998, 2001) for example writes about what happens to a visual form: 'Once manifest in the world it begins a career and accumulates a series of linkages and social embeddings' (1998: 18), describing how visual research methods explore visual forms and representations and how they construct and mediate social relationships. He says there are three broad sets of activity in socially oriented, visual research:

1. *Making* visual representations: studying societies and cultures through making images about them;
2. *Examining* pre-existing visual representations: studying images for information about societies and cultures;
3. *Collaborating* with social actors to produce visual representations about societies and cultures.

This suggests exciting possibilities for art therapy research that could, for example, involve practitioners and users visually exploring the histories and cultures of places, services, systems and organisations. Banks (2001) also describes a visual method in social research called photo elicitation which usually occurs in interviews, using photos that may be archival or contemporary, belonging to the interviewer or to the research subjects, or taken from magazines in order to prompt memories and associations in a manner akin to reminiscence work, to art therapy's retrospective review and to Kopytin's (2004) description of taking and using photographs in art therapy. All these add a visual dimension to longitudinal outcome studies.

Banks suggests that research interviews be filmed, and research extended, to include a later showing of the film to the subject with another, accompanying interview about the response to the original film, this being filmed too in an iterative, longitudinal research process. This kind of socially oriented, visual research is inherently collaborative between the different image makers and subjects, but photographs and video can also be an aspect of any project's documentation and be part of its dissemination, for example, through exhibition. Still or moving images can be made in order to remember, to show others, to record that which cannot be described in words, but Banks points out that the making processes of TV, film and to some extent photography too, are reliant on technologies that many people have little access to. The technologies of production are socially embedded and so power relations and social control should be considered in this kind of research.

Such methods offer rich potential for art therapy research that have only just begun to be explored. McClelland (1992, 1993) for example video-recorded and reviewed individual art therapy sessions with her clients, and Hosea (forthcoming) video-recorded key moments in a painting group for young children and their parents, subsequently showing them the video and interviewing them about their experiences in the group while watching the video. Other art therapists have used video as an observational tool: Evans and Dubowski (2001) have drawn on the micro-analysis of video recordings of art therapy sessions to develop a template for practice with autistic children; Damarell (forthcoming) videoed a single art therapy session with people who have learning difficulties to explore the relationship between making art and thinking; and Tipple (2003) analyses video-recordings of art therapy assessments to examine how the dominant discourses in a setting construct a client during the assessment process. Other studies have given the camera to the client/participants and, through film, photography and interviews, enabled collaboration with the therapist/researcher and the co-construction of visual and oral narratives about gender transition (Barbee, 2002) and, in another project, about the move from residential to independent living by young, deaf American Indians (Eldredge and Carrigan, 1992). The voices and stories of the individuals are powerfully conveyed in these projects, photography and video being media for self-representation and the camera a reflexive tool through which the co-researchers engaged in dialogue. Thus the making of images about a research topic and subsequent discussion of them in an iterative process of making and talking, inquiry and display, enables art itself to enter the heart of the research process and become a means of data collection and analysis.

An art-based approach to art therapy research has been proposed by McNiff (1998). He speaks to the importance of art therapists using a research language that remains true to our primary discipline of art and values subjectivity, the imagination and introspection. McNiff rightly points out that insufficient attention has been paid to the visual qualities of images and to the practicalities and effects of art making in art therapy research. This relates to the hands on approach to inquiry in art history, to the documentation of making through still photography and video and accompanying texts and narratives by the artist. McNiff suggests that art therapists investigate the particularities of their individual expression in an experimental and experiential way, extrapolating data about how art is made and meaning is created. Mahony's (2001, forthcoming) research does just this in an heuristic, interdisciplinary project that investigates her own art making in and outside an art therapy group, illustrating the complex and critical reciprocity between the clients' and the art therapist's art. Sibbett's (2005c) 'arts-based authoethnography' is another example of an art-based method that expands heuristic research into the visual domain. Rose (2001) also suggests, and I agree, that it is helpful for the researcher to visually explore how s/he looks at or audiences an image, and to include this in the critical reflection about, and interpretation of, art works. Collaborative documentation of art-making processes that are both visual and text based could provide powerful evidence about the interior of art therapy and its link to outcomes. Lanham's (2002) account of collaborative work with his students about art-making processes is an interesting example. Making images that address all kinds of research topics, taking photographs, curating displays, documenting responses and presenting the research through exhibition, installation and performance offer many layers of exciting possibility (see Bagley and Cancienne, 2002).

This was brought home to me at a conference on 'Art-based Research Methods in Education' (at Queens University, Belfast in 2005) that explored the use of the arts in the collection, analysis and presentation of social and educational research. One of the keynotes, Carl Bagley (2005), orchestrated a particularly striking representation of his research. One could say that the project itself was traditional, having used interviews and participant observation to investigate a new intervention, but its representation through the arts gave the findings an immediate accessibility. Bagley had asked a visual artist, a scriptwriter/director and a musician to work together and present his research to the conference through their art forms. Their performance began with small groups of delegates being invited into the performance space via a narrow corridor littered with disposable nappies, plastic toys and a toaster exuding a smell of freshly burnt toast. We entered a darkened theatre cleared of stage and seats where there were ambient sounds of a radio, music and voices, with large images and videos being projected on to the walls behind actors as they repeatedly played out various tableau, surrounded by more nappies, toys and shabby furniture with endless washing up and the kettle always boiling. Gradually all the delegates entered the space. Every so often our attention would be directed to one of the tableaus, much in the manner of medieval mystery plays with strolling players moving in the space and interacting with the audience. Occasionally our guide would try to get his actors together to 'start' from half-made starting lines taped to the floor, but not everyone or everything was ready so it never quite happened, until eventually it did. Then it stopped. This was a powerful evocation of Bagley's research into local experiences of the government's 'Sure Start' scheme that conveyed the participants' social deprivation, hopelessness and frustration and their brief optimism when the programme eventually began but almost immediately ceased. It showed how research and the arts could enhance each other through an experience that stimulated thought and affect. A million miles from EBP you might say, but this risky representation illustrated how affect-laden, visual and other kinds of research material can be conveyed to audiences in ways that are neither dry nor distant (Elkins, 2000).

Visual research methods can be visual and textual, practical and scholarly, heuristic and analytic, clinical and social. Visually oriented art therapy research goes beyond case-based looking to art-based research. Art making can be a means of generating data. Art therapists and their clients can respond visually to a research topic, question or series of questions; different forms of display and audiencing can invite new understandings; and artworks can be interrogated within art historical and phenomenological frameworks that sit more comfortably with our primary discipline than those that equate the formal elements of visual representation with pathology. I think art-based and visual methodologies offer significant potential for new and interesting kinds of art therapy research about the profession and its practices. As yet we have barely scratched their surface.

Case studies

The implicit showing and telling – the narrative, display, reflection and theorising of a case study – is often key to presentations about art therapy and at the heart of many of its texts. Case studies are familiar to art therapists and are some of the most accessible and immediate methods of practice-based research.

Case studies or *case reports* describe 'unusual or exemplary' single cases (Higgins, 1996: 58). Research case studies are often based in narrative and written retrospectively; they can also be done concurrently and can combine quantitative and qualitative material (McLeod (1994, 2001) gives useful guidance about this). Researchers/practitioners can collaborate with clients, their families and the multidisciplinary team, and can investigate their own clinical work or that of others. Such studies can include, not to say privilege, the client's voice, providing the ultimate in 'first-hand' evidence. In such studies everything to do with the case – all the visual material and process notes plus other related texts such as referral documents, ward notes, letters, journals, follow-up demographics and so on – is data. Whatever form they take the data are interrogated in the light of the literature, the methods, theories and processes that underpin the looking at and thinking about the visual and text-based data, all being explicit and transparent. Case studies like these, while in narrative form, need a specific focus and must be systematic. Direct and clear links need to be made between a client's presenting problems, the particular kind of art therapy intervention made, and its short- and long-term outcomes.

The detailed case study that forms the backbone of Schaverien's (1992) research shows one approach to single-case research that draws on a phenomenological investigation of art therapy's artefacts. Other examples include O'Brien's (2003, 2004) narrative description of her work with an abused child and Zammit's (2001) collaborative case study with an artist/therapist with cancer. An allied approach by Herrmann (forthcoming) used a visual method; this involved the creation of a photographic display of the visual archive of a single case that allowed the distillation of an immense amount of visual material which identified and then focused on a particular aspect of the client's imagery. Waldman (1999) took a slightly different approach to her investigation of the use of clay within a particular period of an art therapy group's life. This too involved archival documentation and included a visual 'mapping' of the group and its artworks, followed by a comparison of this with process notes so as to identify periods of time when clay was used and experiences of abuse were explored. This led to theorising about the mind–body axis being activated through the physicality of clay that enabled abusive experiences to emerge and be explored in the group. Extending the use of such visual methods into curating different kinds of visual presentation – of single or multiple cases – could expand the framework of research-based case studies beyond the usual chronological narrative into forms and structures of writing and visual display that could capture the shifts and plateaus, the three dimensionality of therapy, that does not always follow a linear trajectory. Curating visual displays of works in a private setting, either for viewing solely by the curator/practitioner or working collaboratively with clients, and perhaps for viewing by different audiences – the practitioner, other art therapists and the team – could compare different genres of artworks thematically and visually, enabling different kinds of audiencing, presentation and dissemination that expand not only the researcher/practitioner's gaze but also that of others outside art therapy. Such research is just beginning (see Mahony, 2001, forthcoming).

Case-study research that draws on visual methods enhances its validity because artworks triangulate with texts of various kinds. Triangulation refers to the use of data from different sources, gathered through different methods. However, the validity of all case-study research is internal, true only within the context of the particular case; the findings cannot be generalised to other populations and settings and so lack external validity. Nonetheless case studies describing work with people from the same population, with similar problems and using the same clinical approach contribute to the cumulative evidence base of the discipline and form the bedrock of all forms of clinical research.

Case series are allied to single case studies and single case experimental studies. Case series are usually based in narrative, using several cases to illustrate, amplify and theorise a particular observation. Casework is not usually described in detail and so case series can lack the rigour of single case studies and experiments, the approach being one where clinical vignettes are used to make a point in a more general way. But here too visual methods of curating and display have much to offer about how we view and what we see in groups of artworks in a way that does not fall foul of pathological reductionism. Case series are an important and useful approach because they encapsulate emergent clinical and/or visual phenomena in a manner akin to pilot studies, often being the way clinicians begin to explore an idea about something they have observed. Ball's (2002) study of an art therapist and five of her cases provides an interesting and methodologically rigorous model.

Cohort studies are a particular kind of case series that require greater rigour and specificity than case series because they aim to document the presence and frequency of certain patterns. This approach to case-based research involves the observation of a defined population who, for example, share a certain characteristic where patterns can be identified, either in retrospect or contemporaneously. The chosen population should be representative and homogeneous, the size of the group varying depending on the population being studied. Cohort studies are often within the narrative tradition but they also draw on discourse and content analysis and could, once again, include visual methods to identify patterns and visualities across a cohort. An interesting example of a small cohort study is the work of Wood (2002) who analysed the written and visual archive of her casework with clients who had AIDs-related dementia, using grounded theory to analyse five cases. Another is Rehavia-Hanauer's (2003) investigation of four years of her casenotes about individual art therapy with ten clients who had eating disorders.

In my view the evidence base of art therapy could be significantly enhanced by research-based case studies within both the narrative and positivist traditions. I agree with McLeod's (1994) suggestion that the strongest case studies are systematic and pluralist, combining qualitative and quantitative data, the essential story-telling with outcomes, and of course including art therapy's added extra of visual material. McLeod advises:

- Using as many sources of information as possible;
- Drawing on a team of researchers so that subjectivity and bias are diminished;
- Developing case series so that initial findings and generalisations from the first cases can be checked against later cases;
- Integrating quantitative and qualitative measures and observations, particularly with regard to the confirmation, contradiction and further articulation of theory.

Gathering a team of practitioners/researchers with the time, skill and resources to undertake large-scale research is not easy, but modest case series and single case-study research are manageable means through which individual practitioners, collaborating with users and colleagues when appropriate, can contribute robust, credible and valid evidence, especially if multiple sources of textual, oral and visual data are integrated and compared in ways that are transparent, consistent and replicable.

Phenomenological, heuristic and hermeneutic research

Phenomenological, heuristic and hermeneutic approaches to research are related but subtly different forms of inquiry that have proved popular with art therapists. In phenomenological research the focus is on the connections between inner and outer events explored primarily through observation and description; heuristic inquiry focuses on the subjective and experiential and on discovery through introspection; hermeneutic research is dialogic and seeks interpretations, usually of texts. These methodologies have a comfortable fit with art therapy because of their exploratory and experiential nature and because the data can arise directly from practice.

Phenomenology

Phenomenology has been described as 'a *radical* way of doing philosophy' (Moran, 2000: 4, emphasis in original) that attempts to access the truth through exhaustive description. This is accomplished through a rich, detailed, thick description of an issue, event, problem, thing or whatever is the subject of the research, as it appears to the experiencer. Often the descriptive account is an end in itself, whether framed as a narrative or organised in categories. In order to perceive the essential structures of the phenomenon the researcher has to go deeply into their topic and see them untainted, in the original. This requires suspension of all the researcher's preconceptions, assumptions and *a priori* explanations in order to consider the phenomenon from every conceivable angle, distinguishing those aspects of it that are to do with particular circumstances from those that are not. Aspects of the phenomenon that are not contingent on circumstances and which remain constant are considered to be the 'essence', the certainties or ultimate truths about the matter under investigation. McLeod (2001) states that phenomenological inquiry underpins all qualitative research.

Phenomenological research therefore focuses on ruthless and systematic observation, exploration and analysis of what something essentially is. It involves the radical suspension of the experiencer's views about the world and the material objects, immaterial systems, thoughts, feelings and experiences that are encountered in the experiencing human being in their area of inquiry. The aim is to seek new ways of seeing and understanding a phenomenon from within and in its own terms, not through externally imposed methods. This implies a rejection of positivist attitudes towards knowledge and all the assumptions that underpin EBP. Moran describes how turning away from an understanding of knowledge that is either empiricist (based in observation or experiment) or representational (existing outside the mind) led Husserl – the principal phenomenological philosopher – to try and create experiential accounts of knowledge that were based in 'concrete, lived human experience … about everything, to capture life as it is lived' so as 'to remain faithful to the deepest experiential evidence' (2000: 5–6, emphasis in original).

When it comes to actually describing how to go about phenomenological research problems arise because of the highly individualistic nature of human experience and the whole approach being 'grounded in the self-reflection of the individual philosopher-inquirer' (McLeod, 2001: 40). The approach is problematic in its attempt to find the essence of a phenomenon that is context-free and not positioned in terms of other studies of similar events, things or problems. This creates acute difficulties when most contemporary qualitative researchers work on a constructivist basis where findings are contextualised and reflect a truth rather than the truth; thus there is little cumulative knowledge in the phenomenological literature, most of the research being 'one-off' studies. Nonetheless McLeod describes attempts to operationalise a phenomenological method and illustrates how phenomenology has been used in psychotherapy and psychological research. This approach to research has been used by art therapists, although it is not always so described. Examples are the work of Schaverien (1992) and Skaife (1995, 2000, 2001), both of whom have contributed to the development of art therapy theory through in-depth description and analysis of casework in different theoretical and philosophical frameworks.

Heuristic research

Douglass and Moustakas (1985) say that if phenomenology requires a kind of detachment from a research topic which eventually results in a definitive description of it, then heuristic research emphasises a personal attachment to a topic and a search for its meaning. Heuristic research is introspective, experiential and intensely personal, involving the researcher in an individual journey of discovery that contributes to theory building and also leads to growth in the researcher's self-knowledge. However, the method is not about the researcher, the focus being the nature of human experience as represented by the experiences of the researcher, often in connection with the experiences of others (e.g. clients). Moustakas describes the necessary commitment to and total immersion of the researcher in their topic in heuristic research, and the reflexive, critical subjectivity that is central to it. He asserts that there is 'an unshakeable connection' (1990: 12) between the external world of the research topic and the individual researcher's experience, his or her reflections, intuitions and internal frames of reference about it being the data that are discovered and explicated. Individuals' experiences are traced and mapped and the correspondences between them explored, for example, through the use of diaries and other kinds of writing, and through creative processes. It is here that art making can either be the subject of a heuristic inquiry or be used to amplify exploration of a topic or research question. Mahony's (2001, forthcoming) research offers a good example.

Moustakas (1990) describes six phases of the heuristic research process: an initial engagement with the topic that is followed by immersion, incubation, illumination, explication and creative synthesis, that is, the communication about what has happened. This outlines a recognisable process that is central to any research or creative work, moving from uncertainty and chaos to discovery, situating the findings in a critical context and then communicating them, but in heuristic research exploration of the imagination and the personal *is* the research. The deliberate stimulation of the imagination aims at building preliminary theoretical constructs; this requires the researcher to not only be imaginative but also logical, to discern general problems or patterns that emerge through an intensive analysis of their own and others' material. Thus heuristic research can include unstructured interviews, or dialogues with the self and with research participants, involving cooperation and openness so that a rich and comprehensive depiction of the topic is achieved. Higgins (1996) discusses how such correspondences emerge and how understanding grows through differing kinds of dialogue. He gives examples of case studies where arts therapists explored the correspondences between their own and their clients' experiences, using active imagination to explore thoughts, feelings, images and associations in order to create an 'inverted perspective' that comes from within the object or dialogue that amplifies meaning, moving beyond what is immediately apparent and contributing to the development of theory. Heuristic research such as this has much in common with narrative case studies, that is, studies that are not 'designed' but draw on in-depth description of practice, analysis of transferential responses, cultural associations and imaginative written and visual explorations.

Heuristic studies can be about a particular piece of casework that is unusual or particularly affecting in some way. The case is likely to offer a clue to something if it is subjected to both imaginative and rigorous inquiry, enabling the gradual development of theory through the study of individuals. Nonetheless the intensely personal nature of heuristic inquiry gives rise to questions of validity, especially within the framework of EBP. This by no means limits the necessity for heuristic studies in art therapy research because validity can be determined by the researcher's exhaustive, continual checking and by their critical reflexivity about the accuracy of their depiction and explication of their own and others' experiences. This can be enhanced by remaining particular about the clients, the therapy and its results, and through returning to the research participants with the 'essence' of the phenomenon being explored that has been derived from the researcher's reflections and analysis of the data.

Hermeneutic research

Hermeneutics – meaning to interpret, especially that from another language – is linked to heuristics and phenomenology in a circle of description, discovery and interpretation. If phenomenology seeks to describe and heuristics seeks to discover through personal introspection then hermeneutics seeks to interpret; neither phenomenology nor heuristics place knowledge in a context whereas hermeneutics is all about context. The origins of hermeneutics are in deciphering ancient manuscripts and so linguistics, language and the historical and socio-cultural locations of the researcher and the researched, the interpreter and the interpreted, are critical. The object of inquiry is usually a text, one that has to be in the public domain but which can include interview material and therapy transcripts as well as books, articles and archival material. The researcher/interpreter unpacks and reconstructs their understanding of a text, amplifying meaning and situating both the text and their interpretation of it in the respective historical and cultural locations. The inherent subjectivity of hermeneutic research is not a distortion but a means of understanding how we make sense of the world; it is a dialectical process that moves back and forth between the interpreter's presumptions and what the data actually reveal. McLeod (2001) says that hermeneutic research acknowledges and works with the particular perspective of an interpretation. Texts are made in one context and interpreted in another; in hermeneutic research the two worlds meet and fuse so that the cultural and historical traditions of the interpreter are enriched. The interpreter is a member of a community and their reading of a text will be shaped by it, but both the text and the interpreter will be changed by hermeneutic inquiry. McLeod gives the example of Cushman's (1995) hermeneutic investigation of the social and cultural factors that have shaped the development of psychotherapy in America over the last 250 years, a study that indicates the potential for hermeneutic study of art therapy texts to explore how the discipline has been (and is being) constructed in different parts of the world.

Phenomenological, heuristic and hermeneutic research enables discoveries that can shift a discipline's discourse but their inherently subjective nature renders them suspect within the orthodox EBP paradigm. This reiterates the fact that the paradigm at large has to become significantly more inclusive than it is at the moment, and that art therapists have to adapt its principles and precepts to a discipline-specific framework that supports the development of pluralistic research in art therapy. There are many questions yet to be asked that involve different kinds of inquiry, not only about art therapy's efficiency and effectiveness but also about its very nature, about what makes it unique.

Historical and archival research

The first step in many research projects is a bibliographic search for literature relevant to the topic and a review of what has been found. This is, in itself, a form of historical research because the review requires the identification and analysis of past work – the literature *is* the data. But data also come from all the physical objects that bear the traces of human activity, usually printed sources but including other kinds of texts and films, videos, slides, tapes (of sound), photos, artworks and so on. These are also the material of retrospective, research-based case studies.

Historical research aims not only to understand the past but also to inform the present; understanding why things are the way they are enables progress and change. Cohen and Manion (1980) describe historical research as a sequence that requires the identification (and limitation) of the area, followed by the collection, selection, organisation, verification, validation and analysis of the data followed by their interpretation; this model applies to archival research of all kinds, from case studies to political biographies. An important task is to differentiate between primary and secondary sources. Primary sources are the original documents – the records, letters, official papers, minutes of meetings, newspapers and so on – that describe what happened and were made at the time of the event being researched. Secondary sources are those that do not have a direct physical relationship to the event being studied, often drawing on primary sources but describing events second-hand. Art therapy historical research might include biographies based on journals, letters and images, for example, Maclagan's (1995) research about the psychoanalyst Pailthorpe and her artist/patient Ruben Mednikoff. Histories of institutions draw on similar data, based on original minutes of meetings, visual material and objects, usually found in government documents, local organisations and personal archives (see Von Zweigbergk and Armstrong (2004) on the history of Bexley Hospital; Cole (1997) on the history of art therapy at Epsom and Ewell Hospitals).

Historical research sometimes draws on the systematised approach of content analysis. Cohen and Manion (1980) describe how content analysis aims to translate a verbal document into quantitative material, using the content of communication to infer meaning and intention. This can be accomplished through simple counting of word-usage rates, for example, to infer emotional states such as anxiety, or through the more sophisticated identification of categories of content. This can elucidate not only the content of documents but also the influence of the social and political contexts, and thus be helpful in the researching of comparative or cross-cultural issues and in the analysis of case notes. A good example is Wood's (2001, 2002) archival research.

Historical research about the profession of art therapy has, interestingly, a relative high profile in the UK. Waller's (1991) work documented the history of the profession, Hogan (2001) explored its socio-cultural origins, and Wood's (2002, forthcoming) research explored the development of theory and practice of art therapy with people who have a history of psychosis. Waller (1998) has also documented the development of art therapy in Europe and I have investigated the development of the profession in Australia (Gilroy and Hanna, 1998; Gilroy, 2000). These projects have drawn on documents and literature in the usual manner of historical research and, because much of the profession's history continues to be embodied in the lived experience of its practitioners, some have been amplified through interviews and questionnaires. Art therapy would benefit from more studies like these, exploring how theories, practices and systems in the profession have originated and developed. This would enable further understanding of the relationship between the social, economic and political systems in which we operate and their influence on art therapy services and practices. Research that explores how the differing approaches in art therapy have evolved could provide evidence about whether or not they continue to meet present needs. Other useful topics could include the study of particular institutions and the development of art therapy within them, and biographical studies of key individuals in the profession's history.

Interviews

What is a research interview? Hitchock and Hughes define them as 'conversational encounters' or 'talk to some purpose' (1986: 79) but others say they are not part of ordinary conversation (Denscombe, 1998) because the interviewee gives their informed consent to take part in something that is specifically for the purposes of research, the conversation is on the record and the focus of the interview is set by the researcher. Interviews are an adaptable method that can follow a structured format or be completely open-ended and fluid, depending on the nature of the project and the research question. They can be structured, semi-structured or unstructured, the key difference being that structured interviews tend to check facts and seek information whereas semi- and unstructured interviews are, by their very nature, exploratory. Structured interviews are very like questionnaires that are done face to face with a prearranged interview schedule of short, direct questions that can have an equally short, immediate response, for example, telephone-based opinion polls and market-research interviews. Semi-structured interviews are also guided by a schedule, one that allows flexibility for the researcher to follow up responses and explore new areas as they emerge. Unstructured interviews can be informal and focused around a topic that is developed by both parties. In these kinds of interview there is discussion, a negotiation, and room for expansion and a relationship to develop between the interviewer and the interviewee. Data from interviews are often detailed and in depth and can address matters that are personal and sensitive. Here rapport and empathy are crucial, and the interviewer has to be very aware of likely sources of bias and the way the whole situation is shaped by the relationship and dynamics between interviewer and interviewee, taking account of age, gender, ethnicity and social status; for instance, interviews with managers or with clients will have different power relationships that may invoke differing kinds of presentation by the interviewer of themselves and their research.

Whatever the nature of interviews they require careful planning. Interviewees need selecting so as to be a representative sample of a given population: this can be random (every 10th client entering a service) or selected (art therapists working in schools within a particular geographical area). They need to be approached, be informed about the topic and give their permission to be interviewed; employers or those responsible for the respondent also need to agree (e.g. Director of Education if interviewing teachers or the consultant or family if interviewing clients). An interview schedule may need to be designed to ensure that carefully worded questions are asked that develop from initial fact finding to more in-depth, exploratory material. Piloting is essential so as to identify unclear questions, ensure that the interview flows and that the kind of material the researcher wants is accessed. How to record the interview also needs consideration: whether to use a tape recorder, or video, or to take notes in the interview or subsequently.

The importance of establishing a rapport with the interviewee goes without saying, but a note of caution must be sounded as it is important that research interviews do not become therapy: the interviewee is there to assist the interviewer, not vice versa. This is particularly delicate when interviewing clients, as King (1996) and McLeod (1994) discuss. The boundaries of the interview need to be established and maintained, ensuring at the outset that the interviewee knows what the encounter and the research are about and making it clear that he or she can chose not to answer questions if they so wish and may stop the interview at any point. Confidentiality and giving the interviewee an opportunity to review the transcript should be discussed as this embodies the reciprocal nature of the relationship: the interviewee is doing something for the interviewer and the exchange must be worthwhile.

Tapes have to be transcribed and transcripts sent to the respondent for checking, reflection and feedback. Description and analysis then go hand in hand as the researcher moves in and out of the data, juxtaposing respondents' answers to the same question while making links and identifying similarities and differences in their responses; this forms the basis of content and discourse analysis. During the process issues, themes and categories gradually emerge, a method Quinn Paton (1982) describes as finding and then working with an 'actively selective point of view'. Once a theme or category has been discovered the researcher actively seeks evidence of it, but then looks for evidence of the opposite as a checking device; these 'units of meaning' are juxtaposed to the research questions to see what light they throw upon them (Glaser and Strauss, 1967). Hitchcock and Hughes (1986) emphasise that such units will have an intrinsic meaning that may not relate to the research topic – they may indicate findings quite different from what was anticipated and have to be accommodated, otherwise research findings are forced into a predetermined pattern that will not reflect the data and be 'grounded' in them.

Interviews are a method than can access complex and sensitive material. They are usually conducted individually and face to face, although telephone interviews and focus groups are other options. Art therapists have used interviews to investigate clients' responses to treatment (Lomas and Hallas, 1998; Theorell et al., 1998; Greece, 2003; Sibbett, 2005a, 2005b), the history of the profession (Waller, 1991) and the processes of art therapy students' occupational choice (Gilroy, 1992b).

Ethnography and observation

Ethnography involves the observation of subjects and events in their natural environment. The researcher/observer is usually also a participant in the setting, being immersed in the local culture and language but, unlike the obtrusive action researcher and the participating collaborative inquirer, tries to be as unobtrusive as possible. Ethnographers participate, watch and listen – hence the method known as participant observation – supplementing their observations with visual data from film, photography, video and audio recording. The observations are then ordered and analysed in order to identify cultural patterns.

The ethnographer aims to ensure naturalism in an undisturbed situation, documenting and describing their experiences objectively but in as much depth and detail as possible, a technique known as thick description. There are one-off, detailed ethnographic descriptions that are not necessarily situated within a wider context, known as the *idiographic approach*. Another approach is known as *nomothetic;* this is when cultures or groups are compared and contrasted, generalisations and links to wider issues are made and theory is developed. In practice elements of both detailed, stand-alone descriptions of real-life situations and generalisations from them can contribute to the study of societies and interactions. Contemporary ethnography has parallels with anthropology, investigating the lives of differing groups and cultures within our society, for example, drug users (Denscombe, 1998).

Fieldwork such as this, wherever it may be, necessarily involves access to all kinds of places and people and negotiation with gatekeepers and ethical, sometimes political, decisions about how open the researcher is going to be about their activity. Ethnographers can gather material covertly which, although it might maintain the naturalism of the setting nonetheless gives rise to ethical issues about informed consent. Denscombe suggests that most ethnographers are overt about their role, despite the potential influence of their presence on the naturalness of the setting.

Inevitably the intensive fieldwork required of an ethnographer involves something of a personal journey. Researcher reflexivity is therefore a key concern, including, for example, remaining marginal to that which is being studied and not being taken over by it, and how the researcher's background will influence their perception, description and analysis of what they observe. The values, beliefs and culture of the researcher cannot be ignored and so introspection becomes a key part of the ethnographic research process. It is recognised that the final research account must therefore include open reflection about the influence of the researcher's self – his or her history, personal details, beliefs and values and so on – on their interpretations of their observations and experiences. The account is therefore 'more than just a description – it is a construction' (Denscombe, 1998: 69), often thought of as a creative work in its own right.

Examples of an ethnographic approach to research are the studies of psychiatric institutions by Goffman (1961) and Rosenhan's (1981) study of pseudo-patients in psychiatric hospitals. Surprisingly few art therapists have used an ethnographic approach. One example is Rees' (1995) research that demonstrated how detailed observation of people with severe learning difficulties in the naturalistic setting of a ward and of their art making in art therapy could inform the pictorial representation of space and territorial issues. Another is Spaniol's (1998) research that describes the process of entering the disability culture of people with mental health problems as if it were an unfamiliar place, that is to say, as an anthropologist or an ethnographer.

Action research

As suggested by the name, action research involves both taking action and generating knowledge about that action. Its origins are in social psychology, organisational science and social policy, particularly the work of Lewin (1951), on institutional, organisational and group dynamics. It is commonly used in organisational development and in education, social and healthcare as a means to review and improve practices and/or to directly address problems.

Action research involves two levels of process: a planned, cyclical and interactive sequence of identifying a problem, planning, taking action and evaluating the action, and the active participation in a project that takes place over time in a group, community or organisation which changes and learns. There are also two approaches. The first studies social and organisational problems in communities and systems, sometimes in a top-down way; here a need for change may have been identified by management who commission a project that involves researchers acting as consultants to an organisation. The second is usually associated with much smaller scale projects undertaken by practitioners to investigate their own practices, that is, it is bottom-up. Hart and Bond (1995) say that the defining characteristics of action research are that it aims at involvement and improvement, is context specific and problem focused and involves participants in a process of change within a research-based relationship; it is a hands-on approach that deliberately seeks change, bringing together research and practice in an applied and practical way. The approach is systematic but evolutionary and flexible, and can involve the whole range of textual, oral and numeric methods including participant observation, interviews, group processes, the study of archives and documents, surveys, journaling and so on. Hart and Bond helpfully describe several examples of such projects in the health and social services, showing how action research can generate significant impetus for change in different settings.

Coghlan and Brannick (2001) describe two action research cycles that operate simultaneously. The first involves an investigation of the context of a problem or project, the environment in which it operates, the external forces upon it and the internal forces within it and articulation of the desired future state, drawing on Lewin's (1951) field theory and force field analysis. Diagnosing the issues, identifying and planning the action/s are followed by an active doing phase, the outcomes of which are examined and fed into the next cycle of diagnosis, planning and action. The second cycle is reflective, one where the researchers reflect and evaluate the project as it continues, creating a dynamic interplay between the learning from the action research cycle as well as the learning about it. Naturally the participative nature of action research makes it a potent process that may involve conflict and real change over time and so continual critical reflection and a narrative about the research are paramount. Coghlan and Brannick say that a good action research project has three main elements: a good story; rigorous reflection on the story; and an extrapolation of knowledge or theory from the story.

Action research in all its forms seeks to challenge and alter the status quo with those who have direct experience of it, asking why things are the way they are and becoming a force for change that contributes to both local knowledge and to the development of social theory. Through action research art therapists could investigate the organisations and teams in which they work, the influence of art therapy upon them and the impact of new areas of service provision. Waller's (1995) research about the impact of the initiation of art therapy groups on a psychiatric system in Bulgaria offers a good example; Ivanova's (2004) study of art therapy workshops with orphans, also in Bulgaria, another.

Collaborative research

Action research involves partnerships with people, be it in a large organisation, with colleagues in a team or with clients; this has been described as democratising the research process (Denscombe, 1998) and enables a respect for participants and inclusion of the insider knowledge of both practitioners and the consumers of services. As it has developed so too has the extent of the collaboration between insider practitioners/users and outsider researchers, evolving into a non-hierarchical approach now known as collaborative, human, participative or cooperative inquiry. This seeks to empower all those involved in a research project to become co-researchers, doing away with the positions of researcher and subject and inviting collaboration. Collaborative inquiry focuses on the inter-relatedness of knowledge and action, the group-based and cyclic nature of the inquiry and the self-reflection of all co-researchers. The subjective nature of experience is actively embraced as key to the generation of knowledge, creating an experiential approach to research. Data might be collected through interviews and focus groups as well as diaries and observations of self and other, but it is the negotiated, cooperative, collective and practical nature of collaborative inquiry that differentiates this research approach from others. The way findings are disseminated also distinguishes it from other methodologies as the public domain is not necessarily entered via the research norms of texts and conferences: knowledge might be disseminated through performance, exhibition and social action (Reason and Rowan, 1981; Reason, 1988, 1994).

The principal notion is that all stages of a collaborative inquiry project should, ideally, be in the hands of a collaborative inquiry group; it should be initiated, designed, investigated, analysed and introduced into the public domain by the co-researchers. This offers exciting potential for user collaboration in all kinds of art therapy research. Faulkner's (2004) guideline about survivor or user-led research describes a project that developed a manual for ethical research from the perspective of users and survivors of mental health services. The project used focus groups, interviews and questionnaires and highlighted the importance of respect, empowerment and equality of opportunity for users throughout the research process, from design through to implementation. Danley and Ellison (1999) also describe participatory action research with people with mental health problems. Here the initiator was, as is often the case with collaborative inquiry, a researcher, but the process aimed to be as inclusive of users as possible through training and support, power sharing and mutual respect.

Collaborative inquiry is often group based. It may begin with an individual initiating a project, the group that is formed to a greater or lesser degree assuming ownership of the research as it proceeds; alternatively a group of co-researchers decide to meet to investigate an aspect of their experience. The project then proceeds with cycles of action and reflection, beginning with negotiation and agreement about the topic to be investigated and how this will be done. Co-researchers then immerse themselves fully in the data collection (action), meeting regularly to explore their experiences and make sense of the data, elaborating their understandings of the topic (reflection). Further cycles of data collection/action and inquiry/reflection involve the collaborative inquiry group in reviewing their original questions and understandings in the light of their experiences, modifying them accordingly and theorising if appropriate. The group-based nature of the process means that it is not without its difficulties; it can be hard to maintain the delicate balance between inquiry and therapy, especially in a model that often leads to personal as well as professional development. Egalitarianism can become problematic if one person has initiated the project, especially if the initiator is a therapist and the inquiry group involves clients. Certainly some, if not all, of the co-researchers need training and/or prior experience of group work. Collaborative inquiry can challenge personal beliefs and values and so must be conducted in a safe, containing environment where honesty can be maintained and the research group can stay on task. Different approaches to collaborative inquiry can be found in McClelland's (1992, 1993) research with clients in individual art therapy and Dudley et al.'s (1998, 2000) group-based inquiries into introductory art therapy groups and experiential art therapy training groups. I am not aware of any user-led art therapy research to date, but Spaniol's (1998) ethnographic entry into the disability culture of people with mental health problems drew on a collaborative approach to articulate clients' perspectives about art therapy.

Research describes a huge range of activities through which it is possible to find things out. There are numerous questions that we need to explore about art therapy and lots of different ways research can be done. This chapter has described the possibilities of qualitative research methods; the next explores the use of quantitative methods. Each offers very different methodological possibilities for exploring the range of research questions art therapists, users, colleagues and employers might ask about art therapy. All will contribute to the construction of a rich and pluralistic evidence base for art therapy.

7

Generating the evidence through quantitative research

Quantitative research covers different forms of small and large-scale experiments from case studies to surveys. EBP positions quantitative methods within an incremental framework that begins with single-case experimental designs and 'natural' experiments, or single group studies, with gradual increases in scale to controlled clinical trials and RCTs that involve hundreds of subjects. Experimental studies like these seek to measure change and clinical effectiveness through increasing degrees of numerical complexity and statistical analysis. Large-scale research requires teams of clinicians and researchers but more modest projects are well within the capabilities of individual practitioners. In this chapter I outline the different kinds of quantitative research and describe some of the processes and methodological issues that arise.

Single-case experimental designs

Individual experimental case studies (N = 1) were developed by behavioural psychologists, 'N' referring to the number of subjects. They differ from qualitative studies first because the researcher or researcher/clinician seeks to control the conditions or setting in which the work is done – this means maintaining a consistent environment and treatment approach – and second because they are designed from the outset as experiments that measure the outcomes of therapy.

The most common experimental case study design is known as the ABA design. This documents the course of change in therapy through what is known as a time series analysis that occurs over three phases. The baseline, A, is measured before treatment begins; the treatment or intervention, B, follows; then the new baseline, A, has the same measures applied again and the 'before and after' distributions are compared. The data analysis does not usually involve inferential statistics, the assumption being that meaningful change will be visible and can be seen on a graph. Variations in the research design describe measures taken at different times, for example, an AB design means that measures are taken when the patient is not being treated (A), and being treated (B); ABAB patterns describe a baseline (A) followed by treatment (B), followed by withdrawal of the treatment and another baseline (A) and the reintroduction of treatment (B). Other designs can compare a different intervention, C, creating more complex, multi-phase designs such as

ABACA or ABCBC. The client's behaviour, symptoms, social relations and so on can be measured each session, once a week, etc. Experimental case studies need not be entirely within the standard format of experimental research; numerical data can sit side by side with visual material and casework narrative that is informed by both the client's and the art therapist's voices so that the process through which the outcomes have been achieved can be seen and understood.

McLeod suggests that experimental case studies offer a reliable, robust and practitioner-friendly research method through which clinical work can be evaluated, their strength being the 'ability to document what "works"' (1994: 111). The main advantages are that they stay very close to clinical practice, provide a direct measure of the effectiveness of a treatment and have the potential (because of the controlled conditions) for systematic replication. Experimental case studies could, I think, enable art therapists to make robust contributions to the evidence base of the discipline in the short term and could easily be undertaken in cooperation with colleagues, using outcome measures appropriate to the sector, for example, of social relationships or educational attainment. There are many examples in the American art therapy literature: Stanley and Miller's (1993) study of short-term art therapy with an adolescent with behaviour problems is one, and Pleasant-Metcalf's (1997) on the use of art therapy to improve academic performance in a school, another.

Natural experiments or single group studies

Natural experiments are appropriate in situations where it would be impractical or unethical to conduct a controlled experiment. They investigate the outcomes of routine practice. In these studies variables can be controlled through naturally occurring events; for example, pre-existing/archival data can be subjected to experimental analysis, that is, compared to other existing data, but more commonly they investigate the outcomes of work with small sample sizes or a single group of clients, using a pre/posttest design in the same way as single case experiments. There are several examples in the American art therapy literature including Saunders and Saunders (2000) longitudinal study of the effectiveness of an art therapy service for children and adolescents and Ponteri's (2001) study of the effectiveness of group art therapy for depressed mothers and their children. Again, experimental studies like these can be enhanced with qualitative data, narrative from clients and art therapists, and visual methodologies too.

Controlled clinical trials

Controlled trials usually develop from cohort studies, paving the way for RCTs. Individual cases, groups or populations with a particular problem who are being treated are matched with individuals or groups without the problem or who are not being treated; the two groups are then compared. These are akin to natural experiments because the data come from routine casework, but are controlled experiments because the study's subjects are matched with others who act as controls in terms of age, gender and symptoms; they are unlike RCTs because clients are not randomised to treatment and non-treatment groups. Controlled studies can be conducted either retrospectively or prospectively. An example is Rosal's (1993) study that measured the effectiveness of art therapy for adolescents with behavioural problems. Such studies can lose the texture of practice but, once again, it need not be so; descriptive and visual data can accompany numerical comparisons, putting flesh on the bones of experimental research. I think this is critical. All too often the process through which the outcomes have been achieved in experimental research are not reported. This works with treatments that can be administered like doses of medication, but interventions that involve relationship and social interaction need accompanying qualitative data that document therapeutic processes and include user views about their experience of what has been important and effective.

Randomised controlled trials (RCTs)

An RCT is a large-scale experiment that measures the results of an intervention before and after it has been introduced, and often for a follow-up period as well. It usually involves huge numbers of subjects who fit explicit, and in medicine usually diagnostic, criteria, who are randomly assigned either to an intervention group or to a 'control' group that might receive a placebo, no intervention (for example through being put on a waiting list), standard care or some other form of intervention that is compared with that being investigated. Different degrees of blindness are part of the procedure that depend on the nature of the trial and the intervention being tested. The randomisation procedure itself is usually blind, that is, the selection procedure prevents the researchers influencing which patients are assigned to which arm of the trial (intervention or non-intervention). RCTs can also include 'all the annoying side' (Finzen, 2002: 26) that comes from qualitative data, and visual material too. The two examples of controlled trials in the British art therapy literature have done exactly this. Sheppard et al. (1998) and Waller (2002) report different aspects of their trial of art therapy groups with people who have dementia presenting findings and describing casework and the dynamic effects of institutions on practice and outcome. Similarly Richardson et al.'s (forthcoming) RCT of art therapy groups with people diagnosed as schizophrenic presents the trial in a standard format in one venue, but in another Jones (forthcoming) allows the reader into his experience as both clinician and researcher. He describes encountering profound distress and social deprivation while recruiting for the trial and explores ethnicity in short-term art therapy groups. The American literature offers more examples of RCTs including Tibbets and Stone's (1990) investigation of short-term individual art therapy with adolescents and Kymiss et al.'s (1996) RCT of a short-term, structured, group-based art therapy intervention with inpatient adolescents. Doric-Henry's (1997) RCT of individual pottery sessions with the elderly similarly includes rich qualitative material about the sessions, the artworks, the institution and the clients and the researcher/clinician's response to all that was involved in her research.

Surveys

Surveys involve asking direct questions of respondents who have been identified for that purpose; they can be many or few, an entire population or a representative sample, chosen randomly or specially selected. Questions can seek different kinds of information in different ways, giving rise to qualitative and quantitative data, the kind of information being sought determining the way it is gathered and how the questions are asked. The centrepiece of a survey is a questionnaire, often seeking factual information from large numbers of respondents through closed questions and ranked responses. They require careful consideration of language, sequencing and pilot studies so that the researcher can be confident that the questionnaire, like all instruments and measures, is reliable, that is to say, it produces the same data every time.

The guiding principle of every questionnaire is to keep the document as short as possible, asking only essential questions and doing so in a succinct, precise way. It is advisable to stick to questions to which the respondent can answer either 'yes' or 'no', can rate their agreement or disagreement with a statement on a 5- or 7-point Likert scale, rank their responses in order, or respond to a particular scenario. Open-ended questions can also be included, inviting general responses and/or personal responses and reactions that would otherwise be missed. The sequence of questions and the layout of the whole document need to be considered. It is a good idea to begin with straightforward, usually factual questions before moving to others that might require more thought. An accompanying letter and instructions also need to be written, an SAE will always help the response rate and sometimes a follow-up reminder is useful too.

The analysis of quantitative survey data usually begins with distilling the raw data into a data matrix, for example, through its transfer on to graph paper or a simple computer spreadsheet. If the number of respondents and variables are relatively small (under 30) and only descriptive statistics are needed then no more than the software available on most PCs is necessary. Anything larger, or using inferential statistics, will need a package such as the Statistical Package for Social Scientists (SPSS) and, although user handbooks are relatively simple, it is helpful to call on the expertise of colleagues well versed in such techniques. There are a number of examples of surveys in the art therapy literature, for example, to do with the profession (Gilroy, 1989), its theoretical frameworks (Karkou, 1999), and practice with particular client populations (Murphy, 1998; Fulton, 2002).

This brief description of different kinds of quantitative research cannot address the complexities of data collection and analysis. I have found it helpful to understand some of the underlying methodological issues. Denscombe (1998) and

Walliman (2001) give accessible descriptions of the use and analysis of quantitative data that I have drawn on for the brief summaries that follow.

Numbers and statistics

Experimental studies and surveys involve the analysis of different kinds of numeric data. Numbers can be assigned to discreet qualities or things that are either present or absent. Nominal scales do no more than enable their number to be counted, for example, the gender of research subjects could be coded as female = 1 and male = 2; ordinal scales use number to rank or position a thought or feeling on a scale, for example from 1 (highest) to 5 (lowest); and interval scales define equal units of measurement between points on a continuum. These different uses of number allow different kinds of statistical analysis.

Statistics are tools that can be used to identify and analyse the relationships between large amounts of data within a matrix that could otherwise not be seen. There are two different kinds: *descriptive* and *inferential*. Descriptive statistics summarise data, for example, through frequency distributions that show how measurements cluster and form patterns that are either normal or skewed. These include the mean, that is, the average score, achieved by adding all the scores together and then dividing by the number of scores; the median, the score representing the mid-population point where 50 per cent of subjects have scored higher and 50 per cent lower; and the mode, which is the most frequent score. Descriptive statistics like these also include the standard deviation. This shows how scores relate to the mean, a low score indicating that scores are clustered near the mean and a high score indicating that they are distributed across the range. Descriptive statistics are usually used in small-scale experiments.

Inferential statistics are used to answer questions or to test hypotheses, working from data about one group to infer material about another, as in RCTs. Inferential statistics assess the degree of probability that difference or change in the scores of different variables is the result of chance. Probability addresses the likelihood of change happening again, that is, that the change occurring in the controlled environment of the experiment with particular people will, given the same conditions and a similar population, be repeated. Thus the effects of intentional differences, that is of different variables, can be demonstrated, and findings from one situation with a relatively small number of people can be extrapolated to another, much bigger population. The conventions are that $p < 0.05$ is a significant level of probability, meaning that there is a 5 per cent or less than 1 in 20 chance of the difference between the variables being due to chance, and $p < 0.01$ is a highly significant level of probability, representing 1 per cent or less than 1 in 100 of the difference being due to chance. The lower the score the higher the probability that change occurred because of the variables being tested in the experiment: there is a real difference, the so-called treatment effect. Other tests include analyses of variance that assess the difference between variables, and correlation that establishes the association between one variable and another.

Validity, efficacy and effectiveness

Experiments differ according to their internal validity and external validity. This refers to the extent to which an experiment has excluded as many likely sources of confounding as possible (internal validity), and the extent of its relevance beyond the laboratory to routine practice in clinical settings (external validity), again as in RCTs. Thus the internal validity of an RCT is strengthened when its results can be attributed solely to the intervention being tested, and threatened when the results can be attributed to factors other than those being tested. However, the strength of an experiment's internal validity is likely to weaken its external validity. An inherent tension thus exists because excluding as many confounding factors as possible inevitably weakens a trial's external validity. Reynolds (2000), for example, describes how clients treated in RCTs of psychological therapies that have strong internal validity frequently differ from those seen in routine clinical practice. This is because clients in a trial are likely to be a homogeneous group with a single diagnosis who have been selected according to very strict criteria, treated by highly qualified and experienced, research-aware clinicians who have been trained to adhere to a treatment manual, have their adherence to it regularly monitored through feedback and supervision, and who work in teaching hospitals. This bears little resemblance to ordinary practice.

The tension is usually addressed through differentiating between efficacy studies and effectiveness studies. Efficacy studies refer to RCTs that have strong internal validity derived from a controlled environment, and effectiveness studies are RCTs and other kinds of experiments in real-world settings. Explanatory and pragmatic RCTs are differentiated in the same way. According to the EBP research cycle efficacy/explanatory studies and effectiveness/pragmatic studies are undertaken at different points, that is, according to Salkovskis's (1995) hourglass model. Efficacy studies are the pinch in the hourglass and effectiveness studies the broadening of the glass that follows.

Variables and outcome measurements

Different kinds of small- and large-scale experiments gather data about whether or not change occurs and try to establish what exactly causes an outcome through the isolation of particular factors, that is, through minimising the variables in the experiment by excluding or standardising some and varying others. Variables are any measure or event that can be defined and compared so as to assess their interaction and determine cause and effect. For example, the relationship with the therapist and the use of art materials (the independent variables that might cause change) could be introduced or varied to see if certain thoughts and feelings, for example self-esteem or negative symptoms (the dependent variables), were effected or changed. Thus a hypothesis (that 20 weeks of individual art therapy will alleviate depression) will be tested to see if the independent variable (the therapy) will effect the dependent variable (the depression) through its presence (for the treatment group) or absence (for the control group). Alongside the hypothesis that a particular situation or intervention is responsible for particular effects there is always the suggestion that the reverse is true, that chance caused the effect. This is the null hypothesis that experiments seek to disprove.

Experimental research seeks to establish that any change is a direct consequence of a specific intervention. This is achieved through measuring an attribute or quality such as anxiety on a high/low continuum, that is, the dependent variables, before and after treatment and at follow-up. These can be gathered through self-report questionnaires or psychometric tests (literally 'measurement of the mind') and routine symptomatic, social, educational and psychological measurements. In small studies and single-case experiments these can be administered either by practitioners, by colleagues or by independent researchers, according to the research design.

Art-based measurements

Some British art therapists are grappling with the design of outcome measures specifically for art therapy (Mottram, 2000) and some have devised scales to measure client expectations (Jones, forthcoming; Richardson et al., forthcoming) and attitudes towards artworks and associated behaviours in art therapy groups (Gilroy, 1995). Few outcome measurements, if any, use art as a tool, although art therapists in the USA have paid significant attention to the development of art-based measurements for the purposes of research, assessment and diagnosis, usually centring around the production of a particular image, for example Gantt and Tabone's 'Formal Elements of Art Scale' (FEATS; 1998). This was developed through consideration of ten years of clients' artworks and assesses how an image is made, not its content (Gantt, 2001, 2004). Feder and Feder (1998) give a useful overview of such art-based assessments, identifying three approaches:

1. *Psychoanalytic*: these look for symbolic representation of unconscious material in art works;
2. *Phenomenological*: these try to give an overview of the client, their behaviour and art-making processes and include consideration of the work itself and what is said about it;
3. *Diagnostic*: these analyse the artwork in terms of its formal elements, that is, the colour, space, composition, visual coherence and so on, considering them as diagnostic indicators.

Here the different *modus operandi* of art therapists in Britain and American come into sharp relief. Many American studies focus on the development and relative usefulness of art-based tools but these are usually – sometimes specifically, sometimes inferentially – situated within the diagnostic model of medicine and psychiatry (e.g. Ulman and Levy, 2001; Lev-Wiesel and Shivero, 2003; Silver, 2003). Two British research studies draw on psychoanalytic and phenomenological models to correlate visual qualities in clients' artworks with shifts in the therapeutic process (Schaverien, 1992; Simon, 1992). All encounter the problem of capturing change and development in art in an art-based way and struggle with the difficulties inherent in translating the gestalt of art making into linear, descriptive text. Whether art-based assessments are useful research tools for art therapists on either side of the Atlantic remains to be seen.

Quantitative research of all kinds is usually replicated and therein lies its strength. Repetition either highlights erroneous results or confirms true results. The findings of several small experiments can be combined to produce the strong, composite, critical mass of outcome research required by EBP orthodoxy that can be represented in systematic reviews. Questions about art therapy's outcomes and efficiency may be driven from the top down but I suspect that, as art therapists discover that quantitative methods are not quite so awful as was supposed and indeed can produce rather interesting results, and that a mixture of quantitative and qualitative research works well, such questions may begin to be driven by curiosity, from the bottom up. There are a number of examples in the art therapy literature of small- and large-scale experimental research and, although there is still only one single case experimental design by a British art therapist (Dalley, 1979, 1980), there are many more in the American art therapy literature. The standard presentation of such studies makes it difficult to retain the texture of practice, although some do, but different kinds of reports can be published in different places for different audiences. Thus it is eminently possible for quantitative research to offer rich, interesting – and, in EBP terms, acceptable – evidence of art therapy's effectiveness.

8 The evidence base for art therapy with adults

This and the following chapter about art therapy with adults, adolescents and children speak to the key question EBP asks of art therapy: 'what works with whom?' They would be very short chapters indeed were I to consider the discipline's existing research according to EBP orthodoxy, but taking a more wide-angled lens to the task, within the levels of art therapy evidence proposed in Chapter 2, enables a more pluralistic representation of the discipline's current evidence base. These, however, are neither critical appraisals nor systematic reviews – those would be other tasks – but summaries of art therapy's research and knowledge, as currently represented in the British and American literatures, that demonstrate effectiveness and articulate what it is that makes art therapy a unique intervention.

It is not surprising that the same variation in practice, outcome and research that Cochrane identified in medicine is evident across the psychological therapies. In the UK these comprise the psychoanalytic therapies, systemic therapies, behavioural therapy, cognitive analytic therapy, psychodynamic counselling and the arts therapies. Parry and Richardson (1996), in their seminal review of psychotherapy services in England, remark on the unevenness of research informing these treatments, although some do have a good critical mass. But despite the volume of both quantitative and qualitative research Roth and Fonagy's (1996) review of the evidence base for the psychological treatment of adults found that only psychodynamic psychotherapy for depression in the elderly was fully empirically validated. Cognitive-behavioural therapy was found to have a relatively robust evidence base and psychodynamic psychotherapy received partial validation for a few conditions. The arts therapies were excluded from these reviews, apart from a passing reference by Parry and Richardson. Since then other reviews have identified a lack of research in long-term work and therapy with the severe and enduringly mentally ill (Reynolds, 2000) but found suggestive evidence that psychoanalysis is effective (Fonagy, 2002). Such reviews can have significant influence on service provision but they have been challenged because of an unquestioning acceptance of EBP's value-laden ideology that excludes qualitative research and other studies that are not in accord with medicine's evidence hierarchies (Jones, 1998; McLeod, 2001). This reiterates the importance of using evidential criteria that reflect the values of the discipline and/or the practice under review.

Reading and searching

This review of the art therapy literature began with a search for research about clinical practice but soon widened to include related rigorous, often descriptive, texts that suggested effectiveness and/or described discipline-specific knowledge about the theory and practice of art therapy. I conducted searches of online databases and hand searches of British and American art therapy journals, although time prevented a full survey of the American literature. It was immediately apparent that the discipline has clearly discernable, discrete 'clusters' of literature. These are not associated with the diagnostic criteria that EBP favours but with clearly identifiable, discrete but broadly based client populations and services in different sectors. This included literature about art therapy with people who have been abused and traumatised, are on the autistic spectrum, who have addictions, dementia, eating disorders, learning difficulties, who are offenders, are in palliative care and who have severe and complex problems. Each cluster has a characteristic configuration: a few research projects, some academically rigorous texts and rich, descriptive writing about clinical work. To my mind these articulate the subtly different theories and approaches that art therapists are developing for various client groups and give clear indications for guidelines and future research in the way that evidence-based disciplines are supposed to do.

This and the following chapter therefore focuses on British and American art therapy literature that addresses research, theory and practice with different client groups. I have excluded research about the profession, its history and educational matters, general theory and descriptions of 'standard' practice (as outlined by Case, 1994) but included literature that fulfils one or more of the following criteria, that is to say it is:

- *Relevant*: describes practice with a specific population, either in terms of diagnosis, presenting problems or service provision;
- *Effectiveness oriented*: addresses or gives indications of effectiveness with a specific population;
- *Methodologically rigorous*: is either quantitative or qualitative research about clinical work; academically rigorous and/or scholarly texts; or rich, 'thick' description of clinical practice.

Limiting this, or any, review of art therapy's evidence base to quantitative, outcome research, even extending it to effectiveness-oriented qualitative research, would be to collude with EBP orthodoxy and drastically curtail the representation of art therapy's current research and knowledge. To restrict the view to that from UK shores alone would be similarly restrictive; despite many differences there is much that British and American art therapists can learn from one another. This is the evidence art therapy has so far.

Abuse and trauma

This cluster describes art therapy with adults who were abused as children, have experienced other traumas or been diagnosed with Post Traumatic Stress Disorder

(PTSD). Trauma is broadly defined as a response to overwhelming threat to the individual such that the person feels helpless and hopeless and surrenders to the terror and proximity of psychic and/or physical death. Trauma, when it is recalled, is often remembered visually and so its external and visual representation, sometimes without speech but witnessed by the art therapist, can assist an eventual reconnection to relationship and an integration of the trauma.

There are several outcome studies, mostly in the American literature, that demonstrate the effectiveness of short-term group and individual art therapy with people who have experienced abuse, war and other kinds of physical assault. For example, Brooke (1995) conducted a controlled study of an eight-week art therapy group for adult, female survivors of sexual abuse as children. Clients completed self-esteem inventories before and after the group and kept a journal in which they did art-based 'homework'. Their self-esteem improved, the findings approaching statistically significant levels. Waller's (1992) controlled clinical trial compared eight weeks of verbal group and individual therapy with group art therapy in the treatment of adult female incest survivors. This demonstrated that a structured series of art therapy interventions provided a safe means of communication which enhanced insight, catharsis and group cohesion and, Waller suggests, prevented early drop-out following catharsis. Three experimental single-case designs of short-term individual art therapy also demonstrated positive outcomes (Howard, 1990; Peacock, 1991; Morgan and Johnson, 1995). Howard, for example, describes nine weeks of individual art therapy with an adult female survivor of physical and sexual childhood abuse experiencing symptoms of PTSD. The Beck Depression Inventory was administered before and after the therapy and the client kept self-monitoring charts throughout; these showed a decrease in depressive symptoms and improvements in self-esteem and sense of autonomy. Peacock's study is of interest too because of the extreme brevity and intensity of art therapy (daily for ten days) and the use of repertory grids that enabled both client and therapist to understand how she construed her world. Even within this very limited timeframe pre and posttherapy measures showed a decrease in symptoms of anxiety and depression and improvements in self-esteem.

The British literature on art therapy with traumatised adults has a more descriptive quality and addresses short- and longer-term interventions. It includes one research study, McClelland (1992, 1993), which investigated a combination of art therapy and process work with clients in altered states of consciousness (ASC). This author established a cooperative inquiry group with two ex-clients who had completed art therapy, their difficulties being the result of prolonged physical and sexual abuse as children. They co-authored a narrative of two inquiry sessions where art materials were used to amplify experiences of ASC, their interactions being videoed and subsequently discussed within a co-operative inquiry framework. This collaborative research demonstrated that the particular combination of process work and different forms of creative expression with acute ASCs was a useful and seemingly effective intervention because, as McClelland states, 'very few clients indeed have been readmitted' (1993: 106).

Although not research, Schaverien's (1998) description of art therapy workshops with descendants of the Holocaust is a rigorous paper that considers whether or not trauma should be directly addressed. She says that concentration camp survivors never attend the workshops she runs because they would be too painful and not therapeutic, the trauma being so great that it causes a numbing anaesthesia that cannot be directly addressed; the scars are carried by their children and grandchildren who are unable to process their and their families' experiences. Schaverien suggests that art therapy is 'a non-invasive technique' (1998: 171) that enables an intense emotional engagement through art making. Events can be externalised and unseen trauma that 'defies articulation' can be witnessed and viewed – by the maker, the group and the art therapist – as if from a distance. Schaverien (1992) draws on her concept of the scapegoat transference to describe how the art object can become an embodiment of traumatic experience, its disposal having elements of a cleansing ritual that works on a deep level.

The overall picture of art therapy with traumatised adults is intriguing. Short-term art therapy interventions and workshops seem to dominate practice, or at least the literature, particularly in the USA where the nature of treatment is determined by the requirements of managed care (see Goodman, 1997), but laboratory and practice-based research, occurring soon after the event or many years later, shows art therapy's effectiveness in reducing the symptoms of PTSD and increasing self-esteem and feelings of autonomy. Several studies infer that encouraging clients to self-monitor and process material outside sessions, whatever the nature and length of art therapy, may be an effective and empowering treatment strategy. However, there is disagreement about whether profound and prolonged traumatic experiences require client and therapist to 'go right into them' (McClelland, 1993: 123) or whether the non-invasive aspects of art making that access, visually articulate and witness experience are more appropriate.

Addictions

The art therapy research literature about clinical work with people addicted to alcohol or drugs focuses on short-term, mostly structured, group-based interventions. For example, Springham (1994) describes an active approach to short-term art therapy groups with substance misusers and an investigation of clients' private and public responses. He draws on theories about narcissism and artists' wish to be seen/not seen in order to demonstrate art therapy's effectiveness as a short-term, 'sobering' experience that assists with clients' clarification of their problems and encourages them to seek longer-term treatment. Springham describes their responses to pre and postgroup questionnaires, comparing these with his observations in the group, he was able to identify differing kinds of defensive strategies that clients employed.

Springham's (1998, 1999) subsequent work draws on his primary research. He demonstrates the usefulness of imagery as an indirect communication to the art therapist about the maker's relationships and develops theory about art therapy and the treatment of drug and alcohol problems and their relationship to narcissism. Springham describes the importance of the image in understanding the presentation of the false, narcissistic self in a group and goes on to explore 'images of entitlement' or 'paradise pictures' that, he suggests, must be confronted in treatment. American research has also considered particular kinds of images that might predict relapse (Dickman et al., 1996) or identify the nature of clients' attachment relationships (Francis et al., 2003), and has shown how art-therapy groups can be effective in helping these clients to acknowledge their problems. Julliard (1995) used an experimental case design to investigate the effectiveness of group art therapy and role play in increasing chemically dependent clients' belief in 'Step One' of a 'Twelve Step Program', the group being offered as part of inpatient, multidisciplinary care. The group involved a mixture of media and topic-led art making and psychodrama, the clients completing daily self-report measures, questionnaires before and after the group and being interviewed after the group had ended. Julliard reports clients' increasing belief in the programme as time went on; prior to the group they felt isolated, disempowered and disconnected but afterwards felt more able to express their feelings, were less isolated, were able to see the possibility of change and, perhaps most significantly, their denial of problems had decreased markedly.

Mahony and Waller (1992) and Karkou and Sanderson (1997) remark on the different approaches to art therapy with this client population. Karkou and Sanderson (1997) describe these as direct (a variety of interventions from drug abuse workers that focus on addictive behaviours) and indirect (the psychodynamic approach that treats the whole person, not just the symptom). Mahony and Waller see it differently and note the differences between the American and British literature; the American literature is larger and describes mostly structured, didactic, sometimes confrontative methods that draw little on psychoanalytic concepts. They remark on the therapeutic nihilism felt by many psychotherapists working with addicts and compare this to art therapists' optimism about their effectiveness. Mahony and Waller also describe the influential work of Albert-Puleo (1980) who developed a particular form of art therapy practice derived from Freudian theories of narcissism; this limits verbal interaction and delays interpretation so that attention and action can be channelled into art making, allowing transference to develop and be addressed at the client's pace. Mahony and Waller (1992) suggest, like Springham (1999), that art therapy has a unique contribution to make to the psychological treatment of these clients because the making of art in art therapy offers an arena for narcissistic withdrawal and self-interest that is not accessible through other psychological services. Art therapy is therefore a more tolerable treatment for this client population than other, more direct, approaches.

These few papers convey the potential for art therapy as a distinctive treatment for clients with addictions. Short-term art therapy groups challenge the assumptions of clients in a manageable way; this links with Karkou and Sanderson's (1997) suggestion that a more task-oriented approach might be appropriate early on in treatment, and distinguishes between longer-term individual and studio-based art therapy where clients can withdraw into narcissistic self-appraisal through art. Problems have, however, been identified in service provision. Mahony's (1994, 1999) survey of the use of art activities in the alcohol services of a large health region found a marked lack of art therapy services and real confusion about what art therapy was. She identified a widespread use of art activities for educative, healing or psychotherapeutic purposes by various members of multi-disciplinary teams, usually as a leisure or craft activity, but offered by staff in the belief that they were 'doing art therapy'. Mahony concluded that clients are misled about the art therapy services they receive and do not have equable access to effective services from trained professionals. Despite an interest in art therapy, misunderstandings continue about its nature and unique properties with clients addicted to alcohol; these are exacerbated by resource problems that inhibit the development of appropriate services.

The evidence base for art therapy with addictions indicates that it offers something significantly different to other psychological services, shows the development of long and short-term approaches, conveys its potential effectiveness and situates practice within a particular theoretical framework. The extent and nature of art therapy service provision for these clients needs to be established as there is clearly room for both the improvement of services and for the development of particular art therapy approaches at different times in the treatment process.

Dementia

Art therapy with people who have dementia has one outcome study that demonstrates its clinical effectiveness. Waller's (2001, 2002; see also Sheppard et al., 1998) seminal work in this area was a small-scale RCT of two, ten-week art therapy groups compared with two, ten-week activity groups. This pilot study showed a significant reduction in the art therapy group members' depression and an improvement in their attentiveness. Clients, whose average age was 80 and who had moderate to severe dementia, were randomly assigned to the groups and a series of tests of cognitive ability, depression and attention were used to measure change throughout the project and at one month follow-up. Staff also observed physiological change affecting daily life, mood change in the groups was assessed and the perceptions of the clients by their carers, key workers and therapists were measured too. Improvements were found in sociability, mental acuity, physical competence and calmness. The research demonstrated that people with dementia responded positively to short-term art therapy groups, findings that are now being explored in a longer-term study.

Interesting qualitative material also emerged about the importance of the institutional context to the effectiveness of the art therapy groups. Two groups were offered in different organisations whose attitudes to art therapy reflected either support or ambivalence. This had a direct impact on group cohesion and the nature of clients' engagement with the art materials: the organisation where art therapy was supported enabled a richer, freer engagement with art materials, the clients in this group showing greater improvement overall (Waller, 2002). Initial findings from a further 18-month qualitative research project of 160 art therapy sessions suggests that 'institutional factors have a high impact on the outcome' (Waller, 2005, personal communication).

Waller et al.'s project followed Byers's descriptive texts (1995, 1998; Wilks and Byers, 1992) that portray difficult but affecting casework which illustrates how 'art therapy groups can be empowering and containing at a time when body and mind are disintegrating' (1998: 130), a theme that is continued in *Arts Therapies and Progressive Illness* (Waller, 2002). Tyler (2002), for example, describes the profound marginalisation of the elderly that is exacerbated when in care and suffering from memory loss. He illustrates, through a series of poignant case vignettes, how his elderly clients were able to address their own and others' mortality. Similarly, Falk (2002) shows how, in the art-therapy group he conducted with adults suffering from Alzheimer's Disease, clients were able to explore their fears of deterioration but also experience the group as an escape and a means of retaining memory. Studies by American art therapists echo those in the UK; for example Stewart's (2004) paper both theorised and illustrated how art therapy can improve the concentration of people with dementia, and Gregoire's (1998) assessment of the functioning and drawing abilities of these clients suggested that copying can assist interaction and form the basis for other creative activities, and so improve clients' engagement in art therapy.

I was interested to note the paucity of studies about art therapy with the non-organically impaired elderly. Doric-Henry's (1997) RCT is a notable exception, although this did not investigate art therapy *per se* but individual pottery sessions with elderly residents in a nursing home. Nonetheless it is an interesting paper because it demonstrated the effectiveness of the sessions in reducing clients' anxiety levels and because the trial included qualitative methods. Other research has demonstrated similar improvements in elderly clients' levels of depression through a mixture of life review and individual art therapy (Schexnadre, 1993); improvements in clients' sensorimotor skills and social interaction following a stroke through the use of clay in an art therapy group, evaluated through video and qualitative questionnaires (Yaretzky et al., 1996); and an increase in the social interaction of those in institutional care as a consequence of textile painting (Weiss et al., 1989). As an aside, it is interesting to note that Yaretzky et al., remarked, like Waller et al., on the influence of staff attitudes towards art therapy on its outcomes.

The sensory nature of art materials and opportunities for self-expression in individual and group art therapy with clients who have dementia can counteract the effects of memory loss, improve communication, enhance self-esteem and reduce depression, and there are indications that this might be so for non-demented elderly clients too. Research has demonstrated the effectiveness of group art therapy; hopefully further investigations will establish the efficacy of group and individual art therapy unequivocally and differentiate the benefits of long- and short-term work. Meanwhile it would be useful to establish the extent and nature of art therapy service provision for both the elderly and for those with dementia in the different sectors of health and social care.

Eating disorders

Art therapy with people who have eating disorders (mostly young adults) comprises qualitative research and a number of rigorous texts (including Wood's (1996) overview of the literature). Authors usually contextualise eating disorders within the social, cultural, aesthetic and gendered constructions of womanliness and femininity and remark on the difficulties of working with this client population, caught as they are in destructive cycles of 'defiance, defence and ambivalence' (Waller, 1994: 76) and a 'desperate unwillingness to change' (Luzzatto, 1994: 60). Waller was the first to research art therapy with this client population and to identify the dialectical dynamics. She took part in a multidisciplinary investigation, the members of her analytic art therapy group being interviewed by a psychologist using personal constructs; this occurred at three-month intervals and a year after the group had ended. Particular interactions within the group and with the art therapist were identified, namely spilling in the group and then withdrawing from it, and idealising and then demolishing the therapist, clients focusing on significant relationships and the construction of identity and what they thought would be an ideal self. Art therapy enabled the women to access core constructs and to express feelings through art rather than through eating or not eating (Waller 1983, personal communication, 2005).

Levens's (1995) and Rehavia-Hanauer's (2003) research developed theory about art therapy's potential to be effective with this client population. Rehavia-Hanauer describes qualitative research that used grounded theory to analyse casenotes of four years of weekly individual art therapy with ten adolescent clients. She identified six conflicts that characterise anorexia nervosa: resistance and attraction to art therapy; the creation and destruction of the art object; a desire to be looked after and an inability to express that desire; dependence and autonomy; the development of female sexuality and identity and the rejection of these; and a need for control coupled with a lack of control. Rehavia-Hanauer argues that art therapy is a particularly suitable form of treatment for this client population because it exposes and embodies these conflicts in a tangible form, reducing them and enabling their negotiation in a manageable, non-intrusive and concrete way through the art making process and object.

Levens proposed that the underlying dynamics of anorexia and bulimia are based on the need to control food, the body and psychological processes through magical thinking, suggesting that art therapy is particularly helpful when magical thinking dominates. She explored the significance of boundaries between the inside and outside of the body, showing how art can 'create the body that has been lost' (1995: 71) so that clients can realise that they have an inside that is theirs. However, as this material is preverbal and clients' thinking tends to be concrete, and because the language used to describe such experiences comes from later stages of development, Levens suggests that 'as if' interactions are inappropriate and indeed can be experienced as invasive, especially early on in the therapeutic relationship. She goes on to say that this incongruity can be addressed through the art therapist lending words and/or suggesting art activities that give these clients a way of articulating and communicating their experience – of giving it form. How art objects are used becomes particularly significant as they offer visual feedback to the maker that reflects disowned projections in a less threatening, digestible way. Levens states that it is important that the art therapist does not take over the client's thinking, as s/he will be pressurised to do, but should encourage the client to explore their artwork, perhaps through fantasy and storytelling and thinking about spatial order, outline and form; this displaces the focus from the client to the object and enables communication through it. Joining the client at this concrete level enables him or her to develop an observing self and move, through art, from acting out through the body to symbolic thought.

Others concur. Schaverien (1989, 1994), Luzzatto (1994) and Waller (1994) agree that transference interpretations can be experienced as threatening: art thus becomes a crucial mediator between client and art therapist. Luzzatto suggests particular art-based interventions that assist the therapeutic process through directly addressing the 'double trap' of eating disorders (or the conflicts Rehavia-Hanauer describes) via the unique double transference of art therapy to therapist and artwork. She suggests that images of a double trap recur; the client is invariably small and vulnerable, within an imprisoning situation and threatened or imprisoned by something persecutory in the external world from which s/he cannot escape. Luzzatto proposes that frightening negative transference can be contained within the image while a benign transference can be maintained through the therapeutic alliance, and that this prevents clients from early termination of therapy. She suggests that the three dimensionality of art therapy enables imaginative responses that can envisage change, giving a short case example of brief, community-based individual art therapy where imagery developed and the client made important lifestyle changes. Luzzatto indicates effectiveness, reporting that these positive changes were maintained and confirmed at a three-year follow-up with the client's GP.

Other approaches to group and individual art therapy with this client population in various settings are also described. Rust (1994) for example outlines year-long, community-based, closed art-therapy groups; she found that introducing some structure into the group with time to make and talk worked better than an open-ended approach, the latter resulting in problems with decision making and a consequent inability to use the group effectively. Schaverien (1994) describes an approach that begins individually, at the bedside, for those on bedrest; having gained a stable weight and ceased bedrest, clients join a group. Schaverien suggests that anorexics respond best to individual work while bulimics and compulsive eaters find groups helpful. She, like others, equates the material, sensory experience of making art with bodily sensations, and adds that anorexics may take a while to engage with art materials while bulimics may 'binge' and make copious amounts of work. Art therapy offers something particular to this client population: what were unconscious enactments through food can become conscious enactments through art. When this occurs a capacity for symbolisation and relationship can develop because art offers a medium through which relationship can be entered, first with the self and then with another, enabling power to be divested from food and invested in art.

Art therapists working with eating-disordered clients have focused on clear and well-formulated theorising about how and why art therapy is an effective intervention. It is particularly worthwhile because of the physical resonances between food and art materials and because art therapy operates at preverbal levels that enable symbolisation and relationship to develop. Detailed narrative and experimental case studies are needed that demonstrate the effectiveness that has been indicated, which establish the suitability of group and individual art therapy for different kinds of eating disorders at different stages of treatment, and begin to explore some of the different approaches art therapists have developed for this client population. The location and extent of art therapy services for eating-disordered clients also needs to be established.

Learning difficulties

Art therapy with people who have learning difficulties has a long history and, relative to most other client populations, a large general literature and some accompanying research. Some early practitioners valued the creative process, non-verbal symbolism and an inherent therapeutic benefit of art making while others based their practice on a 'developmental approach' (e.g. Stott and Males, 1984). This sought to enable clients to move through the stages of drawing development as children do, the aim being to generalise from this to improvements in other areas of functioning and behaviour. This is allied to the research of Dubowski (1984, 1990) who compared the non-representational marks of young children to those of severely disabled clients.

In contrast to the structured and/or developmental model of art therapy is descriptive literature that develops a psychotherapeutically oriented approach which uses insight and interpretation to address challenging behaviours and facilitate clients' capacity to think. For example, both Fox (1998) and Stack (1998) describe casework that demonstrates the importance of long-term group and individual work with autistic adults. They show how a capacity for symbol formation can be achieved through understanding and renegotiating early stages of development in art therapy, and describe how the use of art materials can enable the development of relationship and a diminution of destructive behaviours. Tipple (1992) gives an account of casework that demonstrates a link between the client's emotional life, bodily movement and non-representational painting that led to a similar lessening of violent and challenging behaviour. Rees's (1995) research, drawing on Dubowski's developmental approach, used ethological methods of meticulous observation to explore the relationship between her clients' non-representational marks and paintings, their social functioning and their use of physical and social spaces. Rees (1995) and Tipple (1992, 1993, 1994) suggest that the art in art therapy offers a potential for relationship with clients who have the most severe difficulties and challenging behaviours because the capacity to represent and symbolise are not prerequisites for communication and expression. Case studies and vignettes have also described how these clients' early experiences of damage, loss and separation can be addressed in art therapy. See, for example, Kuczaj's (1998) reports of work with the loss continuum and bereavements of learning-disabled clients, and Lomas and Hallas (1998) who give an interesting account of interviews with people with learning disabilities who attended a community-based art-therapy group; this enabled them to consider how the group and their countertransference responses had reflected the clients' feelings of anger, disempowerment and helplessness about their social and environmental circumstances.

There are two outcome studies in this literature, both case-study based. Bowen and Rosal (1989) outline their use of guided imagery and storytelling in a single-case experimental design of ten weeks' individual art therapy with a young man who had mild learning difficulties and behavioural problems. Pre and posttreatment psychological tests and 'work production averages' showed that his behavioural difficulties and feelings of helplessness decreased and his sense of control and accomplishment increased. The dual approach of Mackenzie et al. (2000) brings cognitive psychology and art therapy together. Their paper describes an integrated model of group and individual work over two and a half years with sex offenders who have learning difficulties, the goals of which were to reduce the offences. The offending behaviours were addressed through cognitive behaviourism and the associated feelings through art therapy that was 'a more successful means of introducing a challenging issue without resistance from group members' (2000: 65). Mackenzie et al.'s evaluation, although without follow-up or detail of the measures, demonstrated effectiveness because, during the life of the group, members did not reoffend.

The literature on art therapy with clients who have learning difficulties describes two approaches: one that is structured and sometimes developmentally based, and another that is psychodynamically oriented. Both appear to mitigate against challenging and offending behaviours and, even for those with the severest of difficulties, enable relationship and the development of a capacity for symbol formation. Given art therapists' long history of work with this client population it would be helpful to establish the nature and extent of current services across the health, justice, social and educational sectors, and to build on research that has indicated art therapy's effectiveness in the treatment of short-term problems and as part of ongoing community-based support.

Offenders

The literature about the pioneering, often sessional work in prisons, prison hospital wings, young offender institutions, within probation and in secure and forensic units is mostly descriptive and sometimes lacks a critical context. It includes one British research study that addresses art therapy's effectiveness in a prison (Riches, 1994) and two American outcome studies (Ackerman, 1992; Gussack, 2004). Nonetheless there has been increasing recognition by the Home Office of the value of art and art therapy in the treatment and prevention of criminal behaviours (Riches, 1994; Liebmann, 1998), no doubt assisted by the development of *Guidelines for Arts Therapists Working in Prisons* (Teasdale, 2002). These aim to promote the arts therapies and delineate the nature of service provision in prisons, giving guidance about the practical and psychological support systems practitioners need to sustain clinical work in what can be toxic and debilitating working environments.

Art therapists have explored whether there is a creative tension or a conflict between art therapy and a prison system that seeks to punish, confine, control and limit risks (e.g. Tamminen, 1998). Although direct attention has not been paid to how differing art therapy approaches might be suited to different settings and client needs, it has been given to how the antecedents of crime might be addressed. Liebmann (1998), for example, developed the use of a cartoon sequence through which individuals on probation could narrativise their offence and gain understanding, Teasdale (1999, 1997) has described a similar storyboard that emerges in art therapy groups, and Riches (1994) described a method that sits between art education and art therapy. Liebmann (1998) explores these varying approaches, usefully distinguishing between the orientation of different institutions and the work art therapists are consequently able to do. There are NHS secure, forensic units and hospitals where the feelings and behaviours of offenders with psychiatric problems are addressed in groups that aim to contain feelings and improve communication (e.g. Sarra, 1998), increase insight, and consequently change criminogenic behaviours and decrease the likelihood of recidivism (e.g. Hagood, 1994; Teasdale, 1995, 1997). There are also probation centres and units offering art as one among several recreational or quasi-recreational activities, although these may not be facilitated by an art therapist, and high security, long-term prisons employ art and art therapy as a means of exploring and counteracting the destructive effects of prison life, supporting the process of adjustment to imprisonment as well as to release.

This last approach was the subject of research that evaluated the work of the Arts and Crafts Centre at HMP Albany. Whether the artworks were highly skilled and product oriented or focused on insight and self-exploration, either helping prisoners to survive their sentence or to effect some personal growth, there were clear therapeutic benefits of working in the Arts Centre. Riches reported a 29 per cent reduction in the discipline reports of prisoners attending the Centre during a 13-month period compared to their records prior to attending. Observations by prison officers corroborated these figures, attesting to the men's improved behaviour in the Centre as compared to that in an adjoining industrial, woodwork centre, and also to improved relationships between prison staff and the men when in the Centre. Wing governors reported similar improvements in the men's behaviour in their living quarters.

Two American studies address the outcomes of group and individual art therapy. Ackerman (1992) used a single-case experimental design to evaluate the effectiveness of brief, individual art therapy in a prison that focused on the development of self-esteem and somatization; the client's somatic complaints decreased and there were improvements in self-concept, self-esteem and emotional expression. A more detailed pilot, single-group study (Gussack, 2004) used a variety of psychological tests and the Formal Elements of Art Therapy Scale (FEATS; Gantt and Tabone, 1998) to explore inmates' artwork. Again the intervention was brief and a mixture of themes, group-based art tasks and structured and unstructured sessions were used. All the measures showed significant change: there were improvements in inmates' attitudes, social skills and acceptance of the organisation and its staff. The absence of a control group meant that these positive outcomes could not be attributed entirely to art therapy, but the findings nonetheless demonstrated the benefits of art therapy in the prison services.

The literature on art therapy with offenders describes a range of provision in organisations that have very different foci: to contain, to rehabilitate and to offer treatment. While there is a common focus in the British and American literatures on decreasing offending behaviours within and outwith institutional care, the nature of art therapy can shift: from exploring the antecedents of crime to countering the effects of long-term incarceration. The nature and extent of art therapy service provision for offenders across all sectors needs to be established, and so too does its interface with other art activities. The effectiveness of relatively long-term engagement in art making and brief, focused art therapy has begun to be demonstrated, but rigorous descriptive, narrative and experimental studies are needed that, first, document and then explore the effectiveness of various approaches to art therapy in different sectors with different kinds of offender. Riches, Ackerman and Gussack all offer useful models that could be replicated which, together with longitudinal studies that establish outcomes beyond prison walls, could greatly enhance the profile of this area of art therapists' work.

Palliative care

There is a relatively large body of literature about art therapy in palliative care and a number of research projects exploring theory, process and outcome that have progressed the evidence base. Practice in this area includes work with the bereaved, staff and carers. I refer the reader to other reviews that document the development and range of practice in the UK (Wood, 1998b, 2005), and to Pratt's (2004) practical guidelines that clarify the different kinds of arts-based activity in palliative care and inform managers about resources and provision.

Wood proposes that art therapy enables people to adjust to changes in their health, body image, circumstances, behaviours and relationships; it also helps to improve self-esteem, maintain identity and offers purposeful, individually expressive and validating activity that improves the quality of life during its last stages. The interrelationship of mind and body and a physical engagement with art materials in art therapy 'enables word-less layers of experience to be rendered in concrete form' (1998b: 35). This has enormous therapeutic potential, for example in the alleviation and psychological control of pain. These themes are developed in the rich descriptions of practice to be found in Pratt and Wood (1998) and Waller and Sibbett (2005). Although the literature is varied and can be anecdotal, it can be seen how practice has had to adapt because of the time constraints of uncertain health and the limitations caused by diminishing abilities and the physical space in which art therapy takes place. For example, Connell describes the ongoing compilation of a 'Group Notebook' by cancer patients that contains an 'extraordinary human testimony' (1998: 78) of images and texts that are perused, discussed and to which contributions are made over the years; Bell (1998) outlines his development of 'domiciliary art therapy' in clients' homes; the facilitation of image making for new clients through open studio sessions (Luzzatto, 2005) and provision of a range of materials including sand and silk painting (Bocking, 2005) are also described; and both Coote (1998) and Wood (1998a) convey the significance of one-off sessions where an enormous amount is expressed and processed in a short space of time. Such brief encounters are also explored in Wood's (2002) archival research which used grounded theory to explore seven years of art therapy case notes with clients who had AIDs-related dementia. She describes her unstinting efforts to connect with her clients through adapting art materials and the conditions in which the therapy took place, echoing other art therapists' descriptions of art therapy occurring not only in art rooms but also in dining rooms, on wards, by the bedside and on living room floors. Wood suggests that art therapy gives these clients a continuity of experience and a way of mobilising an autonomous, active part of the self in the midst of the most distressing experiences and unpredictable circumstances.

Active and structured approaches to short-term group art therapy in palliative care, sometimes including multidisciplinary work, have also been developed and their outcomes measured. For example, Luzzatto (2000, 2005) and Luzzatto and Gabriel (1998, 2000) describe ten-week, theme-centred groups that encourage the use of art materials and aim to facilitate self-expression. Clients ending these groups completed a brief postgroup questionnaire and reported increases in feelings of peace, freedom and in their self-awareness (Luzzatto, 2000). Schut et al. (1996) conducted an RCT that investigated the outcomes of a combination of art therapy and behaviour therapy in the treatment of clients who had complicated bereavement reactions following different types of loss (of a spouse, child or parent). They describe how the art therapy component enabled the exploration, representation and symbolic disposal of chaotic feelings while the behavioural component enabled clients to order, understand and cognitively restructure their emotions.

There are several, again very different, research papers about art therapy in palliative care that consistently report improved mood, self-esteem and quality of life, and a lessening of fear and isolation in the face of serious illness and pain. This includes art therapy with people who were in intensive care (Rockwood and Graham-Pole, 1997) and undergoing hemodialysis (Weldt, 2003); a mixture of interviews and case narrative describing art therapy and patients undergoing bone marrow transplants (Greece, 2003); the use of process description, regular questionnaires and long-term follow up interviews to evaluate the usefulness of art therapy for people who had chronic illnesses and somatic symptoms (Theorell et al., 1998); and an interview-based study of 30 textile artists who regarded continuing involvement with their practice as important in their ability to cope with a range of chronic physical illness (Reynolds, 2002). Not only was their work stimulating, productive and expressive, it was also transformational in that it allowed the women to overcome the pain and fear associated with their illnesses.

Hardy (2001: 24) suggests that it is important to distinguish between the 'restorative' qualities of art making in art therapy and therapy that seeks insight and understanding of the client's internal world, for example to assist the resolution of prediagnosis issues and grief that become intensely engaged when the client is dying (e.g. Schaverien, 2000, 2002). While this is an important distinction it is not always readily apparent. Zammit's (2001) narrative and collaborative case study, for example, is about a psychiatrist and psychotherapist diagnosed with cancer who used art to explore and understand the relationship between mind, body and spirituality and who, after a terminal diagnosis, became cancer-free. This extraordinary story is interesting not only in terms of the treatment of physical illnesses (an integrated approach to body and mind), outcome (art was healing) and art therapy practice (Zammit suggests a series of foci on the illness, insight, emotional expression, goals and spirituality), but also methodologically. Here narrative, interviews, observation, documentation and visual methods meet and are explored cooperatively by artist and researcher. Sibbett's (2005c) arts-based, autoethnographic research also includes moving testimony and representation of her own experience of cancer and that of others, accessed through interviews, focus groups, questionnaires and art reviews. She explores liminality in art therapy and the experience of cancer (Sibbett, 2005a, 2005b, 2005c), construing it as a transitional space characterised by ambiguity and being suspended in time. She suggests that art therapy enables experiences of flow, of being absorbed and in a state of reverie that enables clients to gain a sense of control and empowerment. Sibbett suggests that the multi-sensory, lived experience of cancer and associated issues concerning the body and self-image can be explored through art therapy.

Art therapy in palliative care has taken the first steps in demonstrating its effectiveness. It has been shown to have an impact on the quality of clients' lives when they are chronically or terminally ill in terms of self-esteem, self-awareness, the alleviation of pain and the ability to address immediate as well as long-standing issues. That this can occur in the most unconducive of physical circumstances (in terms of the client's health and the setting in which therapy occurs) attests to the power and effectiveness of art therapy. Narrative and experimental research have evidenced the significant impact that art therapy can have on coping with illness, imminent death and bereavement, and rich descriptive writing and personal testimonies convey the lived, human experience of serious illness and the important contribution that art therapy makes to patient care. Art therapy and cognitive approaches again seem to make a powerful combination.

Severe and complex problems

Clients who come into this category include those diagnosed as schizophrenic, psychotic, bipolar, personality disordered, phobic, compulsive and chronically depressed. Many of these disorders are co-morbid and difficult to explore as discrete entities. However, it is interesting to note the relatively large body of research literature on art therapy with clients who have psychotic, schizophrenic and related disorders, but the marked absence of literature about practice with other members of this client population.

Depression

I was surprised that I could only identify one piece of research that specifically addressed art therapy with depressed clients. Although the clients in Ponteri's (2001) study were not chronically depressed I include it here because of the methods used to explore the effect of group art therapy on depressed mothers and their children. Four mother–child dyads attended an art therapy group for eight weeks; pre and postgroup assessments were conducted, play sessions were videoed, and the mothers completed self-reports, questionnaires and took part in postgroup interviews. Various art therapy 'directives' and art-based games facilitated mother–child interaction, and psychoeducational activities for the mothers and separate space for their children's play were also provided. Ponteri reports that all clients showed increased levels of self-esteem and a more positive self-image, and half were able to interact more positively with their children.

Personality disorders

Again, there is a notable absence of research about art therapy with personality-disordered clients. Greenwood (2000) is the only author to directly address this area of practice, although others have explored art therapy with these clients within discussion of practice with other populations (e.g. addictions, offenders) and drawn on these experiences to inform discourse about other issues (Dudley, 2004, personal communication, 2005). Nonetheless there are descriptions of practice. Greenwood discusses the difficulties in long-term individual art therapy with an adult client diagnosed as personality disordered who had been neglected and abused as a child. The therapy was long term but felt limited, the client finding Greenwood's attempts to think and understand intolerable. Teasdale (1995) also points to the difficulties of art therapy with personality-disordered clients, this time in prisons, and the importance of art therapists resisting notions of themselves as crusaders in the face of extreme difficulty and destructiveness.

Given these problems I was interested to hear more positive reports of art therapy with this client population. This came about coincidentally through consultation with the Expert Panel advising on the guidelines being developed at Oxleas NHS Trust. An enquiry to the Panel about practice with clients who have borderline personalities or personality disorders elicited responses that suggested that, over time, artworks could hold the extraordinarily powerful and destructive projections from clients who believe they are hated and are experienced as hating. The experts suggested that directing clients to use art materials can militate against destructive behaviours and offer a non-threatening means through which clients can relate to the art therapist (Dudley, 2005, personal communication; Wilks, 2005, personal communication). The establishment of clear boundaries is considered critical, especially as negative reactions, acting out and aggression towards the therapist can occur and the therapy is likely to be sabotaged and defended against (Greenwood, 2005, personal communication). The non-verbal or preverbal benefits of image making can mediate in the tension between confrontation and empathy, enabling an eventual experience of the symbolic when art works are observed and shared. 'Art can soften the often highly charged reactive processes' (Dudley, 2005) and, in group, individual or open studio work, enable clients to slowly enter relationship. Expert opinion therefore indicates that art therapy has much to offer to this client population. Rigorous description and documentation of practice and service provision with personality-disordered clients – in day hospitals, therapeutic communities and offender institutions – is urgently needed so that research can begin to demonstrate and explore the pivotal, mediating role of art therapy in ameliorating destructive tendencies and fostering development that expert opinion has indicated is effective.

Psychotic and related disorders

Wood (1997a, 1999a, forthcoming) has documented and researched British art therapists' longstanding clinical practice with this client population. Others have used different methods to explore theories and practices (Greenwood and Layton, 1987, 1991; Killick, 1991,1995, 1997, 2000; Killick and Greenwood, 1995; Saotome, 1998; Mahony, forthcoming) and have investigated art therapy's effectiveness through an RCT (Jones, forthcoming; Richardson et al., forthcoming). An apparent absence of parallel research and literature about art therapy with this client population from colleagues in the USA is intriguing, perhaps precluded by the long-term nature of much of this work and the imperatives of managed care.

Wood's historical research (1997a, 1999a, forthcoming) identified four stages of practice development. Art therapy began with an approach based on the premise that art is inherently healing and developed through periods informed by social psychiatry, psychoanalysis and group analysis, reaching the present period that, Wood suggests, is characterised by increasing attention to the influence of popular and visual culture. She differentiates between the supportive, long-term and even open-ended art therapy needed by many of these clients who live in the community, often in the most deprived and disadvantaged socio-economic conditions, and the approaches developed by art therapists working with clients in the acute, inpatient stages of illness.

The difficulties these clients experience have been described as a blurring between inner and outer realities, or conscious and unconscious states, that results in a blankness where the capacity for thought and relationship are profoundly damaged. Authors therefore agree that not only is the formation of a containing relationship the first task of art therapy but that the nature of the physical space in which therapy takes place is also a critical factor (Greenwood and Layton, 1987, 1991; Killick, 1995, 1997, 2000; Wood, 1997b, forthcoming; Saotome, 1998). Killick was able to demonstrate this in her research that investigated the theoretical underpinnings of her work. Clients attended an open studio all day, every day, and had their own space in which to work. Killick showed how the making of art in this environment could address the creative interplay between the different realms of clients' experience. Art therapy proceeded on the premise that clients' work was 'sealed' and only accessible by and through them; neither the form nor the content of the work were addressed, simply what happened as it was made and once it was finished. Killick suggested that repeated attention to the tangible, functional aspects of making art and storing it lessened the catastrophic anxieties that characterise psychosis and allowed the client to experiment with different degrees of relatedness to the art therapist. This enabled a mediation between the concrete and the symbolic that, in time, restored clients' capacity to symbolise. As one of Killick's clients said: 'People like me need places like that art room. Places which allow the mind to heal' (quoted in Killick, 2000: 113).

Killick (1997) acknowledged that changes in service provision during the 1990s nowadays preclude working with such intensity, although some aspects of her approach can be seen in community-based practice described by other authors. For example, Mahony's (forthcoming) heuristic research describes a long-term, outpatient group where the focus was on the making of art. Greenwood and Layton's (1987, 1991) case study based papers also minimise the role of insight and interpretation in their community-based art-therapy group, but they explain how making art and talking and thinking about it focused on situating individual art works within the groups' visual and social matrix. They suggest that the projection of psychic material into objects and images through the art making process helps clients to strengthen their psychological boundaries and manage their unconscious material in a creative way, a process supported by the group as everyone links the parts (the individual artworks) to the whole. Greenwood and Leyton emphasise the social processes in the group and its extension to interactions before and after which, together with a side-by-side, transparent, empathic and playful therapeutic approach, enable the development of the client's self in relation to others. Long-term, supportive art therapy such as this enabled clients to develop mature defences such as sublimation (through art) and humour, and to function as well as possible in the community and in the long term.

Wood (1997b) agrees that art therapy with this client population is supportive and operates at a relatively low intensity over prolonged periods of time. She describes how giving these clients time to make, remake and digest their art parallels artists' development of their work over time and enables a sense of agency which transfers to other areas of clients' lives. However, although she acknowledges that the particular therapeutic milieu that art therapy offers might be unusual in the current NHS, there is 'considerable pragmatic acceptance amongst my managers ... (for) ... long-term work' and 'economically sensible reasons for offering it' (1997b: 43). This, coupled with indications of positive change consequent upon art therapy from inductive, practice-based research, is important evidence of art therapy's effectiveness. For example, Greenwood and Layton (1987, 1991) propose that members' commitment to the group was evidence of its positive outcome, given the difficulties of engaging this client population with mental health services. They also say that three members of their group who had recurrent psychotic episodes had both their frequency and the duration of their inpatient admissions reduced. Similarly, Mahony says that her group resulted in significant improvements in clients' mental health such that 'several said they thought it unlikely they would need mental health services again' (forthcoming).

Saotome's (1998) investigation of art therapy practice with these clients drew attention to their social deprivation and the importance of relationships in the group to their lives. Wood's research similarly highlights the social and economic deprivation of clients living in the community (1999a, forthcoming). It is therefore interesting that unexpected findings from the sole experimental study with this client population – Richardson et al.'s (forthcoming) seminal RCT – included indications of the acceptability of art therapy groups for these clients, documented the improved participation of those from ethnic minority groups and gave rise to powerful qualitative material about clients' life circumstances (Jones, forthcoming). The trial examined the incremental benefits of short-term group art therapy over the standard package of mental health care, measuring its benefits according to clients' symptoms, interpersonal function and the quality of their lives before and after the group and at six-month-follow-up. The results provided qualified support for art therapy's effectiveness but there were statistically significant improvements in clients' negative symptoms. Given that the group's brevity did not reflect the norms of routine practice, these results are encouraging. Interestingly, the model of art therapy used in this RCT – short-term group interactive art therapy – has not hitherto been discussed in relation to work with these very damaged clients. Jones (forthcoming) gives a more detailed qualitative description of this research, the groups and what it was like to be both clinician and researcher. Like Greenwood and Layton (1987, 1991) and the guideline about art therapy with clients prone to psychotic states (Brooker et al., forthcoming), Jones suggests that the art therapist's capacity to think with clients about their artworks and to sometimes offer an interpretation, can be an important aspect of the art therapy process with this client population, even in the very short term.

Art therapists have demonstrated that they offer clients with complex difficulties a non-threatening means of entering and maintaining relationship that can, eventually, enable symbolisation and the development of mature defences. For clients whose capacity for thought is profoundly damaged art therapy can offer a mediating experience that enables a sense of agency to develop in their lives that can be sustained through long-term individual and group art therapy. Outcome research has demonstrated the effectiveness of what, in the routines of practice, would be considered an extremely short-term art therapy group for these clients. Thus there are good indications that art therapy is an effective intervention that enables people with severe, enduring and complex problems to reduce and manage their symptoms and hence reduce their use of other mental health services. This is important evidence supporting art therapy services for people whose difficulties often preclude them from other forms of psychological intervention. To develop the evidence base further the discipline needs systematic research that documents practice and provision for both short-term acute and long-term community-based art therapy with this client population that can involve relationships and different interventions that extend over many years.

Thus is the evidence base for art therapy with adult clients being constructed. Effectiveness has been demonstrated or indicated with some client groups and specialist interventions have been researched and developed for short- and long-term art therapy with different populations in different services and sectors. Much remains to be done, but clearly art therapy's research and knowledge base about clinical work with adults is sufficient to enable the development of evidence-based guidelines and focused, strategic research. What of the evidence base for art therapy with children and adolescents?

9 The evidence base for art therapy with children and adolescents

A review of the evidence base for art therapy and the psychological therapies with children and adolescents is problematic because clients are often described in a generic way that makes it difficult to organise the literature according to discrete populations or services. Children's problems tend to be clustered as 'emotional', 'behavioural' or to do with 'conduct', diagnostic descriptors being inappropriate to education, social services and justice systems that neither use such terminology nor organise children according to disorders. Problems such as truancy, vandalism and at-risk behaviours require intervention by systems other than healthcare, delinquency for example including behaviours that violate the law and overlap with psychiatric and educational difficulties. Developmental change and variation bring additional factors into the frame that have to be incorporated into multi-agency and cross-sectoral practice and research to address the episodic, recurring nature of problems.

There are more than 500 therapies used in the treatment of children and adolescents (Kazdin, 2000) but little evidence either for or against the effectiveness of psychodynamic therapies. Wiesz and Kazdin (2003) note that behavioural and cognitive-behavioural treatments account for 70 per cent of the published outcome studies, but that non behavioural treatments are the most favoured in practice. Carr (2000), Fonagy et al. (2002) and Kazdin and Weisz (2003) conducted reviews of psychological treatments for children and adolescents similar to Roth and Fonagy's (1996) review of psychological treatments for adults. Fonagy et al. report that there is clear evidence supporting specific (rather than generic) cognitive-behaviourism for general anxiety and phobias, depression, conduct disorders in older children and for some physical symptoms, and that there is some evidence that systemic family therapy is effective with anorexia and depression, physical symptoms and conduct disorders. Clearly there are significant gaps in this literature, not least addressing the non-behavioural treatments preferred by practitioners.

There is an academically rigorous British literature that addresses the theory and practice of art therapy with children and adolescents, some of which applies to practice with clients of all ages. Case (1995, 2000, 2003, 2005) for example contributes significantly to understanding about silence in therapy, the multiple transferences that move between images and therapist, and the use of materials and equipment. There is some exploration of practice with children from particular populations and settings, for example about art therapy with very young children (Meyerowitz-Katz, 2003), those in mainstream (Welsby, 1998) and special education (Boronska, 1995), and in child and adolescent mental health services (e.g. Dalley, 1993). Authors have also described approaches to practice, for example, Dalley (1993) and Prokoviev (1998) concur about the need for clearly defined periods of art making and discussion and for interventions that contain behaviour and maintain boundaries in art therapy groups with children, that is in a different way to art therapy groups with adults. Alongside this rich descriptive material from art therapists in the UK is qualitative research (e.g. Evans, 1998; O'Brien, 2003, 2004; Tipple, 2003) but to date no outcome research. The American literature also has rigorous descriptive studies (e.g. Henley, 1994) and qualitative research (e.g. Ball, 2002), but it also has a notable body of outcome studies (e.g. Tibbetts and Stone, 1990; Saunders and Saunders, 2000).

Generally speaking, art therapists work with a huge range of children and adolescents in all kinds of settings and in all kinds of ways. The problem of differing systems and discourses in the art therapy literature parallels that of the psychological therapies and makes it difficult to cluster the art therapy literature according to particular groups of children and adolescents. I have therefore focused on texts that begin to form a critical mass, either about effectiveness or about a specific population, that is, children diagnosed with ADHD, on the autistic spectrum and who have been abused. I have used the same criteria for selecting British and American texts about children and adolescents as I have in the previous chapter reviewing the existing evidence for art therapy with adults.

Outcome research

Quantitative and qualitative research has investigated art therapy's effectiveness in the treatment of behavioural, conduct and educational problems. These exclusively American studies are noteworthy not only because they attempt early intervention and seek improvement in children's academic achievements and behaviour but also because they involve collaboration with teachers. Research has included combinations of education and art therapy, teacher-based evaluations of children's learning and behaviour and, in early studies, what is described as 'art-based counselling'. White and Allen's (1971) study, for example, was the first to investigate the outcomes of 'art counselling' through a single-group controlled study in a residential summer school for preadolescent boys. The group participated in a visual arts course designed to help the boys to better understand themselves and the world around them; those in the treatment group showed significantly more improvement in their self-concepts compared with those in the non-treatment group, the changes remaining stable at 14-month follow-up. Onizo and Onizo's (1989) RCT used a similar model of art activity in a quasi-counselling setting within mainstream education. This study sought to improve the self-esteem of children with Hawaiian ancestry. Once again the sessions were structured with the aim of encouraging the children to explore the art materials and express themselves and, in so doing, to improve their self-esteem. Children in the treatment group scored significantly higher in tests measuring self-esteem than children in the control group, and felt better about themselves in relation to school and to their peers. The improvements seemed to their teachers to remain stable at 3-month follow-up.

Allied to these studies is the more recent research of Carr and Vandiver (2003), Rousseau et al. (2003) and Ivanova (2004). These use different kinds of structured, sometimes educational and therapeutically oriented, art-based interventions to address trauma, grief and cultural dislocation in different settings: in a crisis centre, a school and residential setting respectively. Mixtures of observation, action research, image making and storytelling were used to demonstrate improvements in self-esteem, concentration, participation and behaviour. The structuring of these sessions or workshops moves between art therapy and art education, an issue addressed directly by Carr and Vandiver. They explored the usefulness of art instruction and found that children were either overwhelmed or impeded by too much instruction, but became chaotic without any. The most useful projects were structured but sufficiently flexible to allow for the children's individual spontaneity and creative expression.

Rosal's (1993) small-scale RCT is also interesting because it too investigated art therapy in an educational setting, this time in a primary school. Pre and postgroup tests, a drawing interview and teachers' evaluations of the children's behaviour compared the outcomes of three groups: art therapy, a combination of group art therapy and cognitive behavioural therapy, and a control group. The antisocial behaviours and conduct disorders of both treatment groups improved. Rosal et al.'s (1997) later study is of similar interest because it investigated how the integration of art therapy and the teaching of English in the classroom might improve academic performance and reduce school drop-out. English was taught through autobiographical writing, the children's learning being explored in monthly art therapy groups that occurred during class time. Pre/postgroup tests found significant improvements in the children's attitudes towards school with none of the children dropping out or failing. Other, smaller scale experimental studies have also demonstrated improvements in self-esteem and academic performance and decreases in problem behaviours, for example Stanley and Miller (1993) and Pleasant-Metcalf (1997) both conducted single-case experimental studies of brief structured art therapy and were able to demonstrate positive outcomes. All these studies either included evaluations or interviews with teachers and/or drew on routine demographic data available in schools, for instance attendance records and teacher reports.

Other controlled outcome studies explore different kinds of art-based therapeutic interventions with adolescents. Chin et al.'s (1980) single controlled outcome study is of a group that used a combination of art, video and social skills to improve the communication and social skills of adolescents in special education. The group met for five, three-hourly sessions over four weeks; the adolescents completed daily checklists, as did teachers and other members of the staff team, and significant increases were reported in the adolescents' self-esteem and interpersonal skills. Kymiss et al. (1996) developed a structured art-therapy intervention and evaluated its effectiveness with groups of adolescent inpatients who had a range of diagnoses. Twelve-week art-therapy groups ran on four separate occasions, each being compared with parallel discussion groups that acted as controls.

Both the treatment and the control groups showed significant improvement, the art therapy group showing the greatest improvement. Although the differences between the groups were not statistically significant, the art works facilitated the development of group cohesion.

A particularly important study was Tibbets and Stone's (1990) small-scale RCT of short-term individual art therapy with seriously disturbed adolescents in a special educational setting. Twenty adolescents, with diagnoses ranging from school phobia to schizophrenia, were randomly assigned to a treatment group and a control group; the treatment group received six weekly individual art-therapy sessions that were neither structured nor directed, while the control group had weekly social-skills training. Pre and posttreatment tests found statistically significant improvements on a variety of measurements for the treatment group, for example, attention span and sense of identity, and statistically significant reductions in depression, anxiety and feelings of rejection. Short-term individual art therapy therefore provided 'an effective means of therapeutic intervention within the school setting' (1990: 145).

Other outcome studies have also demonstrated positive outcomes. Saunders and Saunders's (2000) research involved collaboration between art therapists, social scientists and evaluators in an investigation of the effectiveness of an art therapy service over a period of three years. Ninety-four clients were tested before they entered individual art therapy and again when it had ended, the outcomes being considered in light of the goals agreed for each individual and the extent to which these were achieved. Interviews with clients, their parents and carers before and after therapy checked behaviour, symptoms and relationships. There were statistically significant reductions in the severity and frequency of symptoms and problem behaviours, and a statistically significant improvement in the positive relationship between client and art therapist that correlated with lengthier periods of therapy.

Another experimental study of very brief work demonstrated the effectiveness of art-based interventions in the reduction of PTSD symptoms following different kinds of traumatic event. Chapman et al. (2001) conducted a randomised cohort study of a single art-therapy session with 85 children and adolescents exhibiting PTSD symptoms following physical trauma such as accidents, woundings and abuse. The session encouraged the development of coherent visual and verbal narratives of the event. Chapman et al. found no significant overall differences between the children who had received art therapy and those who had not, but there were reductions in avoidance symptoms at 1-week and again at 1-month follow-ups. They concluded that art therapy may alleviate symptoms of acute stress and allow traumatic experiences to be processed.

The literature also addresses art therapy with children in palliative care. Dolgin et al.'s (1997) single-group experimental study of two groups of children and adolescents who had siblings with cancer used a mixture of art therapy, group discussion and psychosocial education to address cancer-related knowledge, mood, communication and intra and interpersonal skills. Art therapy was said to facilitate interaction, mutual support and communication between the group members, for example, self- and parent-reported mood states showed significant positive improvement that remained evident at 6–8 week follow-up. Similar brief, structured art therapy interventions are also described in the treatment of grief. For example, Orton (1994) used a single-case experimental design to measure changes in grief reaction and coping skills following 10 weeks of individual art therapy with an adolescent mother and reported a decline in anger, guilt and sadness and an increase in positive outlook, and in the UK, Pratt (1998) describes using photographs and mask making with adolescents who have lost a parent.

Ball's (2002) qualitative outcome study is especially interesting, both in terms of its methodology and its findings. Ball situated her research within a move away from large-scale outcome studies towards research that involves the intensive analysis of significant episodes or single sessions of therapy. Her investigation was of moments of change in the art therapy process. She observed an art therapist working individually with five seriously emotionally disturbed children over a one-year period, accompanied by a number of interviews with the therapist. Ball reports her intensive and systematic analysis of the verbal and non-verbal behaviours of the art therapist and her clients and of the artworks the children made, and describes her immersion in the objects, images, interviews and conversations. Ball differentiates between the foci and modes of interaction between therapist and client and explores how these changed over time. She describes how the art therapist channelled the children's chaotic behaviour into art making so that they learned how thoughts and feelings could be visually organised, processed and related to inner experience; this gradually enabled meaning to be explored, particularly in key moments when the children were able to observe and reflect on their artwork, interactions and behaviour. Ball also identified shifts in early dissonances between child and art therapist as boundaries were established and later resonances when therapist and child 'match' each other. She concluded that the interactions between the art therapist, the children and their art making revealed increases in the children's ability to symbolise their experiences through images and words, to regulate their emotions and behaviour, and to reflect about themselves.

The emerging picture of art therapy's effectiveness with children and adolescents from this literature is encouraging. Small-scale RCTs, controlled group studies and single-case experimental designs have demonstrated art therapy's positive outcomes, mostly in educational and mental health settings. Two issues emerge: first, the collaboration with parents and teachers and the usefulness of demographic data about school attendance, classroom behaviour and academic attainment to address outcomes; second, the use of structured art-therapy approaches that can operate at the interface with art education. Practice and systems may differ on either side of the Atlantic but there is potential, as far as British art therapists are concerned, for the replication of our American colleagues' researches as well as for productive learning about methodology.

Attention Deficit Hyperactivity Disorder (ADHD)

American and British papers on art therapy with ADHD children all describe different ways of structuring group and individual art therapy that help children regulate their behaviour: through the initial drawing of a mandala at the beginning of individual sessions (Smitheman-Brown and Church, 1996); a structured, socially oriented art-therapy group and a 'therapeutic curriculum' in a summer camp (Henley, 1998, 1999); and by moving between different physical spaces and using games and art activities for various stages of an art therapy group's process (Murphy et al., 2004). This last paper is of particular interest because it includes evaluation of the children's behaviour by parents and referrers before and after the group: positive changes were found in children's self-esteem and self-control and their ability to function in a social environment. Henley's (1999) paper is also of interest in terms of the treatment approach – a mixture of art and other activities in small and community-based groups that were themed to allow underlying material relating to the children's problems to emerge and be thought about – and methodology: every facet of each child's experience was recorded through process notes that provided a daily clinical picture that was subsequently analysed. Henley discovered that focusing on the groups and the camp as a community required and enabled the children to negotiate conflict in a cooperative way.

Autistic spectrum disorders

There are a number of robust texts in the American and British literatures that indicate art therapy's effectiveness with children and adolescents on the autistic spectrum and several research projects that propose different theoretical frameworks and treatment approaches. Kornreich and Schimmel (1991), for example, describe three years of individual art therapy with an autistic boy that resulted in a marked decrease in stereotypical behaviours and improvements in social and family relationships and academic performance. Henley (2001) refers to casework in an earlier paper (1994) and describes a child's art then, and following four years of individual art therapy. He suggests that the child's art documented his developmental and emotional progress and represented a successful sublimation through art; this occurred alongside improvements in the child's relationships with adults and a diminution in his social anxiety. Authors agree that art therapy can move clients with autistic spectrum disorders beyond stereotypical behaviours and encourage sensory, perceptual and cognitive development.

Evans (1998) researched a model of art therapy practice that develops the use of particular art therapy interventions which, she proposes, is effective in progressing the autistic child's development. She shows how the sensations and feelings evoked through encountering new materials and making art can be shaped in a way that facilitates the autistic child's communication skills and relationship with the art therapist. An allied chapter (Evans and Rutten-Sarins, 1998) and subsequent book (Evans and Dubowski, 2001) describe the research in more detail. Evans and Rutten-Sarins show how the successful attunement of body language coupled with a use of art materials in a series of purposeful interactions and interventions by the therapist can echo behaviours and care in early infancy, enabling a developmental progression in art therapy which in turn makes possible the autistic child's emotional and cognitive development. Evans and Dubowski describe the importance of minute-by-minute analysis of the assessment, made available through video-recording; this enables fleeting communicative cues to be identified that would otherwise remain beyond the therapist's awareness, from which a template of individual therapeutic strategies can be developed. This approach, based on early infant/caregiver interactions, builds the capacity to symbolise, is an effective means of establishing a therapeutic relationship and offers a 'communicative scaffolding' (2001: 101) for further development.

Tipple's (2003) research challenges the norms on which Evans's model is based. His research investigates the assessment of children on the autistic spectrum, moving away from cognitive, developmental and psychoanalytic constructs towards an intersubjective, socially based understanding of their art. Tipple discusses how subjects are identified and constructed by the discourses that describe them. He draws on art history to demonstrate how art is influenced by the circumstances of its production and the barter that occurs between an artist and their audience. Tipple takes this analogy into the assessment of autistic children, describing how the verbal and other exchanges between child and therapist construct the imaginary and intersubjective space between them and have a direct influence on what happens and what is made. He concludes that the art therapy literature (with autistic children and, inferentially, with other client populations too) contains normalising judgements which conform to diagnostic formulations about early infant/caregiver relationships that are reworked in art therapy, suggesting that such judgements organise and legitimise knowledge in a way that precludes the influence of social context.

McGregor (1990) researched the exceptional drawing abilities of some autistic children. He explored the perceptual, cognitive and emotional functioning and development of these children, considering their art in relation to the development of children's drawing and of special talents. He too extends the theoretical base beyond psychoanalysis and developmental psychology to theories of perception, representation and visual analysis, suggesting that autistic children who display extraordinary drawing abilities are able to produce fully formed representations without the preliminary scribbles and experiential understandings that are part of child development. He proposed that these representations are viewer centred, meaning that these unusual children have a sensitivity to and memory for detail and objects that predisposes them to become accomplished draughtsmen because they are always able to see things as a series of lines and forms as if for the first time, that is, in much the same way as an artist might do. This is not because a particular visual strategy for conveying a 3D world in a 2D form has been chosen, rather that the autistic child is perceptually unable to draw anything other than surfaces, and these from a frozen viewpoint. This offers an interesting theoretical counterpoint and potential for other forms of developmental intervention in the treatment of this client population that, surprisingly, seems to have fallen off the art therapy radar.

So where does this leave the evidence base for art therapy with children on the autistic spectrum? Casework description suggests that long-term group and individual art therapy is effective because the particular attributes of art making promote cognitive and emotional development, enable relationship and lead to a lessening of destructive behaviours. This could be established through further narrative case studies, longitudinal and retrospective studies and experimental case studies too. Research has developed different treatment approaches and deconstructed the social contexts of practice and art making that construe clients and their art solely in diagnostic terms. Establishing the extent of art therapy service provision for this client population would be a useful base from which to explore different approaches appropriate to different settings, and to examine their relative effectiveness.

Child sexual abuse (CSA)

The literature on art therapy with sexually abused children comprises different kinds of research and a number of rigorous descriptive texts. Murphy's (1998) survey-based research reviewed British art therapy practice with CSA. She discovered that most UK art therapists worked across the age range, from preschool to early adulthood, offering individual and group art therapy for varying lengths of time. A few practitioners were involved in diagnosis and disclosure but most remained unconvinced about 'graphic indicators' of abuse and the usefulness of images as forensic evidence. Most British practitioners worked non-directively but thought that structuring the time in groups was helpful, although the use of particular art materials or themes was not. Murphy's research identified distinctive art-based responses from these clients that indicate the kind of environment necessary for art therapy; for example, children may need to make messes and develop a positive, sensuous awareness of art materials, images are likely to be spoiled, destructive behaviour has to be contained and clear boundaries maintained.

These issues were also explored by Hagood (2000). She drew on experience of working with sexually abused adults, adolescents and children in various settings in Britain and America. Hagood's research offers good evidence for those art therapists resisting pressure to provide artworks within disclosure processes. Her longitudinal study involved the collection of 306 drawings by non-abused children who were between the ages of 5 and 10 years; these were gathered over a period of 18 months and examined to see if particular characteristics associated with CSA were evident. These visual 'characteristics', or sexual abuse indicators (SAIs), included items such as the absence of hands, legs drawn apart or firmly pressed together, detached heads and phallic-looking arms and noses, these representations being contextualised within a review of the developmental stages of children's drawing. The children's drawings were scored according to developmental criteria and the presence of SAIs, the children being controlled for age. Two-thirds of the SAIs were not found in the work of non-CSA children; one-third were found in the representations of younger children but these decreased significantly as the child grew older and were clearly associated with the child's developmental stage. The use of art to detect or provide evidence of CSA or other trauma is therefore called into serious question.

Hagood attempts to integrate the different approaches to abuse, therapy and to art therapy in Britain and the United States. The consequent eclecticism can be confusing, but I was interested to note her discussion of art-based themes and games to contain her clients, particularly with regard to the making of mess which, she suggests, can be counterproductive. It is interesting to note that the most recent text (from the American literature) is an outcome study that uses just such themes to identify, contain and process feelings. Pifalo (2002) describes three, 10-week art therapy groups with differently aged children and adolescents. Tests before and after each group showed an overall reduction in clinical symptoms of trauma and statistically significant reductions in levels of anxiety, overt dissociation and posttraumatic stress. This single-group experimental study had encouraging outcomes that clearly indicated the effectiveness of a short-term, structured art therapy group with children and adolescents who had been sexually abused.

Brown and Latimer (2001) and Buckland and Murphy (2001) indicate the effectiveness of art therapy groups with CSA, the former with adolescents and the latter with young children. Buckland and Murphy give a moving account of a six-month group with young abused girls that ran in tandem with a group for their parents. The accounts of the groups, followed by the co-therapists' commentary, illuminate art therapy group processes with this client population. Brown and Latimer suggest that the efficacy of art therapy for survivors of CSA 'is in its capacity to evoke emotional rather than intellectual responses' (2001: 186) which counter the repression of memories, dissociation and splits between feeling and thinking. Interestingly their model of practice, illustrated through a case study, brings together art therapy and cognitive analytic therapy (CAT), echoing Hagood's (2000) call for the cognitive, behavioural and addictive components of CSA to be addressed alongside the dynamic issues. Brown and Latimer argue that while art therapy brings into awareness, contains and processes emotional material, CAT enables a restructuring of distorted perceptions and thinking about guilt and shame. They state that group members' self-harm and other destructive behaviours were reduced during the first six months of the group.

Individual art therapy with CSA has also been well described. A heuristic case study is that by O'Brien (2003). She draws on Thomas's (1998) conceptualisation about how the raw trauma of abuse has to be re-presented in art therapy in a direct, non-symbolic/metaphoric way akin to an evacuation, before it can be represented in symbolic form and become able to be thought about. She develops this in a later paper (O' Brien, 2004) that draws further on the case, identifying three research questions and exploring these through the literature. O'Brien describes how the right side of the brain is damaged by very early, preverbal traumatic experiences, linking this with art making – another right-brain activity. She says that the sensual nature of paint and clay and the making of mess activates certain parts of the brain, providing 'a visceral reminder of experience' (2004: 11) so that 'gradually physical states can become thoughts' (2004: 12). She develops the hypothesis that making art in art therapy stimulates right-brain neurological structures that enable early trauma to become known. O'Brien also indicates effectiveness: although not fully reported, she states that pretreatment tests indicated the child's developmental delay and mild learning difficulties but after four years of individual art therapy there was no indication of learning difficulty. O'Brien suggests that this demonstrates that the child's learning had been blocked by emotional distress and that the distress was alleviated by art therapy.

This literature indicates the clinical effectiveness of art therapy with sexually abused children through convincing accounts of group and individual art therapy, and an American outcome study has demonstrated the effectiveness of a short-term, structured intervention. There are recurrent issues in descriptions of clinical work, notably the importance of clients being able to make a mess (although the value of this is contested) and for it to be literally and metaphorically contained. The conditions necessary for practice can therefore be determined and could be developed into practice guidelines and/or auditable standards that could be considered in the context of cross-sectoral service provision. British and American art therapists work differently, but a dual art therapy/cognitive-behavioural approach in British practice points to transatlantic parallels that are worth investigating, particularly given the success of Pifalo's (2002) research. Certainly the links between art making and neurological activity break new ground, and the notion of 're-presentation' or evacuation through art that enables subsequent thought and a diminution in destructive behaviours is a productive line of inquiry that could be pursued.

Generally speaking British and American art therapists work rather differently, but there is perhaps more agreement in this literature about practice with children and adolescents than may have been anticipated. Authors seem to agree that a degree of structure and sometimes 'direction' are needed to contain and channel behaviour into making art, this being the means through which children and adolescents can learn to manage their experiences and behaviour. Art therapists in the USA often work in intensive, short-term ways that have to be actively managed and which can be embedded in social or educational interventions. In the UK art therapists seem able to work in the longer term and, in groups at least, develop themes and use different kinds of activity to guide children through the beginning, middle and end of a session. Differing systems and cultures of education and mental health inevitably influence practice, and care must be taken in generalising from research and practice in one setting to another, especially when children's problems are described in a non-specific way. Perhaps Ball's (2002) qualitative outcome study articulates an underlying pattern of the art therapy process with children that could be drawn upon. Acting-out behaviours are contained through being channelled into art materials; once a child has learned this, art making can be sustained and dialogue and the discovery of meaning can ensue; then an ability to observe and reflect on the self through art making can be developed. Developing, documenting and evaluating consistent practice with different populations in educational, justice, social and healthcare settings would enable the construction of a strong evidence base for practice in this area.

The key question that EBP asks of art therapy is which client population benefits from which approach in which setting? As has been shown, art therapy has a body of descriptive literature and inductive research that informs the answer to this question and has begun to tease out why and how art therapy is effective with clients of all ages in the various sectors where art therapy services are provided. The ice of outcome research has been broken and the results are encouraging. The incorporation of psychosocial, educational and behavioural approaches with art therapy seem to make effective combinations, as some researchers and practitioners have demonstrated. The challenge for art therapists on both sides of the Atlantic is to stay open to innovation and development in their practice and not adhere rigidly to any art therapy mainstream – be it analytic, diagnostic or studio based – and to research both new and more established practices in a pluralistic way. Art therapy has not, as yet, provided unequivocal evidence of effectiveness in any of its many applications and will continue to be undervalued, and indeed be at risk, until outcomes are much more thoroughly addressed. Effectiveness is paramount in our policy-driven times, but it is critical that this be investigated through both quantitative and qualitative research. Outcome research of any kind only makes sense when positioned alongside qualitative research that goes beyond the boundaries of EBP orthodoxy to demonstrate not only that art therapy works but also how and why its unique processes enable clients to see the world differently and become able to effect changes in their lives.

Endnote

Art therapists can tow the EBP line and use its methods to demonstrate what we know to be true: that art therapy is an effective treatment. We need to do the particular kind of research that EBP requires, and we need to do so soon. We need much more inductive, research – both quantitative and qualitative – to build towards the critical mass of hypothetico-deductive research that will demonstrate the effectiveness of different art therapy approaches in particular settings with specific client populations. We need to engage with the whole paradigm and meet the challenges it represents through strategic research and quality assurance initiatives.

But we also need to take risks with the construction of art therapy's evidence base. When the aim is to effect policy there needs to be hard data and rigorous, robust literature, but we should resist exclusively 'scientific' notions of research, difficult though it is to change canonical beliefs about what research and the 'best' evidence are and what it therefore means for disciplines to become evidence based. We need to do research that goes beyond the orthodox hierarchies of medicine and into the social and the visual. We also need to present art therapy's differing forms of evidence and argue that it be judged according to the values and norms of the discipline. We can make some risky representations too. We can disseminate our evidence and differing researches in different venues to different audiences: through visual display, narrative and performance as well as through text. Visual and oral languages are not incompatible practices; they run in parallel with and complement each other. Why then must we always translate from the visual to the oral, and to text? Display and the performative allow a social inclusion that invites in a wider audience who can become immersed in the material and find meaning as forms of evidence and its dissemination are extended and enlivened.

Using non-EBP-conformist research methodologies may, of course, have consequences. It may mean that content is ignored. Art therapists must make sure that we maintain a politically aware engagement with the paradigm and its practices. EBP is embedded in the systems and organisations where art therapists work but it is sustained through our attitudes towards it. EBP is in our working worlds, in our minds and in our hands. We can challenge the paradigm and add our voice to those who contest its fundamental assumptions. We can trouble both the edges and the heart of EBP's territory. To engage solely with the research and governance procedures of orthodox EBP or to limit art therapy research to social and visual methods, would result in a partial evidence base – either way something would be lost. We can generate the evidence that EBP requires, but we can do so in ways that make it our own.

We need the facts, we need the figures, but we need the stories and the pictures too.

Initial appraisal checklist

Please tick Yes/No/Don't Know for each question

	Yes	No	Don't Know
1.1 Is the text research based?			
1.2 If yes: is there an explicit research methodology?			
1.3 Are the methods of data collection and data analysis fully described?			

	Yes	No	Don't Know
2.1 Is the text academically rigorous?			
2.2 Are the ideas, theories, facts and other information adequately described, referenced and properly presented in a bibliography?			

	Yes	No	Don't Know
3.1 Does the text seem truthful and believable?			
3.2 Is the material sufficiently well described for you to believe it?			
3.3 Is the material sufficiently well described for you, potentially, to replicate the author's processes of thought and action?			

	Yes	No	Don't Know
4.1 Is the text helpful?			
4.2 Does it make sense in terms of your own experience?			
4.3 Does it contribute to your thinking about your own clinical practice?			

5 What are the key findings?

   1

   2

   3

	Yes	No	Don't Know
6 Is the paper/chapter relevant to (the topic)?			

Critical appraisal checklist

Check for validity:

	Yes	No	Don't Know
1.1 Is the text research based?			
1.2 If yes: does it address a clear research question?			
1.3 Was there ample description of the context and the respondents/patients?			
1.4 Is the intervention under investigation clearly defined?			
1.5 Was the method appropriate to the research question?			
1.6 Were the methods of data collection and analysis clearly described?			
1.7 Were the respondents appropriate to the topic being investigated?			
1.8 Was the setting(s) appropriate to the topic being investigated?			
1.9 Are the outcomes/findings of the research clearly described?			
1.10 Did the authors make their role in the research clear?			
1.11 Was the data independently assessed?			
1.12 Are the findings replicable?			
	Yes	No	Don't Know
2.1 If the text is NOT research based, is it 'academically rigorous'?			
2.2 Does the text have clearly stated aims and objectives?			
2.3 Are the ideas, theories, facts and other information adequately described and referenced in a properly presented bibliography?			
	Yes	No	Don't Know
3.1 Is the text contextualised within the existing literature?			
3.2 Is the literature review appropriate to the topic?			
3.3 Is the literature review comprehensive and up to date?			
3.4 Does it draw on a range of sources, i.e. does it present more than one point of view?			

	Yes	No	Don't Know
4.1 If a case study, was the process and content of the work adequately described?			
4.2 Was there adequate description of the institutional context?			
4.3 Was there sufficient description of the patient's background?			
4.4 Was there sufficient description of the referral process to art therapy?			
4.5 Was practice appropriately integrated with theoretical discussion of the case?			

	Yes	No	Don't Know
5.1 Were ethical issues considered?			
5.2 Was ethical consent sought from appropriate bodies and/or individuals?			
5.3 Have confidentiality and anonymity been respected?			

	Yes	No	Don't Know
6.1 Were illustrations of artwork included?			
6.2 Were the illustrations adequately discussed?			
6.3 Did the illustrations make sense in relation to the text?			

Check for applicability:

7.1 What are the key findings of the text?
  1
  2
  3

	Yes	No	Don't Know
7.2 Do the results/findings address the research questions/aims and objectives of the text?			
7.3 Are the results/findings discussed in the context of the literature review?			

	Yes	No	Don't Know
8.1 Is there enough detail to assess the credibility of the results/findings?			
8.2 Is there enough detail for you to believe that what the author says is true?			

	Yes	No	Don't Know
8.3 Is there enough detail for you to assess the author's interpretation of the results/findings?			
8.4 Were all the clinically important outcomes considered?			
8.5 Were there any other outcomes or findings that you would expect the author to have addressed?			
8.6 If yes, does this affect your view of the applicability research/paper?			
9.1 Are the findings/results likely to be clinically important?			
9.2 Can the findings be applied to your clinical work?			
9.3 Do they help you gain insights into your work?			
9.4 Are your patients comparable to those in the study/paper?			
9.5 Is your setting comparable to that in the study/paper?			
9.6 Do you have the skills to deliver the intervention investigated/described?			

References

Ackerman, J. (1992) 'Art therapy intervention designed to increase the self-esteem of an incarcerated paedophile', *American Journal of Art Therapy*, 30: 143–9.

Albert-Puleo, N. (1980) 'Modern psychoanalytic art therapy and its application to drug abuse', *The Arts in Psychotherapy*, 13: 53–9.

Allard, S. (2002) 'A user/survivor perspective: what's behind the evidence?', in S. Priebe and M. Slade (eds), *Evidence in Mental Health Care*. Hove: Brunner-Routledge.

Andrews, R. (2004) 'Between Scylla and Charybdis: the experience of undertaking a systematic review in education', in G. Thomas and R. Pring (eds), *Evidence-based Practice in Education*. Maidenhead: Open University Press.

Anisfield, N. (1995) 'Godzilla, Gojiro – evolution of the nuclear metaphor', *Journal of Popular Culture*, 29 (3): 53–62.

Ansdell, G., Pavlicevic, M. and Proctor, S. (2004) *Presenting the Evidence: A Guide for Music Therapists Responding to the Demands of Clinical Effectiveness and Evidence-based Practice.* London: Nordoff Robbins Music Therapy Centre.

Aveline, M. and Watson, J. (2001) 'Making, a success of your psychotherapy service: the contribution of clinical audit', in C. Mace, S. Moorey and B. Roberts (eds), *Evidence in the Psychological Therapies*. Hove: Brunner-Routledge.

Bagley, C. (2005) 'Twisting the tale: exploring the use of arts-based approaches in the (re)presentation of educational research'. Keynote presentation at the Arts-based Methods in Educational Research Conference, Queens University, Belfast.

Bagley, C. and Cancienne, B. (2002) *Dancing the Data*. New York: Peter Lang.

Baker, M. and Kleijnen, J. (2000) 'The drive towards evidence-based health care', in N. Rowland, and S. Goss (eds), *Evidence-based Counselling and Psychological Therapies*. London: Routledge.

Ball, B. (2002) 'Moments of change in the art therapy process', *Arts in Psychotherapy*, 29: 79–92.

Ball, C., Sackett, D., Phillips, B., Haynes, B. and Strauss, S. (1998) *Levels of Evidence*. Available at: www.cebm.jr2.ox.ac/docs/levels/html

Banks, M. (1998) 'Visual anthropology: image, object and interpretation', in J. Prosser (ed.), *Image-based Research: A Sourcebook for Qualitative Researchers*. London: Falmer Press.

Banks, M. (2001) *Visual Methods in Social Research*. London: Sage.

Barbee, M. (2002) 'A visual-narrative approach to understanding transsexual identity', *Art Therapy: Journal of the American Art Therapy Association*, 19 (2): 53–62.

Barkham, M. and Mellor-Clark, J. (2000) 'Rigour and relevance: the role of practice-based evidence in the psychological therapies', in N. Rowland and S. Goss (eds), *Evidence-based Counselling and Psychological Therapies*. London: Routledge.

Baruch, G., Fearon, P. and Gerber, A. (1998) 'Evaluating the outcome of a community-based psychoanalytic psychotherapy service for young people: one-year repeated follow-up', in R. Davenhill and M. Patrick (eds), *Re-thinking Clinical Audit: The Case of Psychotherapy Services in the NHS*. London: Routledge.

Bell, S. (1998) 'Will the kitchen table do? Art therapy in the community', in M. Pratt, and M. Wood (eds), *Art Therapy in Palliative Care: The Creative Response*. London: Routledge.

Bocking, M. (2005) 'A "don't know" story: art therapy in an NHS medical oncology department', in D. Waller and C. Sibbett (eds), *Art Therapy and Cancer Care*. Maidenhead: Open University Press.

Bolton, D. (2002) 'Knowledge in the human sciences', in S. Priebe and M. Slade (eds), *Evidence in Mental Health Care*. Hove: Brunner-Routledge.

Boronska, T. (1995) 'The werewolf and the wrestling ring: exploring unconscious process through the use of metaphor', *Inscape*, 1: 19–25.

Bowen, C. and Rosal, M. (1989) 'The use of art therapy to reduce the maladaptive behaviours of a mentally retarded adult', *Arts in Psychotherapy*, 16: 211–18.

Bower, P. and King, M. (2000) 'Randomised controlled trials and the evaluation of psychological therapy', in N. Rowland and S. Goss (eds), *Evidence-based Counselling and Psychological Therapies*. London: Routledge.

British Association of Art Therapists (BAAT) (2005) *Newsletter*. Summer: 20.

British Psychological Society (BPS) (1990) *Ethical Principles for Conducting Research*. Leicester: BPS.

Brooke, S. (1995) 'Art therapy: an approach to working with sexual abuse survivors', *Arts in Psychotherapy*, 22 (5): 447–66.

Brooker, J., Cullum, M., Gilroy, A., McCombe, B., Ringrose, K., Russell, D., Smart, L. and Waldman, J. (forthcoming) *The Use of Art Work in Art Psychotherapy with People Who Are Prone to Psychotic States*. London: Goldsmiths College and Oxleas NHS Trust.

Brophy, P. (2000) 'Monster island: Godzilla and Japanese science fiction/horror fantasy', *Post-Colonial Studies*, 3 (2): 39–42.

Brown, A. and Latimer, M. (2001) 'Between images and thoughts: an art psychotherapy group for sexually abused children', in J. Murphy (ed.), *Art Therapy with Young Survivors of Sexual Abuse: Lost for Words*. London: Routledge.

Brown, B., Crawford, P. and Hicks, C. (2003) *Evidence-based Research: Dilemmas and Debates in Health Care*. Maidenhead: Open University Press.

Buckland, R. and Murphy, J. (2001) 'Jumping over it: group therapy with young girls', in J. Murphy (ed.), *Art Therapy with Young Survivors of Sexual Abuse: Lost for Words*. London: Routledge.

Bury, T. (1998) 'Evidence-based healthcare explained', in T. Bury and J. Mead (eds), *Evidence-based Healthcare: A Practical Guide for Therapists*. Oxford: Butterworth Heinemann.

Bury, T. and Jerosch-Herold, C. (1998) 'Reading and critical appraisal of the literature', in T. Bury and J. Mead (eds), *Evidence-based Healthcare: A Practical Guide for Therapists*. Oxford: Butterworth Heinemann.

Buttery, Y. (1998) 'Implementing evidence through clinical audit', in T. Bury and J. Mead (eds), *Evidence-based Healthcare: A Practical Guide for Therapists*. Oxford: Butterworth Heinemann.

Byers, A. (1995) 'Beyond marks: on working with elderly people with severe memory loss', *Inscape*, 1: 13–18.

Byers, A. (1998) 'Candles slowly burning', in S. Skaife and V. Huet (eds), *Art Psychotherapy Groups: Between Pictures and Words*. London: Routledge.

Byrne, P. (1995) 'From the depths to the surface: art therapy as a discursive practice in the postmodern era', *Arts in Psychotherapy*, 22: 235–9.

Cabinet Office (2003) 'What do we already know? – guidance notes on systematic reviews', in *The Magenta Book: A Guide to Policy Evaluation*. London: Cabinet Office. Available at: www.policyhub.gov.uk

Cape, J. (1998) 'Clinical practice guidelines for the psychotherapies', in R. Davenhill and M. Patrick (eds), *Re-thinking Clinical Audit: The Case of Psychotherapy Services in the NHS*. London: Routledge.

Cape, J. (2000) 'Clinical effectiveness in the UK: definitions, history and policy trends', *Journal of Mental Health*, 9 (3): 237–46.

Cape, J. and Parry, G. (2000) 'Clinical practice guidelines development in evidence-based psychotherapy', in N. Rowland and S. Goss (eds), *Evidence-based Counselling and Psychological Therapies*. London: Routledge.

Carolan, R. (2001) 'Models and paradigms of art therapy research', *Art Therapy: Journal of the American Art Therapy Association*, 18 (4): 190–207.

Carr, A. (ed.) (2000) *What Works for Children and Adolescents: A Critical Review of Psychological Interventions with Children, Adolescents and their Families*. London: Routledge.

Carr, M. and Vandiver, T. (2003) 'Effects of instructional art projects on children's behavioural responses and creativity within an emergency shelter', *Art Therapy: Journal of the American Association of Art Therapists*, 20 (3): 157–62.

Carrier, R. (1991) *Principles of Art History Writing*. Philadelphia, PA: Pennsylvania State University Press.

Carroll, N. (1981) 'Nightmare and the horror film: the symbolic biology of fantastic beings', *Film Quarterly*, 34: 374–412.

Case, C. (1994) 'Art therapy in analysis: advance/retreat in the belly of the spider', *Inscape*, 1: 3–10.

Case, C. (1995) 'Silence in progress: on being dumb, empty or silent in therapy', *Inscape*, 1 (1): 26–31.

Case, C. (2000) 'Our lady of the queen: journeys around the maternal object', in A. Gilroy and G. McNeilly (eds), *The Changing Shape of Art Therapy: New Developments in Theory and Practice*. London: Jessica Kingsley.

Case, C. (2003) 'Authenticity and survival: working with children in chaos', *Inscape*, 8 (1): 17–20.

Case, C. (2005) 'Observations of children cutting up, cutting out and sticking down', *Inscape*, 10 (2): 53–62.

Chapman, L., Morabito, D., Ladakakos, C., Schreier, H. and Knudson, M. (2001) 'The effectiveness of art therapy interventions in reducing post traumatic stress disorder (PTSD) symptoms in paediatric trauma patients', *Art Therapy: Journal of the American Association of Art Therapists*, 18 (2): 100–4.

Chin, R., Chin, M., Palombo, P., Palombo, C., Bannaasch, G. and Cross, P. (1980) 'Project outreach: building social skills through art and video', *Arts in Psychotherapy*, 7: 281–4.

Cochrane, A. (1972) *Effectiveness and Efficiency: Random Reflections on Health Services*. London: Nuffield Provincial Hospitals Trust.

Coghlan, D. and Brannick, T. (2001) *Doing action research in your own organization*. London: Sage.

Cohen, L. and Manion, L. (1980) *Research Methods in Education*. London: Routledge.

Cole, P. (1997) 'The former lunatic asylums of the "Epsom cluster": the changes, the closures and the concurrent evolution of art therapy services', unpublished MA Final Report, Goldsmiths College.

Connell, C. (1998) 'The search for a model which opens up: open group at the Royal Marsden Hospital', in M. Pratt and M. Wood (eds), *Art Therapy in Palliative Care: The Creative Response*. London: Routledge.

CORE System Group (1998) *CORE System (Information Management) Handbook*. Leeds: Core System Group.

Coole, J. (1998) 'Getting started: introducing the art therapy service and the individual's first experiences', in M. Pratt and M. Wood (eds), *Art Therapy in Palliative Care: The Creative Response*. London: Routledge.

Crombie, I., Davis, H., Abraham, S. and Florey, C. (1993) *The Audit Handbook: Improving Healthcare through Clinical Audit*. Chichester: Wiley.

Cushman, P. (1995) *Constructing the Self, Constructing America: A Cultural History of Psychotherapy.* New York: Addison-Wesley.

Dalley, T. (1979) 'Art therapy in psychiatric treatment: an illustrated case study', *The Arts in Psychotherapy*, 6: 257–65.

Dalley, T. (1980) 'Assessing the therapeutic effects of art: an illustrated case study', *The Arts in Psychotherapy*, 7: 11–17.

Dalley, T. (1993) 'Art psychotherapy groups', in K. Dwivedi (ed.), *Group Work with Children and Adolescents: A Handbook.* London: Jessica Kingsley.

Damarell, B. (forthcoming) 'Shaping thoughts: An investigation into the cognitive significance of image making for people with learning disabilities', in A. Gilroy (ed.), *Messages from Art Therapy Research: from Research into Evidence.*

Danley, K. and Ellison, M. (1999) *Handbook for Participatory Researchers.* Boston: Centre for Psychiatric Rehabilitation.

Davies, P. (2004) 'Systematic reviews and the Campbell Collaboration', in G. Thomas and R. Pring (eds), *Evidence-based Practice in Education.* Maidenhead: Open University Press.

Davenhill, R. and Patrick, M. (eds) (1998) *Re-thinking Clinical Audit: The Case of Psychotherapy Services in the NHS.* London: Routledge.

Denscombe, M. (1998) *The Good Research Guide for Small-scale Social Research Projects.* Buckingham: Open University Press.

Department of Health (DoH) (1989) *Working for Patients: Working Paper 6.* London: DoH.

Department of Health (DoH) (1991) *NHS R&D Strategy.* London: DoH.

Department of Health (DoH) (1997a) *The New NHS: Modern Dependable.* London: DoH.

Department of Health (DoH) (1997b) *New National Research Programme.* London: DoH.

Department of Health (DoH) (1998) *A First Class Service: Quality in the NHS.* London: DoH.

Department of Health (DoH) (1999) *National Service Framework for Mental Health: Modern Standards and Service Models.* London: DoH.

Department of Health (DoH) (2000) *Meeting the Challenge: A Strategy for the Allied Health Professions.* London: DoH.

Department of Health (DoH) (2001a) *NHS Priorities and Needs. R&D Funding: A Position Paper.* London: DoH.

Department of Health (DoH) (2001b) *Research Governance Framework for Health and Social Care.* London: DoH.

Department of Health (DoH) (2003) *Progress with the Implementation of the Research Governance Framework in the Field of Social Care.* London: DoH.

Department of Health (DoH) (2004) *Organising and Delivering Psychological Services.* London: DoH.

Derrida, J. (1982) *Margins of Philosophy.* New York: Harvester Wheatsheaf.

Dickman, S., Dunn, J. and Wolf, A. (1996) 'The use of art therapy as a predictor of relapse in chemical dependency treatment', *Art Therapy: Journal of the American Association of Art Therapists*, 13 (4): 232–7.

Dixon-Woods, M. and Fitzpatrick, R. (2001) 'Qualitative research in systematic reviews', *British Medical Journal*, 323 (7316): 765–6.

Dixon-Woods, M., Fitzpatrick, R. and Roberts, K. (2001) 'Including qualitative research in systematic reviews: problems and opportunities', *Journal of Evaluation of Clinical Practice*, 7: 125–33.

Dolan, B. and Norton, K. (1998) 'Audit and survival: specialist inpatient psychotherapy in the National Health Service', in R. Davenhill and M. Patrick (eds), *Re-thinking Clinical Audit: The Case of Psychotherapy Services in the NHS.* London: Routledge.

Dolgin, S., Saner, E., Zaidel, E. and Zaiger, R. (1997) ' A structured group intervention for siblings of children with cancer', *Journal of Child and Adolescent Group Therapy*, 7: 3–18.

Donabedian, A. (1980) *The Definition of Quality and Approaches to its Assessment*. Ann Arbor, MI: Health Administration Press.

Doric-Henry, L. (1997) 'Pottery as art therapy with elderly nursing home residents', *Art Therapy: Journal of the American Association of Art Therapists*, 14 (3): 163–71.

Douglass, B. and Moustakas, C. (1985) 'Heuristic inquiry: the internal search to know', *Journal of Humanistic Psychology*, 25: 39–55

Doyal, L. (2004) *The Ethical Governance and Regulation of Student Projects: A Draft Proposal*. London: Central Office for Research Ethics Committees. Available at: www.corec.org.uk

Dubowski, J. (1984) 'Alternative models for describing the development of children's graphic work: some implications for art therapy', in T. Dalley (ed.), *Art as Therapy: An Introduction to the Use of Art as a Therapeutic Technique*. London: Tavistock Publications.

Dubowski, J. (1990) 'Art versus language (separate development during childhood)', in C. Case and T. Dalley (eds), *Working with Children in Art Therapy*. London: Routledge.

Dubowski, J. (2001) 'Developing a research strategy for the arts therapies', in L. Kossolapov, S. Scoble and D. Waller (eds), *Arts–Therapies–Communication: On the Way to a Communicative European Arts Therapy*. Munster: Lit Verlag.

Dudley, J. (2004) 'Art psychotherapy and the use of psychiatric diagnosis: assessment for art psychotherapy', *Inscape*, 9 (1): 14–25.

Dudley, J., Gilroy, A. and Skaife, S. (1998) 'Learning from experience in introductory art therapy groups', in S. Skaife and V. Huet (eds), *Art Psychotherapy Groups: Between Pictures and Words*. London: Routledge.

Dudley, J., Gilroy, A. and Skaife, S. (2000) 'Teachers, students, clients, therapists, researchers: changing gear in experiential art therapy groups', in A. Gilroy, and G. McNeilly (eds), *The Changing Shape of Art Therapy: New Developments in Theory and Practice*. London: Jessica Kingsley.

Duff, L., Kelson, A., Marriott, S., McInotosh, A., Brown, S., Cape, J., Marcus, N. and Traynor, M. (1996) 'Clinical guidelines: involving patients and users of services', *Journal of Clinical Effectiveness*, 1 (3): 104–12.

Eby, M. (2000) 'Producing evidence ethically', in R. Gomm and C. Davies (eds), *Using Evidence in Health and Social Care*. London: Open University Press and Sage.

Eccles, M., Freemantle, N. and Mason, J. (1998) 'North of England evidence based guidelines development project: methods of developing guidelines for efficient drug use in primary care', *British Medical Journal*, 316: 1232–5.

Edwards, D. (1999) 'The role of the case study in art therapy research', *Inscape*, 4 (1): 2–9.

Eldredge, N. and Carrigan, J (1992) 'Where do my kindred dwell? Using art and story-telling to understand the transition of young Indian men who are deaf', *Arts in Psychotherapy*, 19 (1): 29–38.

Elkins, J. (2000) *Our Beautiful, Dry and Distant Texts: Art History as Writing*. London: Routledge.

Evans, K. (1998) 'Shaping experience and sharing meaning: art therapy for children with autism', *Inscape*, 3 (1): 17–25.

Evans, K. and Dubowski, J. (2001) *Art Therapy with Children on the Autistic Spectrum: Beyond Words*. London: Jessica Kingsley.

Evans, K. and Rutten-Saris, M. (1998) 'Shaping vitality affects: enriching communication', in D. Sandle (ed.), *Development and Diversity: New Applications in Art Therapy*. London: Free Association.

Evidence-based Medicine (EBM) (1995) 'Editorial', *Evidence-based Medicine*, 1 (1): 5.

Evidence-based Medicine Working Group (1992) 'Evidence-based medicine, a new approach to teaching the practice of medicine', *Journal of the American Medical Association*, 268 (17): 2420–5.

Exworthy, M. and Halford, S. (eds) (1999)*Professionals and the New Managerialism in the Public Sector*. Buckingham: Open University Press.

Falk, B. (2002) 'A narrowed sense of space: an art therapy group with young Alzheimer's sufferers', in D. Waller (ed.), *Nameless Dread: Arts Therapies and Progressive Illness*. Hove: Brunner-Routledge.

Faulkner, A. (2000) *Strategies for Living: A Report of User Led Research into People's Strategies for Living with Mental Distress*. London: Mental Health Foundation.

Faulkner, A. (2004) *The Ethics of Survivor Research: Guidelines for the Ethical Conduct of Research Carried out by Mental Health Service Users and Survivors*. Bristol: Policy Press.

Feder, B. and Feder, E. (1998) *The Art and Science of Evaluation in the Arts Therapies*. Springfield, IL: Chas C. Thomas.

Feldman, M. and Pugh, K. (1998) 'Kaizen and the process of audit in an NHS psychotherapy unit', in R. Davenhill and M. Patrick (eds), *Rethinking Clinical Audit: The Case of Psychotherapy Services in the NHS*. London: Routledge.

Finzen, A. (2002) 'Influence of evidence on mental health care over the last 200 years', in S. Priebe and M. Slade (eds), *Evidence in Mental Health Care*. Hove: Brunner-Routledge.

Fonagy, P. (2002) 'The outcome of psychoanalysis: the hope for the future', in S. Priebe and M. Slade (eds), *Evidence in Mental Health Care*. Hove: Brunner-Routledge.

Fonagy, P. and Higgitt, A. (1989) 'Evaluating the performance of departments of psychotherapy', *Psychoanalytic Psychotherapy*, 4: 121–53.

Fonagy, P., Target, M., Cottrell, Phillips and Kurtz (2002) *What Works for Whom? A Critical Review of Treatment for Children and Adolescents*. New York: Guildford Press.

Foucault, M. (1977) *Discipline and Punish*. Harmondsworth: Penguin.

Fox, L. (1998) 'Lost in space: the relevance of art therapy with clients who have autism or autistic features', in M. Rees (ed.), *Drawing on Difference: Art Therapy with People Who Have Learning Difficulties*. London: Routledge.

Francis, D., Kaiser, D. and Deaver, S. (2003) 'Representations of attachment security in the bird's nest drawings of a clients with substance abuse disorders', *Art Therapy: Journal of the American Association of Art Therapists*, 20 (3): 125–37.

Freshwater, D. and Rolfe, G. (2004) *De-constructing Evidence-based Practice*. Milton Park: Routledge.

Fulton, J. (2002) 'Art therapy and chronic illness: an enquiry into aspects of service provision for patients with atopic skin disease', *Inscape*, 7 (1): 2–15.

Gantt, L. (1997) 'Prescriptions for the future: research', *American Journal of Art Therapy*, 36: 31–5.

Gantt, L. (1998) 'Talk, talk, talk, when do we draw? Research', *American Journal of Art Therapy*, 37: 57–65.

Gantt, L. (2001) 'The Formal Elements Art Therapy Scale: a measurement system for global variants in art', *Art Therapy: Journal of the American Art Therapy Association*, 18 (1): 50–5.

Gantt, L. (2004) 'The case for formal art therapy assessments', *Art Therapy: Journal of the American Art Therapy Association*, 21 (1): 18–29.

Gantt, L. and Tabone, C. (1998) 'Formal elements of art scale (FEATs)'. Morgantown, WV: Gargoyle Press.

Gilbody, S. and Sowden, A. (2000) 'Systematic reviews in mental health', in N. Rowland and S. Goss (eds), *Evidence-based Counselling and Psychological Therapies*. London: Routledge.

Gilroy, A. (1989) 'On occasionally being able to paint', *Inscape*, Spring: 2–9.

Gilroy, A. (1992a) 'Research in art therapy', in D. Waller and A. Gilroy (eds), *Art Therapy: A Handbook*. Buckingham: Open University Press.

Gilroy, A. (1992b) 'From the origins of an interest in art to occasionally being able to paint. The occupational choice and career development of art therapists', unpublished DPhil thesis, University of Sussex.

Gilroy, A. (1995) 'Changes in art therapy groups', in A. Gilroy and C. Lee (eds), *Art and Music: Therapy and Research*. London: Routledge.

Gilroy, A. (1996) 'Our own kinds of evidence', *Inscape*, Winter: 52–60.

Gilroy, A. (2000) 'In search of an Australian art therapy', *International Networking Group of Art Therapists*, 13 (1): 3–11.

Gilroy, A. and Hanna, M. (1998) 'Conflict and culture: an Australian perspective', in A. Hiscox and A. Calisch (eds), *Tapestry of Cultural Issues in Art Therapy*. London: Jessica Kingsley.

Glaser, B. and Strauss, A. (1967) *The Discovery of Grounded Theory: Strategies for Qualitative Research*. Chicago: Aldine.

Glut, D. (1978) *Classic Movie Monsters*. Metuchen, NJ: Scarecrow Press.

Goffmann, E. (1961) *Asylums*. Harmondsworth: Penguin.

Goldner, E. and Bilsker, D. (1995) 'Evidence-based practice in psychiatry', *Canadian Journal of Psychiatry*, 40 (2): 97–101.

Goodman, R. (1997) 'Managed care', *American Journal of Art Therapy*, 36: 35–41.

Goss, S. and Rose, S. (2002) 'Evidence-based practice: a guide for counsellors and psychotherapists', *Counselling and Psychotherapy Research*, 2 (2): 147–51.

Greece, M. (2003) 'Art therapy on a bone marrow transplant unit: the case study of a Vietnam veteran fighting myelofibrosis', *Arts in Psychotherapy*, 30: 229–38.

Greenwood, H. (2000) 'Captivity and terror in the therapeutic relationship', *Inscape*, 5 (2): 53–61.

Greenwood, H. and Layton, G. (1991) 'Taking the piss', *Inscape*, Winter: 7–14.

Greenwood, H. and Layton, G. (1987) 'An out-patient art therapy group', *Inscape*, Summer: 12–19.

Gregoire, P. (1998) 'Imitation response and mimesis in dementia', *Art Therapy: Journal of the American Association of Art Therapists*, 15 (4): 261–4.

Gussack, D. (2004) 'Art therapy with prison inmates: a pilot study', *Arts in Psychotherapy*, 31: 245–59.

Hagood, M. (1994) 'Group art therapy with adolescent sex offenders', in M. Liebmann (ed.), *Art Therapy with Offenders*. London: Jessica Kingsley.

Hagood, M. (2000) *The Use of Art in Counselling Child and Adolescent Survivors of Sexual Abuse*. London: Jessica Kingsley.

Hammell, K. (2001) 'Using qualitative research to inform the client-centred evidence-based practice of occupational therapy', *British Journal of Occupational Therapy*, 64 (5): 228-34.

Hammersley, M. (1992) *What's Wrong with Ethnography? Methodological Explorations*. London: Routledge.

Hammersley, M. (2004) 'Some questions about evidence-based practice in education', in G. Thomas and R. Pring (eds), *Evidence-based Practice in Education*. Maidenhead: Open University Press.

Hardy, D. (2001) 'Creating through loss: an examination of how art therapists sustain their practice in palliative care', *Inscape*, 6 (1): 23–31.

Hart, E. and Bond, M. (1995) *Action Research for Health and Social Care: A Guide to Practice*. Buckingham: Open University Press.

Hartley, C. (2005) 'The development of a profile of children's health services in England', *BAAT Newsletter*, May: 8–9.

Hastings, A. (1996) 'Bambi and the hunting ethos', *Journal of Popular Film & Television*, 26 (2): 53–9.

Hawtin, A. (2003) 'Presentation', *Art Therapy Practice Research Network Newsletter*, April: 10–12.

Healey, K. (1998) 'Clinical audit and conflict', in R. Davenhill and M. Patrick (eds), *Rethinking Clinical Audit: The Case of Psychotherapy Services in the NHS*. London: Routledge.

Health Professions Council (HPC) (2003a) *Standards of Proficiency*. Available at: www. hpc.org

Health Professions Council (HPC) (2003b) *Standards of Conduct, Performance and Ethics.* Available at: www.hpc.org

Healthcare Quality Quest (1997) *Getting Audit Right to Benefit Patients.* Hampshire: Healthcare Quality Quest Ltd.

Henley, D. (1994) 'Art of annihilation: early onset schizophrenia and related disorders of childhood', *American Journal of Art Therapy,* 32 (4): 99–107.

Henley, D. (1998) 'Art therapy in a socialization program for children with Attention Deficit Hyperactivity Disorder', *American Journal of Art Therapy,* 37: 2–12.

Henley, D. (1999) 'Facilitating socialization within a therapeutic camp setting for children with attention deficits utilizing the expressive therapies', *American Journal of Art Therapy,* 38: 40–50.

Henley, D. (2001) 'Annihilation anxiety and fantasy in the art of children with Asperger's Syndrome and others on the autistic spectrum', *American Journal of Art Therapy,* 39: 113–21.

Herrmann, U. (forthcoming) 'The tangible reflection: a single case study investigating the meaning of sculpture for body image development with a congenitally blind client', in A. Gilroy (ed.), *Messages from Art Therapy Research: From Research into Evidence.*

Higgins, R. (1996) *Approaches to Research.* London: Jessica Kingsley.

Hill, D. (1958) 'The face of horror', *Sight and Sound,* 28: 6–11.

Hitchcock, G. and Hughes, D. (1986) *Research and the Teacher.* London: Routledge.

Hogan, S. (2001) *Healing Arts: The History of Art Therapy.* London: Jessica Kingsley.

Hosea, H. (forthcoming) '"The brush's footmarks": parents and infants paint together in a small community art therapy group', in A. Gilroy, (ed.), *Messages from Art Therapy Research: From Research into Evidence.*

Howard, R. (1990) 'Art therapy as an isomorphic intervention in the treatment of a client with PTSD', *American Journal of Art Therapy,* 28: 79–86.

Huet, V. (1997) 'Challenging professional confidence: arts therapies and psychiatric rehabilitation', *Inscape,* 2 (1): 14–19.

Huxley, P. (2002) 'Evidence in social care: the policy context', in S. Priebe and M. Slade (eds), *Evidence in Mental Health Care.* Hove: Brunner-Routledge.

Ivanova, A. (2004) 'Therapeutic art practices with orphan children in Bulgaria', *Art Therapy: Journal of the American Association of Art Therapists,* 21 (1): 13–17.

Jackson, J. (2001) 'A lawyer's view of evidence', in C. Mace S. Moorey and B. Roberts (eds), *Evidence in the Psychological Therapies.* Hove: Brunner-Routledge.

James, P. and Burns, T. (2002) 'The influence of evidence on mental health care developments in the UK since 1980', in S. Priebe and M. Slade (eds), *Evidence in Mental Health Care.* Hove: Brunner-Routledge.

Jones, C. (1999) 'Social work: regulation and managerialism', in M. Exworthy and S. Halford (eds), *Professionals and the New Managerialism in the Public Sector.* Buckingham: Open University Press.

Jones, K. (1998) 'Review of "What works for whom? A critical overview of psychotherapy research"', *Inscape,* 3 (2): 75–6.

Jones, K. (forthcoming) 'Art fer a pee: an exploratory Randomised Controlled Trial of group based art therapy as an adjunctive treatment with people with a diagnosis of schizophrenia', in A. Gilroy (ed.), *Messages from Art Therapy Research: from Research into Evidence.*

Juilliard, K. (1995) 'Increasing chemically dependent patients' beliefs in step one through expressive therapy', *American Journal of Art Therapy,* 33: 110–19.

Julliard, K. (1998) 'Outcome research in health care: implications for art therapy', *Art Therapy: Journal of the American Art Therapy Association,* 15 (1): 13–21.

Kalat, D. (1997) *A Critical History and Filmography of Toho's Godzilla Series.* North Carolina: McFarland and Co Inc.

Kane, E. (2002) 'The policy perspective: what evidence is influential?', in S. Priebe and M. Slade (eds), *Evidence in Mental Health Care*. Hove: Brunner-Routledge.

Kaplan, F. (2001) 'Areas of inquiry for art therapy research', *Art Therapy: Journal of the American Art Therapy Association*, 18 (3): 142–48.

Karkou, V. (1999) 'Art therapy in education: findings from a nationwide survey in arts therapies', *Inscape*, 4 (2): 62–70.

Karkou, V. (2002) 'Review of L. Kossolapow, S. Scoble and D. Waller (eds) *Arts-Therapies-Communication: On the Way to a Communicative Art Therapy*', *Inscape*, 7(1): 43–5.

Karkou, V. and Sanderson, P. (1997) 'An exploratory study of the utilisation of creative arts therapies (CAT) in treating substance dependence', *Journal of Contemporary Health*, Spring: 56–60.

Kazdin, A. (2000) *Psychotherapy for Children and Adolescents: Directions for Research and Practice*. New York: Oxford University Press.

Kazdin, A. and Weisz, J. (eds) (2003) *Evidence-based Psychotherapies for Children and Adolescents*. London: Guilford Press.

Killick, K. (1991) 'The practice of art therapy with patients in acute psychotic states', *Inscape*, Winter: 2–6.

Killick, K. (1995) 'Working with psychotic patients in art therapy', in J. Ellwood (ed.), *Psychosis: Understanding and Treatment*. London: Jessica Kingsley.

Killick, K. (1997) 'Unintegration and containment in acute psychosis', in K. Killick and J. Schaverien (eds), *Art, Psychotherapy and Psychosis*. London: Routledge.

Killick, K. (2000) 'The art room as container in analytical art psychotherapy with patients in psychotic states', in A. Gilroy and G. McNeilly (eds), *The Changing Shape of Art Therapy*. London: Jessica Kingsley.

Killick, K. and Greenwood, H. (1995) 'Research in art therapy with people who have psychotic illnesses', in A. Gilroy and C. Lee (eds), *Art and Music: Therapy and Research*. London: Routledge.

King, E. (1996) 'The use of the self in qualitative research', in J. Richardson (ed.), *Handbook of Qualitative Research Methods for Psychology and the Social Sciences*. Leicester: British Psychological Society.

Kopytin, A. (2004) 'Photography and art therapy: an easy partnership', *Inscape*, 9 (2): 49–58.

Kornreich, T. and Schimmel, B. (1991) 'The world is attacked by great big snowflakes: art therapy with an autistic boy', *American Journal of Art Therapy*, 29: 77–84.

Kuczaj, E. (1998) 'Learning to say "goodbye": loss and bereavement in learning difficulties and the role of art therapy', in M. Rees (ed.), *Drawing on Difference: Art Therapy with People Who Have Learning Difficulties*. London: Routledge.

Kuhn, T. (1970) *The Structure of Scientific Revolutions*. Chicago: Chicago University Press.

Kymiss, P., Christenson, E., Swanson, A. and Orlowski, P. (1996) 'Group treatment of adolescent inpatients: a pilot study using a structured art therapy approach', *Journal of Child and Adolescent Group Therapy*, 6: 45–52.

Lanham, R. (2002) 'Inscape revisited', *Inscape*, 7 (2): 48–59.

Laugharne, R. (2002) 'Evidence: the postmodern perspective', in S. Priebe and M. Slade (eds), *Evidence in Mental Health Care*. Hove: Brunner-Routledge.

Le Guin, U. (1979) 'American science fiction and the other', in S. Wood (ed.), *The Language of the Night: Essays on Fantasy and Science Fiction*. New York: Berkley Books.

Lev-Weisel, R. and Shivero, T. (2003) 'An exploratory study of self-figure drawings of individuals diagnosed with schizophrenia', *Arts in Psychotherapy*, 30: 13–16.

Levens, M. (1995) *Eating Disorders and Magical Control of the Body*. London: Routledge.

Lewin, K. (1951) *Field Theory in Social Science*. New York: Harper.

Liebmann, M. (1998) 'Art therapy with offenders on probation', in D. Sandle (ed.), *Development and Diversity: New Applications in Art Therapy*. London: Free Association.

Lomas, H. and Hallas, P. (1998) 'It's a mystery: accounts of an art therapy group for people with learning difficulties', in M. Rees (ed.), *Drawing on Difference: Art Therapy with People Who Have Learning Difficulties*. London: Routledge.

Lutts, R.H. (1992) 'The trouble with Bambi: Walt Disney's Bambi and the American vision of nature', *Forest and Conservation History*, 36: 160–71.

Luzzatto, P. (1994) 'Art therapy and anorexia. The mental double trap of the anorexic patient: the use of art therapy to facilitate psychic change', in D. Doktor (ed.), *Arts Therapies with Clients with Eating Disorders: Fragile Board*. London: Jessica Kingsley.

Luzzatto, P. (2000) 'The creative journey: a model for short-term group art therapy with posttreatment cancer patients', *Art Therapy: Journal of the American Art Therapy Association*, 17 (4): 265–9.

Luzzatto, P. (2005) 'Musing with death in group art therapy with cancer patients', in D. Waller and C. Sibbett (eds), *Art Therapy and Cancer Care*. Maidenhead: Open University Press.

Luzzatto, P. and Gabriel, B. (1998) 'Art psychotherapy', in Holland et al. (eds), *Psycho-Oncology*. New York: Oxford University Press.

Luzzatto, P. and Gabriel, B. (2000) 'The creative journey: a model for short-term group art therapy with post-treatment cancer patients', *Art Therapy*, 17 (4): 265–9.

Lyotard, J. (1984) *The Postmodern Condition: A Report on Knowledge*. Manchester: Manchester University Press.

Mackenzie, K., Chisholm, D. and Murray, G. (2000) 'Working with sex offenders who have a learning disability', *Inscape*, 5 (2): 62–9.

Maclagan, D. (1995) 'The biter bit: subjective features of research in art and therapy', in A. Gilroy and C. Lee (eds), *Art and Music: Therapy and Research*. London: Routledge.

McClelland, S. (1992) 'Brief art therapy in acute states', in D. Waller and A. Gilroy (eds), *Art Therapy: A Handbook*. Buckingham: Open University Press.

McClelland, S. (1993) 'The art of science with clients: beginning collaborative inquiry in process work, art therapy and acute states', in H. Payne (ed.), *Handbook of Inquiry in the Arts Therapies: One River, Many Currents*. London: Jessica Kingsley.

McDonald, R. and Blizard, R. (1988) 'Quality assurance of outcome in mental health care: a model for routine use in clinical settings', *Health Trends*, 20 (4): 111–14.

McGreal, J. (1993) 'Bambi', *Sight and Sound*, 3 (8): 56–7.

McGregor, I. (1990) 'Unusual drawing development in children: what does it reveal about children's art?', in C. Case and T. Dalley (eds), *Working with Children in Art Therapy*. London: Routledge.

McLeod, J. (1994) *Doing Counselling Research*. London: Sage.

McLeod, J. (1999) *Practitioner Research in Counselling*. London: Sage.

McLeod, J. (2000) 'The contribution of qualitative research to evidence-based counselling and psychotherapy', in N. Rowland and S. Goss (eds), *Evidence-based Counselling and Psychological Therapies*. London: Routledge.

McLeod, J. (2001) *Qualitative Research in Counselling and Psychotherapy*. London: Sage.

McNiff, S. (1998) *Art-based Research*. London: Jessica Kingsley.

Mace, C. and Moorey, S. (2001) 'Evidence in psychotherapy: a delicate balance', in C. Mace, S. Moorey and B. Roberts (eds), *Evidence in the Psychological Therapies*. Hove: Brunner-Routledge.

Mahony, J. (1994) 'Perceptions of art therapy and its absence in alcohol services', *Inscape*, 1: 15–18.

Mahony, J. (1999) 'Art therapy and art activities in alcohol services: a research project', in D. Waller and J. Mahony (eds), *Treatment of Addiction: Current Issues for Arts Therapies*. London: Routledge.

Mahony, J. (2001) 'Three commentaries: looking – experiences at three exhibitions', *Inscape*, 6 (2): 51–62.

Mahony, J. (forthcoming) 'Artefacts related to an art psychotherapy group', in A. Gilroy (ed.), *Messages from Art Therapy Research: from Research into Evidence*.

Mahony, J. and Waller, D. (1992) 'Art therapy in the treatment of alcohol and drug abuse', in D. Waller and A. Gilroy (eds), *Art Therapy: A Handbook*. Buckingham: Open University Press.

Males, J. (1980) 'Art therapy: investigations and implications', *Inscape*, 4 (2): 13–15.

Mann, T. (1996a) *Clinical Audit in the NHS: Using Clinical Audit in the NHS–a Position Statement*. Wetherby: NHS Executive.

Mann, T. (1996b) *Clinical Guidelines: Using Clinical Guidelines to Improve Patient Care within the NHS*. Wetherby: NHS Executive.

Margison, F. (2001) 'Practice-based evidence in psychotherapy', in C. Mace, S. Moorey and B. Roberts (Eds), *Evidence in the Psychological Therapies*. Hove: Brunner-Routledge.

Margison, F., Loebl, R. and McGrath, G. (1998) 'The Manchester experience: audit and psychotherapy services in north-west England', in R. Davenhill and M. Patrick (eds), *Re-thinking Clinical Audit: The Case of Psychotherapy Services in the NHS*. London: Routledge.

Maxwell, R. (1984) 'Quality assessment in health', *British Medical Journal*, 288: 1470–2.

Mead, J. (1998) 'Developing, disseminating and implementing clinical guidelines', in T. Bury and J. Mead (eds), *Evidence-based Healthcare*. Oxford: Butterworth-Heinemann.

Menther, I. and Muschamp, Y. (1999) 'Markets and management: the case of primary schools', in M. Exworthy and S. Halford (eds), *Professionals and the New Managerialism in the Public Sector*. Buckingham: Open University Press.

Meyerowitz-Katz, J. (2003) 'Art materials and process: a place of meeting. Art psychotherapy with a four-year-old boy', *Inscape*, 8 (2): 60 9.

MIND (2003) *Your Choices Survey: Report of Findings*. London : MIND.

Moran, D. (2000) *Introduction to Phenomenology*. London: Routledge.

Morgan, C. and Johnson, D. (1995) 'Use of a drawing task in the treatment of nightmares in combat-related post-traumatic stress disorder', *Art Therapy: Journal of the American Association of Art Therapists*, 12 (4): 244–7.

Mottram, P. (2000) 'Towards developing a methodology to evaluate outcomes of art therapy in adult mental illness'. Paper presented at the Theoretical Advances in Art Therapy Conference, Birmingham.

Moustakas, C. (1990) *Heuristic Research: Design, Methodology and Applications*. Thousand Oaks, CA: Sage.

Mulhall, A. (1998) 'Nursing, research and the evidence', *Evidence-based Nursing*, 1 (1): 4–6.

Murphy, J. (1998) 'Art therapy with sexually abused children and young people', *Inscape*, 3 (1): 10–16.

Murphy, J. Paisley, D. and Pardoe, L. (2004) 'An art therapy group for impulsive children', *Inscape*, 9 (2): 59–68.

Murphy, M., Black, N., Lamping, D., McKee, C., Sanderson, C. and Askham, J. (1998) 'Consensus development methods and their use in clinical guideline development', *Health Technology Assessment*, 2 (3).

National Institute for Clinical Excellence (NICE) (2003) *Research and Development Strategy Consultation Document*. London: NICE.

Needham, G. (2000) 'Research and practice: making a difference', in R. Gomm and C. Davies (eds), *Using Evidence in Health and Social Care*. London: Sage.

Newland, M. (1969) 'Bambi meets Godzilla', on *Hardware Wars and Other Film Farces*. Burbank, CA: Warner Home Video.

Noreiga, C. (1987) 'Godzilla and the Japanese nightmare: when *Them!* is U.S.', *Cinema Journal*, 27 (1): 63–77.

O'Brien, F. (2003) 'Bella and the white water rapids', *Inscape*, 8 (1): 29–41.

O'Brien, F. (2004) 'The making of mess in art therapy: attachment, trauma and the brain', *Inscape*, 9 (1): 2–13.

Olsen, C. (1995) 'Consensus statement: applying structure', *Journal of the American Medical Association*, 273 (1): 72–3.

Onizo, M. and Onizo, S. (1989) 'Art activities to improve the self-esteem among native Hawaiian children', *Journal of Humanistic Education and Development*, 27: 167–76.

Orton, M. (1994) 'A case study of an adolescent mother grieving the death of her child due to sudden infant death syndrome', *American Journal of Art Therapy*, 33: 37–44.

Panofsky, E. (1972) *Studies in Iconology: Humanistic Themes in the Art of the Renaissance*. New York and London: Harper and Row.

Parloff, M. (1982) 'Psychotherapy research evidence and reimbursement decisions: Bambi meets Godzilla', *American Journal of Psychiatry*, 139: 718–27.

Parry, G. (1992) 'Improving psychotherapy services: applications of research, audit and evaluation', *British Journal of Clinical Psychology*, 31: 3–19.

Parry, G. (1995) 'Bambi fights back: psychotherapy research and service improvement', *Changes*, 13 (3): 164–7.

Parry, G. (1996) 'Service evaluation and audit methods', in G. Parry and F. Watts (eds), *Behavioural and Mental Health Research: A Handbook of Skills and Methods*. Hove: Erlbaum (UK) Taylor and Francis.

Parry, G. (2000a) 'Evidence-based psychotherapy: an overview', in N. Rowland and S. Goss (eds), *Evidence-based Counselling and Psychological Therapies*. London: Routledge.

Parry, G. (2000b) 'Developing treatment choice guidelines in psychotherapy', *Journal of Mental Health*, 9 (3): 273–81.

Parry, G. (2001) *Treatment Choice in Psychological Therapies and Counselling: Evidence Based Clinical Practice Guideline*. Wetherby: NHS Executive.

Parry, G. and Richardson, A. (1996) *NHS Psychotherapy Services in England: Review of Strategic Policy*. Wetherby: NHS Executive.

Payne, D. (1995) 'Bambi', in E. Bel, L. Haas and L. Sells (eds), *From Mouse to Mermaid: The Politics of Film, Gender and Culture*. Bloomington, IN: Indiana University Press.

Peacock, M. (1991) 'A personal construct approach to art therapy in the treatment of post sexual abuse trauma', *American Journal of Art Therapy*, 29: 100–9.

Pifalo, T. (2002) 'Pulling out the thorns: art therapy with sexually abused children and adolescents', *Art Therapy: Journal of the American Association of Art Therapists*, 19 (1): 12–22.

Pleasant-Metcalf, A. (1997) 'The use of art therapy to improve academic performance', *Art Therapy: Journal of the American Art Therapy Association*, 14 (1): 23–9.

Ponteri, A. (2001) 'The effect of group art therapy on depressed mothers and their children', *Art Therapy: Journal of the American Art Therapy Association*, 18 (3): 148–57.

Power, M. (1994) *The Audit Explosion*. London: Demos.

Power, M. (1997) *The Audit Society: Rituals of Verification*. Oxford: Oxford University Press.

Power, M. (1998) 'The audit fixation: some issues for psychotherapy', in R. Davenhill and M. Patrick (eds), *Re-thinking Clinical Audit: The Case of Psychotherapy Services in the NHS*. London: Routledge.

Pratt, M. (1998) 'The invisible injury: adolescent griefwork', in M. Pratt and M. Wood (eds), *Art Therapy in Palliative Care: The Creative Response*. London: Routledge.

Pratt, M. (2004) *Guidelines for the Arts Therapies and the Arts in Palliative Care Settings*. London: Hospice Information.

Pratt, M. and Wood, M. (eds) (1998) *Art Therapy in Palliative Care: The Creative Response*. London: Routledge.

Priebe, S. and Slade, M. (2002a) *Evidence in Mental Health Care*. Hove: Brunner-Routledge.

Priebe, S. and Slade, M. (2002b) 'Evidence in the twenty-first century: the way forward', in S. Priebe and M. Slade (eds), *Evidence in Mental Health Care*. Hove: Brunner-Routledge.

Pringle, E. (1996) 'Evidence-based practice: exploring the implications for research within the therapy professions', *British Journal of Therapy and Rehabilitation*, 3 (12): 669.

Prokoviev, F. (1998) 'Adapting the art therapy group for children', in S. Skaife and V. Huet (eds), *Art Psychotherapy Groups: Between Pictures and Words*. London: Routledge.

Prosser, J. (ed.) (1998) *Image-based Research: A Sourcebook for Qualitative Researchers*. London: Falmer Press.

Quinn Paton, M. (1982) *Practical Evaluation*. Thousand Oaks, CA: Sage.

Reason, P. (ed.) (1988) *Human Inquiry in Action: Developments in New Paradigm Research*. London: Sage.

Reason, P. (1994) *Participation in Human Inquiry*. London: Sage.

Reason, P. and Rowan, J. (eds) (1981) *Human Inquiry: A Source Book of New Paradigm Research*. Chichester: Wiley.

Rees, M. (1995) 'Making sense of making space: researching art therapy with people who have severe learning difficulties', in A. Gilroy and C. Lee (eds), *Art and Music: Therapy and Research*. London: Routledge.

Rehavia-Hanauer, D. (2003) 'Identifying conflicts of anorexia nervosa as manifested in the art therapy process', *Arts in Psychotherapy*, 30: 137–49.

Reid, J. (2003) *Choice Speech to the New Health Network*. London: DoH.

Reynolds, F. (2002) 'Symbolic aspects of coping with chronic illness through textile arts', *Arts in Psychotherapy*, 29: 99–106.

Reynolds, S. (2000) 'Evidence based practice and psychotherapy research', *Journal of Mental Health*, 9 (3): 257–66.

Richardson, P. (2001) 'Evidence-based practice and the psychodynamic psychotherapies', in C. Mace, S. Moorey and B. Roberts (eds), *Evidence in the Psychological Therapies*. Hove: Brunner-Routledge.

Richardson, P., Evans, C., Jones, K., Rowe, A. and Stevens, P. (forthcoming) 'An exploratory randomised trial of group based art therapy as an adjunctive treatment in severe mental illness', *Journal of Mental Health*.

Riches, C. (1994) 'The hidden therapy of a prison art education programme', in M. Liebmann (ed.), *Art Therapy with Offenders*. London: Jessica Kingsley.

Robinson, S. (2002) 'What gets measured, gets delivered?', *Psychoanalytic Psychotherapy*, 16 (1): 37–57.

Rockwood, M. and Graham-Pole, J. (1997) 'The use of the creative arts in an intensive care setting', in R. Rebollo Pratt and A. Tokuda (eds), *Arts Medicine*. Patterson Harbour, MI: Benton Printing.

Rosal, M. (1993) 'Comparative group art therapy research to evaluate changes in locus of control in behaviourally disordered children', *Arts in Psychotherapy*, 20: 231–41.

Rosal, M., McCulloch-Vislisel, S. and Neece, S. (1997) 'Keeping students in school: an art therapy program to benefit 9th grade students', *Art Therapy: Journal of the American Association of Art Therapists*, 14: 30–6.

Rose, G. (2001) *Visual Methodologies: An Introduction to the Interpretation of Visual Materials*. London: Sage.

Rosenhan, D. (1981) 'On being sane in insane places', *Science*, 179: 250–8.

Roth, A. (2002) 'Applying the evidence in psychological therapies', in S. Priebe and M. Slade (eds), *Evidence in Mental Health Care*. Hove: Brunner-Routledge.

Roth, A. and Fonagy, P. (eds) (1996) *What Works for Whom? A Critical Review of Psychotherapy Research*. New York: Guildford.

Roth, A., Fonagy, P. and Parry, G. (1996) 'Psychotherapy research, funding and evidence-based practice', in A. Roth and P. Fonagy (eds), *What Works for Whom? A Critical Review of Psychotherapy Research*. New York: Guildford.

Rousseau, C., Lacroix, L., Bagilishya, D. and Heusch, N. (2003) 'Working with myths: creative expression workshops for immigrant and refugee children in a school setting', *Art Therapy: Journal of the American Art Therapy Association*, 20 (1): 3–10.

Royal College of Speech and Language Therapists (1996) *Communicating Quality: Professional Standards for Speech and Language Therapists*. London: Royal College of Speech and Language Therapists.

Rust, M.-J. (1994) 'Bringing "the man" into the group: art therapy groupwork with women with compulsive eating disorders', in D. Doktor (ed.), *Arts Therapies with Clients with Eating Disorders: Fragile Board*. London: Jessica Kingsley.

Rustin, M. (2001) 'Research, evidence and psychotherapy', in C. Mace, S. Moorey and B. Roberts (eds), *Evidence in the Psychological Therapies*. Hove: Brunner-Routledge.

Salkovskis, P. (1995) 'Demonstrating specific effects in cognitive and behavioural therapy', in M. Aveline and D. Shapiro (eds), *Research Foundations for Psychotherapy Research*. Chichester: Wiley.

Saotome, J. (1998) 'Long-stay art therapy groups', in S. Skaife and V. Huet (eds), *Art Psychotherapy Groups: Between Pictures and Words*. London: Routledge.

Sarra, N. (1998) 'Connection and disconnection in the art therapy group: working with forensic patients in acute states on a locked ward', in S. Skaife and V. Huet (eds), *Art Psychotherapy Groups: Between Pictures and Words*. London: Routledge.

Saunders, E. and Saunders, J. (2000) 'Evaluating the effectiveness of art therapy through quantitative outcomes-focused study', *Arts in Psychotherapy*, 27 (2): 99–106.

Schaverien, J. (1989) 'Transference and the picture: art therapy in the treatment of anorexia', *Inscape*, Spring: 14–17.

Schaverien, J. (1992) *The Revealing Image*. London: Routledge.

Schaverien, J. (1993) 'The retrospective review of pictures: data for research in art therapy', in H. Payne (ed.), *Handbook of Inquiry in the Arts Therapies: One River, Many Currents*. London: Jessica Kingsley.

Schaverien, J. (1994) 'The picture as transactional object in the treatment of anorexia', in D. Doktor (ed.), *Arts Therapies with Clients with Eating Disorders: Fragile Board*. London: Jessica Kingsley.

Schaverien, J. (1998) 'Inheritance: Jewish identity, art psychotherapy workshops and the legacy of the Holocaust', in D. Doktor (ed.), *Arts Therapists, Refugees and Migrants*. London: Jessica Kingsley.

Schaverien, J. (2000) 'Individuation, countertransference and the death of a client', *Inscape*, 3 (2): 55–63.

Schaverien, J. (2002) *The Dying Patient in Psychotherapy: Desire, Dreams and Individuation*. London: Palgrave Macmillan.

Schexnadre, C. (1993) 'Images from the past: the life review scrapbook technique with the elderly', in E. Virshup (ed.), *California Art Therapy Trends*. Chicago: Magnolia Street.

Schmiedeback, H. (2002) 'Evidence in mental health: a historical analysis', in S. Priebe and M. Slade (eds), *Evidence in Mental Health Care*. Hove: Brunner-Routledge.

Schore, A.N. (1994) *Affect Regulation and the Origin of the Self: The Neurobiology of Emotional Development*. Mahwah, NJ: Lawrence Erlbaum Associates.

Schut, H., de Keiser, J., van Bout, J. and Stroebe, M. (1996) 'Cross-modality grief program: description and assessment of a new program', *Journal of Clinical Psychology*, 52: 357–65.

Scott, E. and Black, N. (1991) 'When does consensus exist in expert panels?', *Journal of Mental Health*, 13 (1): 35–9.

Sebba, J. (2004) 'Developing evidence-informed policy and practice in education', in G. Thomas and R. Pring (eds), *Evidence-based Practice in Education*. Maidenhead: Open University Press.

Seth-Smith, F. (2003) 'Art and music therapy clinical audit at Central North West London NHS Mental Health Trust', *Art Therapy Practice Research Network Newsletter*, April: 37–8.

Sheppard, L., Rusted, J., Waller, D. and McInally, F. (1998) *Evaluating the Use of Art Therapy for Older People with Dementia*. Brighton: Alzheimer's Society.

Shore, C. and Wright, S. (2000) 'Coercive accountability: the rise of audit culture in higher education', in M. Strathern (ed.), *Audit Cultures*. London: Routledge.

Sibbett, C. (2005a) '"Betwixt and between": crossing thresholds', in D. Waller and C. Sibbett (eds), *Art Therapy and Cancer Care*. Maidenhead: Open University Press.

Sibbett, C. (2005b) 'Liminal embodiment: embodied and sensory experience in cancer care and art therapy', in D. Waller and C. Sibbett (eds), *Art Therapy and Cancer Care*. Maidenhead: Open University Press.

Sibbett, C. (2005c) 'An art therapist's experience of having cancer: living and dying with the tiger', in D. Waller and C. Sibbett (eds), *Art Therapy and Cancer Care*. Maidenhead: Open University Press.

Silver, R. (2003) 'Cultural differences and similarities in responses to the Silver Drawing Test in USA, Brazil, Russia, Estonia, Thailand and Australia', *Art Therapy: Journal of the American Art Therapy Association*, 20 (1): 16–20.

Silverman, D. (2000) *Doing Qualitative Research: A Practical Handbook*. London: Sage.

Simon, R. (1992) *The Symbolism of Style*. London: Routledge.

Skaife, S. (1995) 'The dialectics of art therapy', *Inscape*, Summer: 2–7.

Skaife, S. (2000) 'Keeping the balance: further thoughts on the dialectics of art therapy', in A. Gilroy and G. McNeilly (eds), *The Changing Shape of Art Therapy: New Developments in Theory and Practice*. London: Jessica Kingsley.

Skaife, S. (2001) 'Making visible: art therapy and intersubjectivity', *Inscape*, 6 (2): 40–50.

Slade, M. and Priebe, S. (2002) 'Conceptual limitations of randomised controlled trials', in S. Priebe and M. Slade (eds), *Evidence in Mental Health Care*. Hove: Brunner-Routledge.

Smith, D. (ed.) (2004) *Social Work and Evidence-based Practice*. London: Jessica Kingsley.

Smitheman-Brown, V. and Church, R. (1996) 'Mandala drawing facilitating creative growth with children with ADD or ADHD', *Art Therapy: Journal of the American Association of Art Therapists*, 13 (4): 252–62.

Sontag, S. (2001) *Against Interpretation*. London: Vintage.

Spaniol, S. (1998) 'Towards an ethnographic approach to art therapy research: people with psychiatric disability as collaborators', *Art Therapy: Journal of the American Art Therapy Association*, 15 (1): 29–37.

Spender, Q. and Cooper, H. (1995) 'The hinterland between audit and research', *ACPP Review*, 17 (2): 65–73.

Springham, N. (1994) 'Research into patients' reactions to art therapy on a drug and alcohol programme', *Inscape*, 2: 36–40.

Springham, N. (1998) 'The magpie's eye: patients' resistance to engagement in an art therapy group for drug and alcohol patients', in S. Skaife and V. Huet (eds), *Art Psychotherapy Groups: Between Pictures and Words*. London: Routledge.

Springham, N. (1999) '"All things very lovely": art therapy in a drug and alcohol treatment programme', in D. Waller and J. Mahony (eds), *Treatment of Addiction: Current Issues for Arts Therapies*. London: Routledge.

Springham, N. and Huet, V. (2004) *Off the Peg Audit Pack*. London: British Association of Art Therapists and the Art Therapy Practice Research Network.

Stack, M. (1998) 'Humpty Dumpty's shell: working with autistic defence mechanisms in art therapy', in M. Rees (ed.), *Drawing on Difference: Art Therapy with People Who Have Learning Difficulties.* London: Routledge.

Stanley, P. and Miller, M. (1993) 'Short-term art therapy with an adolescent male', *Arts in Psychotherapy*, 20: 397–402.

Stewart, E. (2004) 'Art therapy and neuroscience blend: working with patients who have dementia', *Art Therapy: Journal of the American Art Therapy Association*, 21 (3): 148–55.

Stott, J. and Males, B. (1984) 'Art therapy for people who are mentally handicapped', in T. Dalley (ed.), *Art as Therapy: An Introduction to the Use of Art as a Therapeutic Technique.* London: Tavistock Publications.

Sturdee, P. (2001) 'Evidence, influence or evalutation? Fact and value in clinical science', in C. Mace, S. Moorey and B. Roberts (eds), *Evidence in the Psychological Therapies.* Hove: Brunner-Routledge.

Tamminen, K. (1998) 'Exploring the landscape within: art therapy in a forensic unit', in D. Sandle (ed.), *Development and Diversity: New Applications in Art Therapy.* London: Free Association.

Target, M. (1998) 'Audit and research', in R. Davenhill and M. Patrick (1998) (eds), *Re-thinking Clinical Audit: The Case of Psychotherapy Services in the NHS.* London: Routledge.

Teasdale, C. (1995) 'Reforming zeal or fatal attraction: why should art therapists work with violent offenders', *Inscape*, Winter: 2–9.

Teasdale, C. (1997) 'Art therapy as a shared forensic investigation', *Inscape*, 2 (2): 32–40.

Teasdale, C. (2002) *Guidelines for Arts Therapists Working in Prisons.* London, Department for Education and Skills.

Theorell, T., Konarski, K., Westerlund, H., Burell, A.-M., Engstrom, R., Lagercrantz, A.-M., Teszary, J. and Thulin, K. (1998) 'Treatment of patients wich chronic somatic symptoms by means of art psychotherapy: a process description', *Psychotherapy and Psychsomatics*, 67: 50–6.

Thomas, G. and Pring, R. (2004) *Evidence-based Practice in Education.* Maidenhead: Open University Press.

Thomas, L. (1998) 'From re-presentation to representation', in D. Sandle (ed.), *Development and Diversity: New Applications in Art Therapy.* London: Free Association.

Tibbetts, T. and Stone, B. (1990) 'Short-term art therapy with seriously emotionally disturbed children', *Arts in Psychotherapy*, 17 (2): 139–46.

Tinker, A. (2001) 'Ethics committees: help or hindrance? The experience of the ESRC Growing Older researchers', *Journal of the British Society of Gerontology*, 11 (3): 16–18.

Tipple, R. (1992) 'Art therapy with people who have severe learning difficulties', in D. Waller and A. Gilroy (eds), *Art Therapy: A Handbook.* Buckingham: Open University Press.

Tipple, R. (1993) 'Challenging assumptions: the importance of transference processes in work with people with learning difficulties', *Inscape*, Summer: 2–9.

Tipple, R. (1994) 'Communication and interpretation in art therapy with people who have a learning disability', *Inscape*, 2: 31–5.

Tipple, R. (2003) 'The interpretation of children's artwork in a paediatric disability setting', *Inscape*, 8 (2): 48–59.

Turnbull, J. and O'May, F. (2002) 'GPs' and clients' views of art therapy in an Edinburgh practice' *Inscape*, 7 (1): 26–9.

Tyler, J. (2002) 'Art therapy with older adults clinically diagnosed as having Alzheimer's disease and dementia', in D. Waller (ed.), *Nameless Dread: Arts Therapies and Progressive Illness.* London: Brunner-Routledge.

Ulman, E. and Levy, B. (2001) 'An experimental approach to the judgement of psychopathology of paintings', *American Journal of Art Therapy*, 40: 82–91.

Van Leeuwen, T. and Jewitt, C. (eds) (2001) *Handbook of Visual Analysis.* London: Sage.

Von Zweigbergk, B. and Armstrong, M. (2004) *The Village on the Heath: A History of Bexley Hospital.* Essex: Dopler Press.

Walby, S. and Greenwell, J. (1994) 'Managing the National Health Service', in J. Clarke, A. Cochrane and E. Mclaughlin (1994) (eds), *Managing Social Policy.* London: Sage.

Waldman, J. (1999) 'The clay buffet: the use of clay in a group of female survivors of childhood sexual abuse'. Unpublished MA Final Report, London: Goldsmiths College.

Waller, C. (1992) 'Art therapy with adult female incest survivors', *Art Therapy: Journal of the American Association of Art Therapists*, 9 (3): 135–8.

Waller, D. (1983) 'Art therapy as a treatment for eating disorders. Report of a research project', in J. Henzell (ed.), *Proceedings of the British Psychological Society International Conference 'Psychology and the Arts'.* Cardiff: University of Cardiff.

Waller, D. (1987) 'Art therapy in adolescence: a metaphorical view of a profession in progress', in T. Dalley, C. Case, J. Schaverien, F. Weir, D. Halliday, P. Nowell-Hall and D. Waller (eds), *Images of Art Therapy: New Developments in Theory and Practice.* London: Tavistock Publications.

Waller, D. (1991) *Becoming a Profession: The History of Art Therapy in Britain 1940–1982.* London: Routledge.

Waller, D. (1994) 'The power of food: some explorations and transcultural experiences in relation to eating disorders', in D. Doktor (ed.), *Arts Therapies with Clients with Eating Disorders: Fragile Board.* London: Jessica Kingsley.

Waller, D. (1995) 'The development of art therapy in Bulgaria: infiltrating the system', in A. Gilroy and C. Lee (eds), *Art and Music: Therapy and Research.* London: Routledge.

Waller, D. (1998) *Towards a European Art Therapy.* Buckingham: Open University Press.

Waller, D. (2001) 'Research report: art therapy and dementia. an update on work in progress', *Inscape*, 6 (2): 67–8.

Waller, D. (2002) 'Evaluating the use of art therapy for older people with dementia: a control group study', in D. Waller (ed.), *Nameless Dread: Arts Therapies and Progressive Illness.* London: Brunner-Routledge.

Waller, D. and Sibbett, C. (2005) *Art Therapy and Cancer Care.* Maidenhead: Open University Press.

Walliman, N. (2001) *Your Research Project: A Step-by-Step Guide for the First-time Researcher.* London: Sage.

Weisz, J. and Kazdin, A. (2003) 'Concluding thoughts. Present and future of evidence-based psychotherapies for children and adolescents', in A. Kazdin and J. Weisz (eds), *Evidence-based Psychotherapies for Children and Adolescents.* London: Guilford Press.

Weiss, W., Schafer, D. and Berghorn, F. (1989) 'Art for institutionalised elderly', *Art Therapy: Journal of the American Association of Art Therapists*, 6 (1): 10–17.

Weldt, C. (2003) 'Patients responses to a drawing experience in a hemodialysis unit: a step towards healing', *Art Therapy: Journal of the American Association of Art Therapists*, 20 (2): 92–9.

Wells, P. (2000) *The Horror Genre: From Beelzebub to Blair Witch.* London: Wallflower Publications.

Welsby, C. (1998) 'A part of the whole: art therapy in a girl's comprehensive school', *Inscape*, 3 (1): 33–40.

Wesseley, S. (2001) 'Randomised controlled trials: the gold standard?', in C. Mace, S. Moorey and B. Roberts (eds), *Evidence in the Psychological Therapies.* Hove: Brunner-Routledge.

Whitaker, R. and Middleton, D. (2003) 'Using the CORE systems outcome measure: a tale of doubt, confusion, persistence, serendipity and some happiness', *Art Therapy Practice Research Network Newsletter*, April: 6–9.

White, K. and Allen, R. (1971) 'Art counselling in an educational setting: self-concept change among pre-adolescent boys', *Journal of School Psychology*, 9: 218–24.

Wilks, R. and Byers, A. (1992) 'Art therapy with elderly people in statutory care', in D. Waller and A. Gilroy (eds), *Art Therapy: A Handbook*. Buckingham: Open University Press.

Wilson, C. (2002) 'A time-limited model of art therapy practice in general practice', *Inscape*, 7 (1): 16–25.

Winnicott, D.W. (1971) *Playing and Reality*. Harmondsworth: Penguin.

Wood, C. (1997a) 'The history of art therapy and psychosis (1938–95)', in K. Killick and J. Schaverien (eds), *Art, Psychotherapy and Psychosis*. London: Routledge.

Wood, C. (1997b) 'Facing fear with people who have a history of psychosis', *Inscape*, 2 (2): 41–8.

Wood, C. (1999a) 'Class issues in therapy', in J. Campbell, F. Brooks, J. Jones and C. Ward (eds), *Art Therapy: Race and Culture*. London: Jessica Kingsley.

Wood, C. (1999b) 'Gathering evidence: expansion of art therapy research strategy', *Inscape*, 4 (2): 51– 61.

Wood, C. (forthcoming) 'The evolution of art psychotherapy in relation to psychosis and poverty', in A. Gilroy (ed.), *Messages from Art Therapy Research: from Research into Evidence*.

Wood, M. (1996) 'Art therapy and eating disorders: theory and practice in Britain', *Inscape*, 1 (1): 13–19.

Wood, M. (1998a) 'The body as art: individual session with a man with AIDs', in M. Pratt and M. Wood (eds), *Art Therapy in Palliative Care: The Creative Response*. London: Routledge.

Wood, M. (1998b) 'Art therapy in palliative care', in M. Pratt and M. Wood (eds), *Art Therapy in Palliative Care: The Creative Response*. London: Routledge.

Wood, M. (2002) 'Researching art therapy practice with people suffering from AIDs-related dementia', *Arts in Psychotherapy*, 29: 207–19.

Wood, M. (2005) 'Shoreline: the realities of working in cancer and palliative care', in D. Waller and C. Sibbett (eds), *Art Therapy and Cancer Care*. Maidenhead: Open University Press.

Yaretzky, A., Levinson, M. and Kimichi, O. (1996) 'Clay as a therapeutic tool in group processing with the elderly', *American Journal of Art Therapy*, 34 (3): 75–82.

Zammitt, C. (2001) 'The art of healing: a journey through cancer: implications for art therapy. *Art Therapy: Journal of the American Art Therapy Association*, 18 (1): 27–36.

Index